ENDURING ART, ACTIVE FAITH

3 Generations Create!

Robert G. Proudfoot

Suite 300 - 990 Fort St
Victoria, BC, V8V 3K2
Canada

www.friesenpress.com

Copyright © 2019 by Robert Proudfoot
First Edition — 2019

All rights reserved.

No part of this publication may be reproduced in any form, or by any means, electronic or mechanical, including photocopying, recording, or any information browsing, storage, or retrieval system, without permission in writing from FriesenPress.

Library and Archives Canada Book ISBN 978-0-9948648-0-2;

Robert Proudfoot acknowledges the following other contributors in addition to Annora and Norma Proudfoot (authors): Alicia Proudfoot (prints and photographs of artwork); Valerie Proudfoot (author); Donna Entz (author); Vincent Friesen, Carolyn Wilson and John Woollard (editors/reviewers); Donald Proudfoot and Rodney MacDonald (photographs).

ISBN
978-1-5255-2817-0 (Hardcover)
978-1-5255-2818-7 (Paperback)
978-1-5255-2819-4 (eBook)

1. Biography & Autobiography, Personal Memoirs

Distributed to the trade by The Ingram Book Company

TABLE OF CONTENTS

INTRODUCTIONS AND ACKNOWLEDGEMENTS	VII
WE ARE SUCH STUFF (ARTIST'S STATEMENT)	IX
AUTHOR'S FOREWORD	X

PART I AFRICAN SAFARIS 1

THE COST OF SHARING CHRIST'S MERCY	3
THE MISFITS' DANCE	8
MAY GOD MAKE OUR MUD LIGHT	19
BEHIND THE LEMON TREES	23
TWO BY TWO	28
ROAD CLOSED UNTIL AFTER PRAYER	39
WHO OWNS THE DESERT'S JEWELS?	49
DANGEROUS GAME	56
THE GUARD	65

PART II WHAT IF?......83

THE PRICE OF BELONGING	85
ESSAY ON FARMING	93
A DAY OF SUMMER SUPPLY AT THE OFFICE WHILE THE SECRETARY TAKES A HOLIDAY	106
LEARNING THE ROPES	112
NIGHT TRAINS	123
THREE TREES – REFLECTIONS ON PLURALISM	179
ICEBERG	182

TEST DRIVE	184
TOTEM POLE	185
TWO SIDES	187

PART III ON A LIGHTER NOTE 189

DRUNK WITH SPRING	191
BIG CHIEF'S SECRET	194
JOYOUS PIANO TUNE	202
BUS DRIVER	212
HOW OLD ARE WE REALLY?	214
TOPSPIN FOLLIES	215
HALF AND HALF	229
THE SPECTATOR IN RETROSPECTION (ARTIST'S STATEMENT)	236

PART IV FAMILY MEMORIES 239

WHAT WE LEFT BEHIND (ARTIST STATEMENT)	241
ROOTS, VINES, AND TENDRILS	242
THE MERCY FLIGHT	258
WHY I WEAR A RED POPPY ON REMEMBRANCE DAY	265
ABOUT THE AUTHOR	272

INTRODUCTIONS AND ACKNOWLEDGEMENTS

The following members of the Proudfoot family and their friends are gratefully acknowledged for contributing to the development of this book. Firstly, let me introduce you to the authors and artists:

- Norma Proudfoot (1926–2015), my mother, for writing essays and short stories on social justice, immigration, nature, changing family dynamics, and fond memories from the family farm that too soon disappeared. She also painted *African Memories*, which graces Part I – African Safaris.
- Valerie Proudfoot, my wife, and our friend, Donna Entz, for thoughtfully considering how followers of different faiths, yet people of the same book, can nurture one another.
- Annora Proudfoot, our daughter, for bravely sharing her heartfelt poetry and mask-making skills.
- Alicia Proudfoot, another daughter, for creating some intriguing artwork to support this collective endeavour.
- Robert Proudfoot, for contributing essays and short stories, several from his years (1988–1991) of working for Mennonite Central Committee in Nigeria or living as a student in Zambia (1969–1973). Robert also provides other essays and short stories on sports, social justice, cross-cultural relationships, and sharing of family history.

The authors and artists also thank our friends from First Mennonite Church community in Edmonton who reviewed and provided feedback on several manuscripts that make up this collection: Donna Entz, Vincent Friesen, Carolyn Wilson, and John Woollard.

We also acknowledge the contribution of photos and location directions for the site of the November 22, 1953, Gateway Aviation airplane crash, provided on September 7, 2010, by Donald Proudfoot (Robert's brother) and Rodney MacDonald (Donald's and Robert's cousin and son of pilot Gordon MacDonald).

(*We Are Such Stuff* 2014)

WE ARE SUCH STUFF (ARTIST'S STATEMENT)

BY ALICIA PROUDFOOT

My work addresses the isolation of family, and how it is hidden away in the urban setting. This print shows how family is contained, with the negative space acting as walls, and though domesticity can imitate the external world through pattern, its attempts to reach out the window are futile. The combination of the *chine colled* stone lithography, and the photographic application emphasize the separation of the familial from city life. The thickness of the hand-drawn marks dominates the image as a desperate space, acting like a growth invading the hazy nostalgia of the photographed outdoors of Lethbridge, Alberta.

AUTHOR'S FOREWORD

Art and spiritual faith are important, timeless avenues for nurturing one's soul. Faith and spirituality are expressed by how and what the artist creates. The artist's creativity inspires those who see, hear, touch, or smell his/her work. Serving hand in hand, faith and art can inspire humankind to make our world a more peaceful and just place, where all God's wonderful creations have their being.

God is the creator of Heaven and Earth, the universe and every living thing in it. He made all things and deemed them good. Isaiah 64:8 testifies, "Yet, O Lord, you are our Father. We are the clay, you are the potter; we are all the work of your hands."[1] In ancient times of Jubal and Tubal-Cain, humans learned to play the harp and flute, to forge tools from bronze and iron. Moses and Miriam exulted the Lord in song after he helped the Hebrews cross the Red Sea, and escape bondage in Egypt. David the shepherd boy sang with a harp to calm King Saul's troubled mind; as king, David composed many psalms, and sang them in praise and supplication to the Lord. Mary magnified the Lord in song upon hearing the angel's message that she would be remembered among women as the mother of Jesus.

Benvenuto Cellini crafted sculptures and ornaments from precious metals for kings and popes of the Middle Ages, yet these imaginations

---

1 Scripture as written in the New International Version of the Holy Bible.

do not remain so well today as does the autobiography he wrote with such energy and dash. We continue to sing enduring hymns and enjoy inspiring orchestral and opera music of famous European composers, amid our more modern jazz, blues, bluegrass, rock and roll, rock, pop, punk, alternative, and rap. We appreciate today's abstract art together with vividly complex paintings by renowned artists like Michelangelo and Van Gogh. Writings of Homer, Chaucer and Dickens, Shakespearean plays, Mozart's musical genius, noted African writers of culture like Achebe and Soyinka, and modern heroes like folk singer Bob Dylan (who won the Nobel Prize for Literature) and Brian Wilson, the amazing music innovator behind the Beach Boys, are just a smattering of art-forms that continue to inspire our long-suffering world.

While our artistic, creative collection offered to you now by three generations of my family may be small, unrefined, and unheralded, we celebrate with our readers a few more examples of how God can work his creativity.

Robert Proudfoot September 7, 2018

PART I
AFRICAN SAFARIS

*"God does not call us to be successful, but rather,
to be faithful in our service to Him."*

Pastor Peter J. Dyck, long-time MCC worker and director in England,
Soviet Union, and other nations, and member of Commission on
Overseas Mission for the Mennonite Church, circa 1988.

(*African Memories*, Christmas 1992)

THE COST OF SHARING CHRIST'S MERCY

BY ROBERT PROUDFOOT

An African stranger came to our door yesterday, sombrely seeking help. Asking not how he had breached security fence and guards of the church compound . . . going against all experienced advice given by our Hausa teacher and hard-bitten *bature*[2] friends, I invited this troubled youth to join us in our cool and quiet parlour in Jos, Nigeria.

He furtively explained, after accepting a glass of cold water and engaging in our customary exchange of greetings, that he had been unable to consult a certain white doctor to whom the hospital had referred him. Thus, our visitor had come to me on matters of vital spiritual importance.

"My question is this, sir?" he asked. "What do I do, sir, since I want to become a Christian?"

The fellow appeared ill at ease as he divulged breathlessly and sweated profusely in the wooden lean-to chair opposite me. My initial reaction was to hide behind the excuse I was neither theologian nor

---

2   Hausa word meaning European or white man.

doctor. Moses (that was the name on the *Jan Kwano*[3] hospital papers he showed me) ducked my offer to introduce him to our local COCIN[4] pastor. He shied away from medical advice that my wife Valerie, a registered nurse, supplied concerning his after-treatment for hepatitis. This stranger accosted me because I was a white man—all *turawa*[5] were wealthy Christian missionaries who knew the way to Jesus!

"If you wish to join our faith, you must first acknowledge *Ubangiji*[6] as creator and repent of your sins before him. Then, you should invite *Yesu Kristi* into your heart," I testified, not wishing to disappoint the needy youth whom the Lord had given me.

Moses quickly confessed his sins. He had fled Ibadan after falling out with his Christian family and stealing 500 naira[7] from his architect father. Then, he had joined a gang of thieves who stole everything from watches to VCRs before he was captured and imprisoned. Moses had contacted hepatitis in prison, and since suffered terribly under its scourge. He had languished near death at times because of his inability to purchase proper medicine and eat nourishing food. Yet, the Lord had sustained Moses while richer men with easy access to help had died from this manageable disease. Moses not only had escaped the death penalty normally prescribed for his violent crimes, but had been transferred to hospital for intensive care after only serving nine months of his sentence. Now a free man, he felt God's presence ever stronger. Tired of

---

3 Hausa nickname for a major hospital in Jos operated with some European doctors and frequented by European patients, known for its distinctive, red (*ja*) metal (*kwano*) roof.

4 Acronym for Church of Christ in Nigeria, founded by European missionaries of the Sudan United Mission, but supported and managed mainly by African Christians by the late 1980s.

5 Hausa word for more than one European or white person.

6 Hausa name for God, as utilized by Nigerian Christians, in deference to *Allah*, the general name for God.

7 Nigerian dollar, which, in the late 1980s, was equivalent to approximately 7 cents US.

the troubles lurking in Jos's gritty streets, Moses longed to return home, and be reconciled with his family and church.

Valerie became so unnerved by this stranger's unsavoury story she felt compelled to warn the *mai gida*[8] of his unsolicited intrusion upon our compound. Moses and I were moving towards prayer when the African landlord and his young men darkened our doorway, demanding that we come forth.

Pastor Alhari, a stately church leader, dressed in embroidered, flowing gown and cap of blue and white, was grumpy for being thus disturbed when he was about to leave his compound to attend an elders' meeting, and he now sternly questioned Moses in local Hausa. When the younger man gazed silently at the ground in bewilderment, apparently less fluent in the lingua franca of northern Nigeria than we recently arrived foreigners, who were struggling to learn it, the *mai gida* guffawed in English, "*Ba Hausa,*[9] you are certainly not a Plateau man! Where do you come from? Who are your people?"

"I come from Ibadan," mumbled Moses gloomily. "My father is chief architect for that city."

Pastor Alhari grilled Moses while I cowered with embarrassment. "Who are you? You are young and well-dressed. Why do you trouble my guests when they are here in Jos for only a short time to learn Hausa, before they go Bornu side to work with our COCIN brethren for God among the *Bare Bari*?"[10]

Moses was rendered speechless. Pastor Alhari ordered him off the property, the callous inference being that this young man intended only to steal or beg money from us naively patronizing *turawa*. Yet, in leaving, Moses solemnly thanked me for hearing him.

Although chastened to the grim fact I had risked life and property entertaining a troublemaker, I refused to believe in my heart that Moses

---

8   Hausa word for the household owner or head.

9   A somewhat derogatory name for a person who does not speak the Hausa language.

10 Hausa name for the Kanuri people of northeastern Nigeria.

meant to harm us—until the next morning when I discovered that my wallet was missing! It had been left carelessly in view during our visit; although I had not seen him act, I assumed Moses had pickpocketed me after taking refreshment in my home.

I could not concentrate on the repetitive Hausa class drills in days following as I grieved over how Moses had scammed me. Tricked by the very poor people I had travelled thousands of miles and shed armour of wealth and technology to help, I prepared to join other *turawa* embittered towards Nigeria's seemingly corrupt, often chaotic attempts to keep pace with the civilized world. Our childlike honeymoon with the fabled Africa of Burton, Livingstone, Leakey, and Schweitzer was over, a mere two weeks after arriving in the country!

I poured out my frustrations upon the wise and sympathetic ear of Athanasius, MCC's[11] Nigerian administrative assistant. Since we were not positive that my wallet, in fact, had been stolen, Athanasius agreed to help me search more diligently for it at our guesthouse before going to the police.

We met Moses walking dejectedly on the street and, in our confusion of seeking God's sometimes strange purpose, directed this wanderer to accompany us back to the guest house—the scene of his crime! Athanasius held Moses in check under one of the compound's shady flame trees while Valerie and I searched again in our dwelling for valuables. We found the wallet intact, tucked as though by an angel inside one of our half-empty suitcases back in the bedroom. We praised God for his faithful answer to desperate prayers!

Returning triumphantly outside, we found Moses giving halting testimony to Athanasius, an intense but patient listener. No further mention of the wallet was necessary; our business at hand was to understand and help Moses. His story rang true about wanting Jesus, so Athanasius and I

---

11 Acronym for Mennonite Central Committee, a service and development organization of the Mennonite Churches that had recruited Valerie and Robert and seconded them to COCIN, to do Christian outreach work in Nigeria, West Africa.

prayed with him, while Valerie poured tea and quoted scripture to guide Moses in his spiritual journey. Moses, not keen to join a local church, opted to return like a prodigal son in desperate peace to his family.

He then expressed his embarrassing need for cash to purchase train fare to southwestern Nigeria. I gave him what naira was in my wallet, but Athanasius counselled Moses to seek useful work from local Christians, instead of begging more handouts, to earn his way home. Moses bade goodbye, then left us quickly, lest his unwanted presence be discovered by the *mai gida*.

We hope that Moses did as he vowed and heeded the sound advice given him, harsh as it seemed to gullible outsiders like us. Were Athanasius, Valerie, and I merciful in prodding Moses to help himself? The Lord only knows the full reasons Moses invaded our lives. We believe God had a purpose for permitting such interaction. We pray that we played a part in helping Moses find his way in life.

THE MISFITS' DANCE

BY ROBERT PROUDFOOT

The fiddler's one-string *goge*[12] scratched the dusty night air. His drummers tumbled into the beat and enchanted the wild-eyed midnight crowd drawn into the deserted marketplace. Pretty young girls beckoned with voluptuous dance and, stirred by their lively rhythm, spectators rewarded these performers with *naira* or paid to strut their own stuff in the ring. Spurred by the raucously approving crowd, more dancers joined in. They freed themselves to create and express, in gyrating response to the *mai goge*'s[13] lead.

These night people were jovially alive as they strolled about, drinking in the cool desert air and greeting each other in the dance or at barbecue pits and sweets tables nearby. They broke the hot, sunlight fetters of a legalistic, religious society that fed upon peer pressure and visual impressions. Young men had changed their peacock hats and embroidered gowns for T-shirts and slacks. Gone were virile perfumes and manikin perfections as they mixed jestingly with their girlfriends and age mates. Women came out, uncovered vivaciously from the treadmill

---

12 A large, one-string bowed instrument played in northeastern Nigeria.

13 Fiddler, owner and player of the *goge* instrument.

drudgery of *purdah*.[14] Children munched on watermelon or sugar cane and played beneath the bandstand's eerie light without fear of being driven away with switches wielded by humourless, burdened adults. In this merry, musical night market, nobody cared if one is Kanuri or Marghi[15], Christian or Muslim, a married, Koranic pillar of society or a labourer, indigenous to the desert's beach, or bumbling, starry-eyed foreigners like Valerie and me.

We were a motley crew, and it's a wonder that Wulgo's stern Islamic establishment tolerated our late-night rowdiness in their orderly, ancient town. I, in the silvery moonlight, recognized many misfits plying the night market whom our fiercely discerning landlord, Abba Mai—a successful shopkeeper, esteemed imam[16] of a mosque he had built beside his house, and named after the traditional *mais*[17] of his Kanuri tribe—judged unworthy and banned from our shared compound. There was young, free-spirited Ali, jocular and witty as he strolled hand in hand with a male friend from university. He filled our parlour with questions about Jesus and accolades for science and Kanem-Bornu history until branded a drug addict. Birma's glowing childhood memories spent with British missionaries who sailed around Lake Chad in a hospital ship, failed washing . . . Birma too often visited my wife when I was out, working at the church mission farm. Thanks to Abba Mai throwing his shoe disdainfully at him, now Birma furtively nodded at me but

---

14 A cultural practice in Islam of screening women from men or secluding women inside their husbands' or fathers' homes. Some married Muslim women are required to wear head coverings (hijab) and long, loose-fitting robes that hide their bodies in public. Some married women in conservative families wear black, full-length body robes from the head down and keep their faces hidden by black veils except for their eyes (burka).

15 An African ethnic group native to southern Bornu State, Nigeria, as well as in Cameroun and Chad.

16 A Muslim prayer leader and/or scholar, particularly an authority of Islamic law.

17 *Mai* is the ancient, traditional name in the Kanuri tribal language for king.

continued to barter over a wristwatch with a shopkeeper who claimed his jewelry came from France via Cameroun, which lay beyond the dry river bed behind my house. Abba Gana once sidled around me like Elvis, dressed in rhinestone shirts and smooth English denim until we learned he had spent time in prison for stealing fancy radios. Had Abba Gana abused the intimacy of friendship simply to case our household for trinkets to lift?

Our eagle-vigilant landlord demanded that we avoid these troublemakers, but we remained eager to engage, at face value, any villager who honoured us with attention in this intricate but bewildering society. In our daily struggle to learn Hausa and *Barebarici*[18] . . . not only to be present to serve through the local church but also to fit into the cosmopolitan West African culture that hosted us, we white Canadians welcomed many locals inside our lives, and bonded with them while trusting God to guide us all, every day. We hoped that Africans sought us for better reasons than just that we were rich foreigners who can help them with money and gadgets. Everyone desired fellowship but would we be so trusting and forgiving in our own fast-paced and impersonal Canadian society? May God help us embrace others, where ever we are!

We foreigners remained liberal and hospitable with the time and possessions that God gave us, acts which Abba Mai and his esteemed ilk found marvelously sweet, yet maddening foolish! We believed God went before us to Nigeria, made a safe space and prepared strangers to receive us. He also blinded our eyes to the ugliness bred by poverty and ignorance that Abba Mai saw every day so righteously in his own culture. Abba Mai, the insightful protector for us blissfully ignorant sheep, hated Mustapha for taking my money "on loan," because he knew this shameless man was both a thief and a rapist. When I, under his stern cross-examination, admitted to being robbed, my landlord vowed that he would bring Mustapha to heel in *one* hour, and return my 200

---

18 Hausa is a prominent lingua franca and market language used by various tribes to communicate in multicultural northern Nigeria. *Barebarici* is the Hausa word for the language of the *Bare Bari* (Kanuri) people.

naira into my hand, but I baffled Abba Mai by refusing such vigilante justice. *Why*, he implored, did I lower myself to befriend—even casually employ—Usman the fruit vendor, who cast evil spells and beat people, even killed his own mother in a fit of demonic rage? I explained to my incredulous arguer that Usman, who keenly knew the art of bartering and was fluent in five local languages, helped me sell many tree seedlings in the market; nobody dared cheat me with Usman working at my side!

What a misfit I was to search for goodness, even in the least of these! A less patient and understanding man than Abba Mai would have, within weeks of our arrival, washed his hands and cast me out of his community. He stuck by me, protected and cared for me, even if he secretly thought me mad. I often met a *mai hauka*[19] wandering the streets of Jos, looking unkempt, sometimes naked but able to converse with me in fluent English. In Canada, such a lunatic would be locked up and medically treated in some morbid asylum or left untreated to survive on the street, but African society showed more compassion by allowing its misfits to be present and function within their community. I was touched by the compassion and forgiveness shown when Colonel Ojukwu, formerly the Igbo rebel leader of Biafra,[20] defeated during Nigeria's brutal civil war, was released from prison twenty years later, into the embrace of his countrymen. I tried to honour such grace where I walked.

❖ ❖ ❖

We came to the remote fishing and farming community of Wulgo to be a Christian presence as well as offer agricultural and medical insights to local, dominantly Muslim society through COCIN's Faith & Farm and Rural Health outreach programs. Preaching Christ's gospel to

---

19 A mad person, possessed by demons or otherwise acting out of control.

20 Biafra, the Igbo-dominated and oil-rich eastern region of Nigeria, fought for independence from 1967 to 1970, when more than 2,000,000 civilians were killed.

unbelievers was not our mandate but were we, by showing compassion and friendship to fellow outcasts, proselytizing them into our faith of infidels? Abba Mai agreed that prophet *Isa*, son of Mary, was highly esteemed in the Koran, but he did not accept that this same Jesus came down from Heaven to save sinners and heal the sick and broken-hearted. Because Wulgo's rotten apples refused to follow the Koran, they were not Abba Mai's friends. He, a devout Muslim so esteemed and wealthy as to have made haj thrice to Mecca, gave no time or solutions for their problems. Neither should we, he admonished us every time such misfits lead us astray!

Abba Mai's stern, headmaster lectures began upon arrival, and continued throughout the three years we lived as slow-learning tenants under his roof. Shortly after a sunrise breakfast one April morning, during our inaugural week at our home away from home, Valerie and I rode our trusty Raleigh bicycles down the road . . . out of town . . . to Jagarawaje, some ten kilometres south of Wulgo, to meet our African Christian workmates at COCIN's farm and adjoining primary health care clinic, founded 30 years ago by the legendary white missionary, Dr. Ali Mission. We *sannued*[21] a long queue of patients in rudimentary Hausa, and watched awhile, impressed, as the African doctor and his male nurses kindly bandaged the wounded, gave medications or injections to the sick, examined babies and their teenage mothers, and performed circumcision on two 12-year-old Muslim lads. Leaving Valerie at the clinic where she was called to serve as a nurse, I toured the farm with Mathieu, my African farmer counterpart. He showed me two large fruit trees that, due to diligent guarding by his three sons, still held the odd mango or guava ripening high in their leafless boughs.

Mathieu sold neem and mango seedlings from the nursery; he encouraged purchasers to use such trees to hold back the encroaching Sahara Desert, while making a little shade and food to improve quality of life for their households. Even in drought, trees could stay wet by drinking one's greywater or drippings from a leaky faucet; if the ambitious *mai*

---

21 Said "hello" to in Hausa.

gida dug a hole behind his house and collected his family's wastewater therein, he could not only make a pond but stock it with fish that could be caught and eaten as needed to improve protein supply on one's dinner plate. Trees purchased from the church's nursery and planted around a fish pond would grow robustly from being well-watered; they would shade the pond, bringing refreshing cool that sweetened life for both humans and fish of the compound.

COCIN's orchard, supplied with good water from an on-site borehole, was a blessed oasis for those who managed it as well as those who purchased fruit and seedlings therein. Songbirds and wildlife lived safely with humankind in the thick underbrush among large, healthy trees that promised prosperity: lemon or banana groves, gum Arabic, date palms and tamarind, cashew or almond nuts, yellow cassia and pink desert rose. All was lush green because of water—a flourishing Garden of Eden—compared to the downtrodden dry grass and leafless, thorny shrubs on surrounding savanna plains.

Mathieu breathlessly extolled that the life-giving well, installed by the British during Ali Mission's time, was *artesian*: clean, fresh water rushed from a deep subterranean aquifer to the surface, under pressure and so hot it must cool one hour in the adjacent dugout before he could irrigate the farm's vegetable gardens or fruit trees. One of my first tasks as new manager should be to construct a sturdy, barbed-wire perimeter fence to keep out marauders that would otherwise damage the borehole valve or herd their sheep and goats among our cash crops. Many bush people, Mathieu cautioned me over a delicious lunch of smoked *banda*[22] and spicy okra draw soup drizzled on red sorghum gruel, believed groundwater should be free-flowing when springing from the earth; it had a holy spirit, being a gift from Allah. We stewards who read the Bible and knew Christ's gospel of salvation, however, must preserve precious water for the good of all.

Seemingly within a blink of an eye or the turn of a head, it was 5:00 p.m.—way past time for the new white people to head back to Wulgo.

---

22 Fish or meat dried over a fire.

Our return was pleasant in the cool of the day; the sun was setting like a giant red ball into the dusty plain, sweeping it with a crimson hue.

"*Barka da zuwa, turawa*"[23] or "*Ranka ya dade*,"[24] African people, some with raised fists, jovially greeted us beside the primary school, at the taxi stand, about the marketplace, and along the dusty street as they strolled, headed homeward or sat outside their houses, casually chatting before evening prayers.

Several men, dressed in flowing, embroidered gowns and colourful hats, milled about the street outside our garage door when we rode up. Abba Mai, noting our arrival with an eagle eye, stepped out from among his colleagues and strode towards me, while the others looked on in askance. He seemed glum as we softly shook our right hands and went through the conventional litany of Hausa cultural greetings— "Good afternoon, how is your family, how is your work, how is your health, how is the heat?"—for which the standard, stoical answer was "I am fine," "We praise God," or "Now is the time for it."

"Mr. Robert?" spoke up Abba Mai directly, in English, after dispensing with all this garnish, "Mr. Robert, I am looking for you now. Where did you go? Until now, we did not see you from morning, Mr. Robert."

"I went to Jagarawaje, to see the *asibiti* and *gona*,[25] where soon Valerie and I will work," I explained calmly, although inwardly surprised at my host's concern.

"That is very far now, Mr. Robert. There are many armed robbers along the road. It is too far for you to go on this bicycle. You must be careful; they can catch you at once by *moto*.[26] Mrs. Robert, you must not ride to Jagarawaje by bicycle . . .. Drive your car—that is better now."

We, chastened but chagrinned, got our landlord's drift but, to make sure, Abba Mai greeted us after supper, accompanied by his junior

---

23 Hausa greeting, "Welcome upon your arrival, white people."
24 Hausa greeting, a polite way of addressing a superior, of "May you have long life."
25 Hausa words for hospital and farm.
26 Hausa word for motor vehicle (i.e. motor).

brother Abubakar—who had received a Western education and could speak English well enough to teach children at the local primary school—to explain that we should inform them if ever we travelled away from the village, as bad people were about who might harm us. They also insisted that we should not bring black strangers into our quarters or hold Christian meetings there, as their family and neighbours would feel disturbed by loud singing and prayers by nonbelievers. We should go indoors by sundown, a wise safety protocol, which nonetheless became a command that even Abba Mai soon realized was hopeless after Valerie and I returned, walking through Wulgo late at night, during a week of rousing evangelistic meetings and fast-breaking celebrations held at our church outside town.

One evening, after enjoying supper and fellowship in the home of our teacher friends Imar and his wife Hannatu, I dropped my Toyota Light Ace keys in the sand, while Valerie and I walked by flashlight towards our house. Abba Mai and his fellow Muslim worshippers were dispersing from the mosque after evening prayers when we met on the street. He balefully asked why my van was parked outside our garage after dark; it should be safely put to bed. When I admitted having lost my keys, Abba Mai press-ganged twelve young men to pick up the dead Light Ace and carry it, like pallbearers moving a coffin, into the garage. My landlord then organized three from this crew to search for the keys. Despite my unbelief, I prayed hard and long for God to help me believe in miracles. Next morning, while I stewed over breakfast after a sleepless night as to how I would drive to the farm for work today, let alone travel three hours to Maiduguri, the Bornu State capital, on the coming weekend to meet my boss at COCIN Faith & Farm office, wryly smiling Abubaker brought me my keys. Lost was found, no questions asked!

My landlord was not impressed a year later when I, against his dire warnings, returned unscathed from a trip to Lake Chad through lawless territory infested with armed robbers. Leaving my pregnant Valerie to rest at home, I travelled 80 km north by hired taxi with Imar, Hannatu, her friend Maryamu, and my visiting MCC colleague John, to harvest Imar's winter vegetable garden. When we failed to return by sunset,

Abba Mai worried to Valerie that we had been apprehended by armed robbers. When we were still not home after he returned from evening prayers, a fuming Abba Mai took out his revolver and demanded that Valerie drive him down the road from Wulgo to Darak, a lakeside fishing port, to search for my lost party. At Wulgo's outskirts, Abba Mai acquired the village hunter and his loaded rifle to join the search expedition. Valerie regaled me, after I awoke from sleep late the next afternoon, how diligently, she, Abba Mai, and the hunter had scoured the Sahelian bush for many tense hours but had not found us or even heard about us from people they met in the way. They returned by one of many rough trails to Wulgo, where Valerie graciously dropped off the hunter, and she and Abba Mai gloomily returned to their compound, deeply troubled for our safety.

Yes, our party had returned safely at dawn but not without our own harrowing adventures to tell! We had harvested Imar's garden, but afterwards, I nearly choked to death on kelp soup served at a Darak restaurant; I survived by extracting something slimy and green from my wind pipe. Starting in mid-afternoon, our group encountered difficulties finding transport back to Wulgo. One taxi could only take us part way, to Allegarno; we then hiked for several kilometres to another village, where the only cab driver available was patching a flat tire on his vehicle. After vigorous haggling between him and Imar, the fellow agreed to take us onward after evening prayers but only for a high price, since we were following a dangerous road after dark; robbery was more possible with two white men on board, and we could damn well pay his price or walk! Anyhow, our rich payment did not meet the fare, which seemed to inflate with each rugged, nervous kilometre taken across the wild countryside. In the black of night . . . in middle of nowhere, we were suddenly dumped out and abandoned by the irate taxi driver. Downcast but determined, we continued our journey through no man's land on foot, with each person shouldering a heavy basket of vegetables and supporting one another with Christ's assuring words or songs. After an hour trekking in the chilly darkness, we saw headlights hurtling from far away and ran towards them. By chance, a transport truck travelling from Darak met us; by the grace of God, the Kanuri driver was from our village and knew me. He offered room in the cab and box and was happy to take all five of us and our heavy loads the rest of the way home, no questions or money asked! The next evening, Abba Mai celebrated our safe return with chilled colas and platters of spicy barbecued meat all round, in his shop.

❖ ❖ ❖

Yet, like ourselves, Abba Mai was a misfit within his own culture. He, the workaholic shopkeeper, wasted little time on such frivolities as prolonged visits, wedding parties, cultural dances, or fishing festivals. He ate indoors, rather than on public sidewalks with neighbours and friends. He played the revered role of imam but refrained from glad-handing the rabble as he swiftly, purposefully moved through the back streets of town: here to slaughter a ram and pray to Allah for the petitions of the man making sacrifice; there to check on his own rams grazing in a walled field behind our house; finally to collect payment from delinquent customers who recently acquired on credit an air compressor ordered via his shop or filled a jug of herbicide from a drum he stored in our rented garage. According to our Christian friend Bitrus, who was custodian at the government girls' (GG) secondary school south of town, Abba Mai previously taught Islamic Studies at GG but left that steady employment after a dispute with the headmaster over what Abba Mai perceived as immoral treatment of students at the school. This proudly fundamental believer was called an "Islamicist" by nominal Muslims; scoffers labelled him *mai fada* (the arguer). Yet, Abba Mai also was a father who loved his children, most obviously doting upon his son Abdu Salaam. One daughter he encouraged to become a college-educated teacher rather than marry as a child according to tribal tradition; he mourned the other who, despite his most fervent prayers, animal sacrifices and help sought from witch doctors, died young of yellow fever.

We Christian aliens, whom he chose to shelter beneath his protective roof, loved and respected Abba Mai for the kindness he showed us . . . his fervent devotion to God, who is the author of kindness. Bitrus recommended Abba Mai to MCC and helped our *shugaba*[27] sign him to provide lodging for coming white development workers. Abba Mai took a calculated gamble on us, misfits from Canada who chose to join with him our rich but mysterious cultures. We found that our common father had prepared a good host in Abba Mai. His home was a safe refuge for us to return to after the rigours of each sun-drenched day. Even in this ancient mud brick town located at the end of Nigeria's road network, a pinhead of humanity deep in the Sahel on the original shore of ever-shrinking Lake Chad, we lived as misfits on the fringe of society but enjoyed life!

The fiddler was bowed out, and his drummers were packing up their instruments. The contented midnight crowd, yearning for sleep, drew hands together in farewell then dispersed for home. These merrymakers may be misfits of tomorrow's society, but tonight, they danced in the mainstream.

(Robert with COCIN friends Pascal (L) and Istafanas (R), all dressed in traditional Bornu attire. Jagarawaje clinic compound 1988)

---

27 Hausa word meaning leader, head, chairman, or president.

MAY GOD MAKE OUR MUD LIGHT

BY ROBERT PROUDFOOT

Living as Canadian Christians in a West African Muslim community was a rich but challenging adventure. We were hailed in Wulgo's bustling market and labyrinth of narrow, sandy streets by regally gowned men, colourfully dressed women, and dusty children marveling after our alien appearance. We were given seats of honour at dramas and dances, lavished with jovial greetings by neighbours eager to teach us their tongue-twisting Kanuri language. We witnessed colourful pageantry from his palace walls as ministers riding horseback paid traditional homage at Durbar to the Kanuri Emir of Kanem-Bornu. Then, we were invited inside his cool and spacious, medieval palace to watch the *Shehu*'s[28] choice rams be slaughtered in solemn remembrance to God's deliverance of Ishmael, Abraham's first son through Sarah's handmaiden Hagar (Gen 22:1-14)[29]. Later, in dignified acknowledgement of our

---

28 *Shehu* is Kanuri name for Emir of Kanem-Bornu.

29 This is the Biblical account of God asking Abraham to sacrifice his son Isaac, but Muslims believe that Ishmael, Abraham's first-born son through Sarah's handmaid Hagar, was put on the altar rather than Isaac. Despite

willingness to greet him and live among his people, the *Shehu* wrote special greetings, offering land and women to his esteemed guests. Our Muslim hosts accepted us through our unguarded efforts to adopt their language, dress, and customs.

We came in peace, not to convert Muslims to Christianity but to quietly promote harmony and understanding between our two great, related religions. Muslims knew that we Christian development workers followed the teachings of the prophet *Isa*, son of *Maryamu*,[30] rather than their prophet Muhammad—peace be upon him—so they exempted us from participating in their religious ceremonies. It was lonely to live next door to our landlord's mosque but, as infidels, we were never permitted to enter it. It was even lonelier to eat and drink at home while the entire town suffered together through the heat of month-long Ramadan, when a devout Muslim was forbidden to drink water or even swallow his saliva by day. When the fast finally broke after sundown, we celebrated a token of spiritual purification in the food that Abba Mai's servant brought us to eat in our own parlour. How were we moved by their faithful works to feed begging boys—who should have been in school but, instead, were disciples of Koranic teachers in the bush? Why did we attend the lavish feast of some rich *alhaji*[31] who, having returned from a pilgrimage to the holy city of Mecca, married his fourth wife—a girl of thirteen? These were not our ways, yet we sought to be present and live peaceably for them within our host community.

Our uncertainty of how to embrace Islam received direction in February 1989 when, during Harmattan winter, we were given the rare

---

which youth was the intended sacrifice, the wonderful miracle is that God, recognizing Abraham's obedience, provided a ram for sacrifice, rather than took either of Abraham's cherished boys. Christians believe that this story foreshadowed God's sacrifice of his own son, Jesus Christ, as atonement for all creation.

30 Hausa names for Jesus and Mary.
31 Title given to a devout Muslim man who makes pilgrimage to Mecca, one of the five pillars of Islam.

privilege to participate in a traditional Kanuri funeral. I was awakened at dawn one blustery morning by Abubakar with solemn information that the visiting Koranic teacher, Abba Mai's "father" for the past quarter century, had died in our landlord's arms after a four-day bout with malaria. I was summoned to fetch the deceased's junior brother, that he might identify the body.

I agreed without hesitation, embracing death's sorrow, which suddenly enveloped our common household. The rising sun spilt over the dusty plain as Abba Mai's worker Yusuf and I sped fifteen grim kilometres to Gombaru, seat of the Local Government Area. Sunlight followed our path as we searched house by house for the old *malami*'s[32] relative. He took our bleak news calmly, even fed us dried fish and sweet potato cakes for breakfast while he prepared for the heavy tasks ahead. Eight scholarly cronies of the dead man filled my MCC van and sombrely accompanied Yusuf and I back to Wulgo. Arriving into a crowd of men gathered for prayer at Abba Mai's mosque, I had barely unloaded my passengers before he dismissed me of further duties.

Hurting for my landlord, smitten by the grief of his wife and dozens of neighbourhood women kneeling on prayer mats within her inner courtyard, my wife Valerie and I also prayed in the privacy of our own chambers for the mourners, and how best we might bring comfort. God's answer came quickly when Abba Mai reappeared in our doorway, requesting that I carry his visitors to the graveside.

Leaving Valerie to mourn with the women, I donned my Kanuri hat and gown in preparation for transporting funeral dignitaries. We loaded and followed the crowd trudging to a field outside town, arriving just as officials lowered the shrouded corpse into its pit. We quietly disembarked, I taking my cues from Abba Mai as we squatted on the ground among other silent observers. We all murmured our approval as the presiding elder consecrated each ball of mud that his assistant molded from grave diggings, then laid these mud balls on the corpse. The remaining earth was shoveled in and the unmarked mound sealed

---

32 *Malami* is a Hausa word for teacher or instructor.

with water to complete the burial. We tarried as the elder offered final prayers to God, then everybody dispersed for home. Before leaving, several villagers thanked me for attending, and affirmed me as a member of their community.

Only later did I realize that my spade had been borrowed to dig the grave and a jerry can of our drinking water used to make mud for burying the body. Did it matter that nobody had asked my permission to borrow these utensils? I was no stranger to death's grief, and felt called to compassionately comfort those who mourned, so I was honoured by Abba Mai's efforts to include me in his suffering.

Relating this experience—rare for Europeans—to a missionary friend working for COCIN's Kanuri Bible Translation Project, I learned that one standard Kanuri response to death was to offer condolences of "May God make his/her mud light." Then, I remembered the ceremonial seal of mud and imagined that entreaties had been made on the dead teacher's behalf, that God might remove all barriers to his soul's ascent to Heaven. I recalled the peace of the Lord's presence I had felt, even in that windswept, sandy graveyard, as I contemplated the departed man's eternity of sweet fellowship in Paradise.

It warmed my heart to realize Muslims' sincere reverence for life, death, and afterlife with the Creator of everything. As Christians, we believe God already made our mud light through Jesus Christ. I felt at one with my Muslim neighbours in their very human drama, and hoped to see them all again someday, in Heaven if not somewhere in this world.

BEHIND THE LEMON TREES

BY ROBERT PROUDFOOT

Aisha got married today. The honourable bridegroom, through his matchmaker emissaries, obliged Aisha's family with bountiful dowry and wedding gifts befitting her regal beauty and social standing: a three-medallion gold necklace, five exquisite Saudi dresses, and a suitcase full of cash! The imam and town crier took only five minutes to publicize this transaction in the mosque square but the couple's wedding ceremony unraveled with dawn-to-dusk tradition.

Aisha's father slaughtered his prize ram at sunrise to implore Allah's blessing upon this special day. Village women gathered outside his door soon after to pound maize for the wedding feast. Many friends ventured inside to plait Aisha's hair, paint her limbs with henna, decorate her youthful face with red polish, highlight her lovely eyes with black antimony, perfume her curvaceous body with exotic Arabia, and dress her to perfection in flowing bridal robes. Wedding gifts, accumulated throughout the morning, were presented to beaming Aisha amid yelping accolades from ladies-in-waiting: the essential brass bed with its frilly, flowery linens; boldly painted enamel dishes, trays, and serving bowls—the woman's collateral against destitution if ever divorced or widowed; and generous measures of rice, sorghum and maize for Aisha's future children who, God willing, would be many. The mystery groom, as custom, deigned not to appear . . . . In the late afternoon, he sent a rowdy cavalcade of revelers in taxis and lorries to fetch his bride to where he and his mates were partying at home in another town.

Aisha left home crying and afraid amid crowds of rollicking well-wishers. She was stuffed into an already jammed taxi like a sack of rice, carried limply sobbing on her mother's back from the motorcade to her husband's parlour, gaudily encouraged by old, red-toothed ladies and chanting children outside the wedding bedroom until midnight . . . .. Her innocence swallowed up by this one-way journey into the unknown, was Aisha not terrified amid her fleeting week of honour? Her husband's friends remained with him for seven days, feasting upon Aisha's perfect cooking and celebrating his joy with endless card games, soulful Arabic music, and bold discussions on worldly affairs. They lounged like kings on coloured mats along the tree-lined street while Aisha entertained her girlfriends indoors, amid attending to the honour and needs of her husband. The others could come and go as they pleased, but the bride must not venture forth, even to visit her parents, for another year!

Adults—a wealthy but much older groom, dickering parents, ambitious family, and matchmakers from both sides—forfeited Aisha's innocent childhood. Although barely 16, Aisha became entertainer, cook, housekeeper, and mother to future children of a strange admirer. She hardly knew his name, let alone understood his business or household wherein, she soon would realize, already lived three wives and twenty children. Aisha could neither read nor write, but her rigorous education from birth in domestic chores carried her well into a cloistered life inside her master's galleys. That she was the junior wife and, therefore, servant to the older housewives did not dull Aisha's starry discovery that she was presently her husband's favourite and, thus, receiver of fine gifts of jewelry and robes from his Lagos business trips. Her honour cloaked in the esteem of this *alhaji*'s Koranic learning and recent pilgrimage to Mecca, Aisha believed that he provided for her through almighty Allah.

Aisha was my friend. She used to greet me daily in the COCIN mission's tree nursery where I worked, when she came to fetch water for her mother. Aisha bantered with me there about many girlish things, not realizing how well she taught me her tongue-twisting Kanuri language. As we strolled hand in hand behind the lemon trees at the back of my nursery, picking fruit and listening to colourful birds singing in leafy boughs, Aisha innocently showed that, despite rigid cultural barriers in Muslim Africa, which separate men and women, she liked me and valued my friendship. She playfully asked for many things from one who loved but respected children—requests that grew from merely lemon fruit to photographs, empty tins and bottles to car rides, casual acquaintance to marriage. The last time we strolled together, our most intimate visit, I sadly walked away when Aisha brazenly picked three small and still green lemons and dropped them down inside her dress, after which she bid me to find *her* fruit!

This most poignant request I was unable to fulfil, for I was already a happily married man, with a plucky wife who worked in the nearby church hospital but had borne me no children. Abba Mai suggested that I marry a second wife who was fertile; Muslim men could take up to four wives, and his community boasted many worthy fillies to choose from! At times, during our long and casual walks behind the lemon trees, I wished again to be single. Aisha, half my age, made me feel young and frisky, a big fish in a small pond, the lauded poet and teller of funny jokes. In this staunchly male-oriented, traditional Muslim culture, I could have gained much stature for marrying Aisha, for then I would have two wives and increased my probability of becoming a father. Despite my Christian faith, Aisha's father would have gladly sold her to the rich white man for a few suitcases full of spare cash. He, valuing Western education, believed that I would provide well for his adventurous teenaged daughter but in a respectful manner; I promised not to break his heart, as locals might, by removing his beloved Aisha from him forever.

Other men cared not for Aisha—or daughters of other men . . . . Valerie and I were eating in a Gombaru restaurant one day when, suddenly, all diners were told to clear out so a Nigerian military general could privately entertain his cronies. MCC colleague John and I had to vacate the common room at a government guest house we were staying at in Maiduguri so that more important men could enjoy three teenaged girls who were stoically waiting nearby. Had I not been approached three times by Ahmed, the African bookkeeper at GG, who promised me that, for a mutually agreed-to finders' fee, he could provide me any of the female students I fancied for a pliable mistress? I was a rich white man . . . a big and important man. The girls I rented would pleasure me well in exchange for gifts and prestige. Nobody else need know about our business. I walked away from this devil and his temptation, far more angrily and resolutely than I could when Aisha offered herself to me. Ahmed should never learn that several of GG's ambitious young ladies visited Valerie and I in our home when, on school break and studying too far away from parents to go home for holidays, they sought a local sanctuary in which to relax, eat wholesome food, speak English, have a bath, and be treated kindly by adults.

I did not know then that, 25 years later, *Boko Haram*,[33] a fundamentalist Muslim group that despised Western education, particularly for girls, would kidnap and assault over 250 female students from Chibuk school, frighteningly similar to GG; nor that civil war between the Nigerian military and *Boko Haram* would render Wulgo and my idyllic farm a no-go zone. Lest I think that women are treated better by Canadian society, I received a rude reminder of our own failings in December 1989 (told to me by my *bahaushe*[34] shopkeeper friend Amadu in Wulgo's market, who had heard the jarring headline news on radio) that gunman Marc Lepine, blaming feminists for ruining his life, had killed fourteen female students or staff, and injured another ten women and four men at Ecole Polytechnique in Montreal. Returned to Canada

---

33 A fundamental Muslim insurgency force that is affiliated with Al-Qaida and is currently waging a guerilla war campaign against the Nigerian government in Bornu State. *Boko Haram* is dedicated to removal of Western education and cultural trappings, and for establishment of an Islamic caliphate in Nigeria.

34 *Bahaushe* is the Hausa word for a male Hausa speaker who is also of the Hausa tribe.

after MCC service in 1991, I was confronted by a sickening explosion of cyber pornography easily accessible on the internet, which exploited untold numbers of nameless young women and men to feed lusts of anonymous pleasure seekers . . . .

Yet, what did God want? What did my wife desire? Is not our Creator a jealous God who made humans in his own image? Valerie and I had made our marriage vows to each other sacred before him in love. Despite Aisha's inroad into my life, Valerie still loved me more and could not accommodate a rival relationship like Aisha could. This was more important than consideration of cultural and religious differences. How would Canada's bigamy laws regard me for importing a shoeless, uneducated child as my second wife when I returned home, finally, after three years of serving people in her West Africa? Although I loved Aisha as a friend, I already had chosen my life partner.

Amid my agony of how to treat Aisha justly, God took her away and allowed another man to marry her in a manner which, in their culture, was strangely fitting. Seemingly without warning—in the blink of an eye—Aisha was swept off her feet and carried into another dimension . . . . Since my many photographs taken of Aisha were probably circulated to this and other suitors for perusal by Aisha's father, I felt both jilted and responsible for the loss of my friend. Yet, time heals. She did not forget me. When we enjoyed the pleasure of a visit by well-dressed, happily married, and more mature Aisha in our village home a year later, Valerie and I introduced her to Mairam, our baby daughter, with sweet smile, blonde hair, and beautiful brown eyes: a princess given a Kanuri name in honour of Abba Mai, who descended from ancient tribal kings. Aisha was delighted for us, and we praised God for knowing what was best for all His people.

TWO BY TWO

BY ROBERT PROUDFOOT

Two young African men greeted me while I rested at home on a hot April afternoon. Although I did not know these pleasant and well-dressed fellows, I surmised that they were strangers in our community, travelers who did not understand local Hausa or Kanuri languages, yet spoke English fluently. I invited them into our shady, inner courtyard, brought them chairs to sit upon, and offered water to drink. While Valerie served us tea and biscuits, the young men introduced themselves as Thomas and Peter, brother evangelists from *Our Sacred Heart of Jesus Christ Church of the Living Word*. They were Christians from Anambra State in southern Nigeria, called by God and ordained by their denomination, to preach the good news of Jesus Christ to Muslims in the north, that such heathen countrymen might yet be saved.

"We want to proclaim the mighty power of our risen Lord to this wicked village," Thomas declared. "We saw your open-air market this morning, located on the main road near the transit station. It would be a very suitable place where to hold a crusade, at which our Christian speakers and singers could present messages of salvation to hundreds of people. We could erect a temporary stage, with electricity provided by

NEPA[35] for our microphones, speakers, organ, and floodlights. After the daily programs end, our team will engage those who come forward in the Holy Spirit. We can pray and counsel, do Bible studies, have worship services, give scriptural tracts . . . ."

When I gazed at him with trepidation, Thomas revealed purposefully, "Mr. Robert, our church is very large, prosperous, and blessed by God, but he has shown us his concern about the worldly spirit dwelling generally in this our homeland, which holds Nigeria back from being a great nation in Africa. The harvest is ready but the workers are few. Nonetheless, our church is sending evangelists, two by two, throughout northern Nigeria to see what can be done, how we can serve God. Our teams went to Sokoto, Kano, Bauchi, Zaria, Kaduna, Katsina and Maiduguri—not only to the big cities but also to small villages, like this Wulgo, where you live."

"We are very pleased and excited to encounter white Christian missionaries ministering right here, in the heart of darkness. Surely, it is God's will that we found you here! He has brought us together, so that you can help us to be successful in this important outreach. Mr. Robert, you could host and give us support, spiritually and materially, during the crusade. Then, you can help our team spread the gospel and follow up with converts long after we leave," Peter prophesied.

"I am interested in your project and would like to help you," I acknowledged. They, however, noted my reticence, which I tried to explain without dampening their zealous fire for serving our same Lord. "It is true, my wife Valerie and I live in this village to be a Christian presence and support COCIN, the local Christian church to which we were seconded by MCC, our Canadian church service organization. God opened a window into the Kanuri Muslim society through our living and working here for the past two years, where we have embraced language, dress, and many customs, thereby joining the local community."

"You must have many helpers among your North American churches who pay your salaries and finance your projects?" Thomas surmised. He

---

35 Nigerian Electrical Power Authority.

was enthusiastic and hopeful yet surprised to see a young white couple managing so well among nonbelievers, without electricity and running water, in this mud-walled, sand-swept medieval village. He offered brightly, "Our crusade could bring you many new converts to Christ."

"We are *not* Christian missionaries per say, but belong to a local Christian congregation that is already worshiping and serving God here," I explained patiently. "Valerie and I both work with Nigerian Christian colleagues at Jagarawaje, where I manage a small tree nursery and market garden for COCIN Faith & Farm, while she serves in the attached clinic for the sister Rural Health Program. We follow these helpful church programs, and do our Christian living as part of the COCIN Wulgo flock. We have cultivated many good friends here, both Christians and Muslims, who care about building bridges of understanding and friendship."

"Can we stay with you good people for a few days, until we can determine a course of action for our impending crusade?" Peter broached.

Both men seemed set on fulfilling their own agendas; like Jesus' disciples, they had come to Wulgo and sought out suitable lodging, without bringing any possessions but the clothing they wore.

"You are welcome to lodge with us, at least for tonight," I agreed. Remembering my landlord's strict rules regarding visitors, however, I recommended that we first go to greet Abba Mai in his shop and then visit the *mai bishara*[36] at our church on the south edge of town. "It is important that these authorities meet you and become informed of your purpose in our community."

I, noting with surprise that it was 4:00 pm, stood up and prepared to leave, so that we could complete our rounds before sunset. Although

---

36 Hausa Christian term for a church evangelist or "bearer of good news". Many small Christian congregations in Muslim-dominated, northeastern Nigeria were led by evangelists hired by COCIN and supported mainly by the goodwill of the host congregations. All of the evangelists in our district served under the spiritual and administrative leadership of a seminary-trained and ordained, Nigerian pastor.

the sky overhead was still bright and cloudless, the air was chilly and shadows covered my compound in the cool of the day.

"Mr. Robert," Thomas, retaining his seat, begged to differ. "Your landlord is a Muslim imam, and therefore, no friend to Christians. Brother Peter and I already met him when a village boy first brought us from the market to the Christian bookstore, after which the friendly Igbo proprietor showed us your landlord's shop. Mr. Abba Mai directed us to your door, but he was not pleased that we desired to visit you. We do not wish to bother this stern man anymore.

"As for your pastor, he is just a bush worker, without seminary training or English. He is not from our church, and therefore does not understand what we are called to do by God in this wicked place. Please sir, give us time to quietly look over this village with you, before we must introduce ourselves to others, and thus raise their suspicions."

"I will take you to the COCIN evangelist", I insisted. As I took the van keys that my wife handed me, she pointed out that we needed to drive to the church now in order to complete our visit before dark. Encouraging my glum visitors to follow me to the garage, I explained, "Malam Jonathan is a fair and congenial fellow, who wants to help all people who come to him in need. Even though Malam Jonathan speaks only Hausa, the language of our congregation, I understand it and will translate for you. We are the only Christian fellowship established in Wulgo, but we attract believers from many kilometres away, even French speakers from neighboring Cameroun, all who desire to worship God and help one another in the ways Jesus taught us. Please come with me now; we can talk further as we travel."

"As God wills," Peter conceded.

"We respect your views, as we understand that you also follow the Lord," Thomas added solemnly.

Both Nigerians smoothly arose and, one after the other, softly shook my hand. Turning to Valerie, they congenially praised her hospitality. Following the ageless custom of civility, Valerie happily accepted their accolades and curtseyed for them. They smiled when she promised a tasty supper of okra draw soup with fish on sorghum gruel for supper.

As I drove my two visitors towards the church, the hot, sandy streets were filled with villagers walking out and about. Men regally dressed in flowing, intricately embroidered gowns and caps strolled gaily with their friends, occasionally stopping to greet acquaintances, shopkeepers, or other men seated upon colorful plastic mats outside their mud-walled homes. Women, their elaborate hairdos covered by shawls, and their bodies wrapped in loose-fitting robes, walked chattily together or quietly behind their men. They toted water in jerry cans or carried plastic bags filled with produce or dry goods, often with babies riding on their backs and sometimes, accompanied by children bearing additional loads home from the market or taxi stand. While I carefully managed the van, my passengers intently took in every view—chaotic, vibrant, but old—along our route. Seated behind, Peter and Thomas kept their distance from me, but occasionally conversed with each other in their own, musically lilting language on topics that I could not fathom.

We were skirting the market and entering a road that I explained led to the church, when Peter interrupted, "Mr. Robert, we will leave you now."

"What?" I replied, dismayed by their abrupt request. "The church is close, less than one kilometre southwest from here. We can reach Malam Jonathan's house in ten minutes."

"Thank you, Mr. Robert," Thomas reiterated. "We must get out here, and review this market by foot for a while."

"Shall I park the van and walk with you? I can introduce you to some of my friends. There is also a small kiosk nearby where the proprietor serves fine ginger tea; we can sit and chat further over tea."

"Thank you, my friend. We can meet later, if God wills," Thomas suggested. He offered a pearly smile, although Peter's sombre eyes suggested there would be no such social opportunity, at least not today!

"Okay, suit yourselves. I will leave you now and continue to the farm, where I must greet Mathieu, who is irrigating our vegetable garden tonight." I good naturedly outlined my changed plans, even as my passengers disembarked and we stood together, shaking hands, beside the van. "I will return home after one hour. Please come for supper and a place to sleep for the night."

"We shall take your invitation under advisement," Peter offered stoically. He did not promise anything, but thanked Valerie and I for our hospitality.

"Yes, thank you, Mr. Robert. God bless you," Thomas chimed in. "If, God wills, we are able to secure this Sodom for a Christian crusade, you are whole-heartedly invited to attend."

"May God bless your efforts and bring us all to that time," I replied. Admonishing the Lord, I touched my heart devoutly, how I had learned from Hausa speakers who followed Christianity or Islam.

I felt sad, yet relieved, as we parted and I drove out of town towards Jagarawaje, I diligently checked with Mathieu but, as he had already left the garden and was shutting off the reservoir gate valve when I arrived, I apologized for not joining him earlier for the work.

"Strangers came from Enugu to visit me this afternoon; I was bound to entertain them. Now, I must return home, as I may need to host my visitors overnight," I explained. Frustration flashed in my eyes that concerned Mathieu.

"Are these men European?"

"No, but they are definitely foreign to this harsh place, like me, even though they are Nigerians."

"Enjoy their company then, and rest with tiredness until the morning. If possible, bring your friends to the farm tomorrow, so that they can see what we do here. Then, they can meet the church elders, and we will discuss their plans together."

"Sounds good," I replied. Appreciating Mathieu's salt-of-the earth wisdom and wishing he could take up his calling to become a pastor, I shook his hand in bidding him adieu, "Until the morning, my friend, may God raise us well."

I sped back to Wulgo at sunset, worried that I would find Thomas and Peter alone with Valerie, all waiting hungrily for supper to be served—optics that Abba Mai would not appreciate. They could be polite, and wait outside for me, but then Abba Mai and his Muslim prayer warriors might find the strange Christian pair lurking in the street, and demand to know their purpose. Perhaps Ezra, their Igbo compatriot who sold Christian literature on the opposite street corner from Abba Mai's shop and mosque, might take them in.

Slowing down as I descended the hill into town and creeping past the bus stop, I noticed that two well-dressed young men, who looked like Thomas and Peter, were boarding a coach about to depart for Maiduguri. They briefly regarded me, but did not reply when I stopped the van nearby and called their names. They resolutely entered the bus and left town.

❖ ❖ ❖

I did not see nor hear from Thomas and Peter again; their proposed Christian crusade for Wulgo never materialized under my watch. I was relieved, yet wondered, to the end of my MCC term and beyond, why such an exciting spiritual intervention did not happen. Had funding and manpower not come together or was *I* a stumbling block, who had discouraged well-meaning evangelists from doing God's work? Why had they come to us? Thomas and Peter had somehow heard of our useful mission presence in the Lake Chad basin and had sought us out from a far. . . . Had they, upon observing our worth for only three hours, deemed Valerie and I adverse to their holy mission and shaken the dust of Wulgo off their sandals at us, before moving on to greener pastures, in search of more receptive spirits? Why was I afraid of possibilities, when nothing was impossible with God?

I was afraid of how local Muslims, particularly devout followers of Prophet Muhammad's God-given teachings like Abba Mai, would react to a three-day blitz of zealous preaching, bold music, and strong scriptural reasoning for conversion to serving Jesus, imposed by "spirit-filled" crusaders from outside their village and tribe. Our local church held regular services on Sundays for its flock of believers; although the congregation participated in "spiritual renewal", offered Bible studies with visiting evangelists, hosted sermons by visiting pastors, and fasted in search of God's leading on certain concerns of faith, we lived quietly in order to survive within the dominantly Muslim society, and would never dream of preaching the gospel in Wulgo's public square. Thomas and Peter deigned not to introduce themselves to Malam Jonathan or the church elders; they refused to learn the experience or programs of our local Christian congregation or consider how we might collaborate in reaching out to Muslims. These zealous strangers would go it alone or not at all! Although from a different culture ourselves, Valerie and I belonged to COCIN as well as were part of local society. We were not great white missionaries come to change Muslims into Christians but humble, gentle people who wanted to be present and care about others in our community. Why should I inflame old hatreds simmering beneath the surface, and thus endanger my fellow Christians, by not only hosting these two visiting evangelists but giving them and their future teams a base of operations, blessing and support, to enable their attempt to take the entire community for Christ?

Valerie and I were supported by our MCC Nigeria country representative, who reminded us that the MCC program in Bornu State had nearly been shut down by the authorities in the mid-1980s, due to a Muslim backlash against a former MCC worker's zealous preaching in public, of the "one true path to God through Jesus Christ." This North American fellow had followed his heart to proclaim salvation to Muslims through Jesus, but his personal mission was not encouraged nor supported by MCC. It was extra-curricular to his MCC assignment to teach secondary school mathematics and science; Muslim students had rioted when they learned he was distributing literature that called followers of Muhammad to repent and convert to Christianity, since Islam "placed them into confusion and error". Had not MCC removed this zealot from Nigeria and apologized profusely to the Education Ministry and Muslim students for his antagonistic slander of their faith, Valerie and I would certainly not be serving in Bornu State, a scant three years later!

My sojourn in multi-cultural Nigeria taught me to remain true to my faith, but also to respect Islam as not only a sister religion, but a moral way of life, and valid path to God for the vast majority of community members. Valerie and I, like the smattering of Nigerian Christians who lived and worked in Wulgo, were vulnerable outsiders, but we all made the effort to befriend and walk with our hosts yet stay humble, because we wished to live in peace and harmony with them. We learned Kanuri language and customs; attended night markets, weddings or travelling shows; shopped locally; observed political rallies—such as elections for the local government assembly or to hear Sani Abacha, a Kanuri from Bornu State[37], stump for federal leadership; enjoyed soccer games and local festivals to celebrate end of Ramadan, bountiful fish catches from Lake Chad, or visits by the *lawan*[38]; took part in community affairs and were thus part of the community fabric. We greeted our fellow villagers everyday as we went about our various activities, but we also interacted while walking to and from church on Sundays. Good Friday was a Christian religious day that Muslims found odd but we could discuss it together, since they regularly worshipped at the Grand Mosque on Friday—their sabbath day.

During Christmas and Easter, Christians strolled through the village, greeting fellow believers for meals and festivities, but we also visited in Muslim homes and they, in our homes. I fondly remember how Malam Jonathan, while visiting us together with several of my Muslim friends, gently explained the Biblical account of Christ's birth using pieces of the nativity scene displayed on our dining room table. This ingenious nativity consisted of wooden figurines—human, animal and angelic—carved by a Maiduguri artisan, depicting Nigerian people and their cultures in celebration. I also enjoyed my annual *hadu*[39] of drinking a cup of freshly brewed coffee with Abba Mai early on Christmas Day, to

---

37 Sani Abacha, a Nigerian Army General and politician of Kanuri ethnicity, became defacto President of Nigeria through a military *coup d'état* in 1993, and ruled the country until his death in 1998.

38 A traditional ruler of Kanuri people and lands in northeastern Bornu State, and a vice regal representative of the *Shehu*.

39 *Hadu* is a Hausa verb meaning to be joined or to meet.

celebrate our friendship and various blessings in this season of goodwill. One Christmas, he helped me butcher a ram that he had chosen for me and blessed as *halal*[40], after which I distributed meat cuts to our various Muslim and Christian friends. Another Christmas, I purchased three sacks of maize seed from the market and gifted one each to Mathieu and Sama'ila – my African coworkers at the farm – as well as to Malam Jonathan. The *mai bishara* was grateful to the point of crying and hugging me for my unexpected generosity, as he and his large family were down to their last *mudu*[41] of sorghum for making *tuo da mia*[42] in the same season of need, when rainy season grain was long finished but winter vegetables were far from ripe.

A beautiful act of justice and grace was acknowledged in all the churches of the Gombaru-Ngala district when a local Muslim businessman returned his building, used for the past 20 years as a general store but originally a church, back to the Gombaru Anglican congregation. This house of worship had been seized and its Igbo parishioners, forced to flee for their lives during a 1966 pogrom, prior to the start of civil war against break-away Biafra in 1967[43]. After shelves stacked with

---

40 *Halal* is a Hausa or Arabic description for any lawful act done according to Islamic law and religion. Livestock to be eaten are ritualistically prayed over before they are slaughtered by having their throats slit, so that the blood drains out from the carcass and can be collected.

41 *Mudu* is a Hausa word for a measuring bowl of a standard size used in selling food grains such as guinea-corn, maize, or rice.

42 *Tuo da mia* is Hausa for a traditional African meal of a starchy gruel (such as made from maize, cassava, or sorghum) with which a thick soup of greens, cowpeas and/or some meat is eaten at noon or supper.

43 The Nigerian civil war (1967 to 1970) pitted the Nigerian federal government of President General Yakubu Gowon against the break-away, Igbo-dominated region of Biafra, led by Lt. Colonel Chukwuemeka Odumegwu-Ojukwu, former Eastern Region Governor in federal Nigeria, who had proclaimed its independence in May 1967. The war followed a power sharing impasse between Gowon and Ojukwu, as well chaotic social upheaval in 1966: assassination of Presidents Abubakar Tafawa Balewa

dry goods were dismantled and piled foodstuffs, relocated into a new shop, beautiful wall murals or stained-glass windows that depicted teachings of Jesus and acts of his apostles were rediscovered and found to be largely intact. They were, once again, able to inspire regathered Christian worshippers.

These sightings of God at work were too precious to lose. I thanked him for the re-grounded Anglican church and prayed that Thomas and Peter, indeed the vibrant and caring members of their church, were blessed by God, for they too were doing good work for the Lord in their various fields. I continued to pray for COCIN's many faithful, as they serve him and fellow Nigerians, particularly now when Bornu State is ravaged by conflict between the Nigerian military and *Boko Haram*. Despite our differences in who we understand Jesus to be, I loved my Christian and Muslim friends equally and honored them, with Jews, as children of the same book. Jesus himself said that he, the good shepherd, has many sheepfolds to care for. May Jesus continue to shepherd us.

---

and subsequently General Johnson Aguiyi-Ironsi in a military coup and counter coup, and a pogrom against Igbos in northern Nigeria, who were seen to have caused and benefited from the first coup. The civil war ended in January 1970 with defeat of Biafran forces, after three years of fighting and starvation, and some 2,000,000 civilian casualties. Ojukwu sought political asylum in Ivory Coast, but was pardoned by the Nigerian government and allowed to return to his country in 1982.

ROAD CLOSED UNTIL AFTER PRAYER

BY ROBERT PROUDFOOT

Something extraordinary happened as we waded through hectic Friday afternoon traffic in downtown Jos. City driving in Nigeria was usually chaotic, but Valerie and I could not understand why vehicles ahead were suddenly scrambling off the main drag. Leary to follow them blindly through the maze of narrow alleys choked with penny vendors and mudwalled shops, I stubbornly forged ahead, and ploughed into a throng of Muslims assembling for prayer!

Men of all ages, many attired in princely hats and flowing gowns, carried their prayer mats and water pots in solemn obedience to the muezzin[44] calling them towards Jos's turreted central mosque. They arrayed, then fervently bowed towards Mecca in oblivion to our embarrassing intrusion. Determined to leave their ritual in peace, I sheepishly reversed, and followed the traffic warden's frantic detour signals. A young cadet smiled beside him, and pompously displayed a sign, which expelled even my foreigner's ignorance. Its righteous warning "Road

---

44 A religious officer of the mosque who, standing in the minaret (tower), summons Muslims to prayer.

Closed Until After Prayer", embellished in Arabic, Hausa, and English, finally sunk in!

We drove more cautiously towards our apartment in Jos's leafy suburbs, admonishing ourselves for forgetting this pillar of Muslim culture. Even amid frantic modernity of Nigeria's tourist, tin mining, and Christian missions centre, was not Muhammad's *sallar Jumma'a*[45] solemnly continuing every Friday as it had done for over 1,000 years? Had we really learned so little about the people we served in Christ's name?

◆ ◆ ◆

Reflecting, more calmly and months later upon this incident, we viewed the road sign's message as verbalizing learning adventures that were daily enriching to our first year of working in Nigeria with MCC. God was very real, despite taking us far from home and placing us into an awesome new culture for his service. Had he not walked with us, we would have been unable to stand on the desert of Lake Chad basin as the only English-speaking *turawa* around! Patience which the Lord taught during our long wait to obtain placement, and clear visa and health hurdles, helped us gradually adjust to strange languages and cultures of our west African neighbors. We learned to live one day at a time in fullness under Christ's direction. As he promised during his beautiful mountain side sermon, Jesus heard our prayers, and knew our needs before we asked him. We rediscovered our mutual father while growing as guests with some of his other children, overseas.

Our journey of faith took us through various cross-cultural experiences. Village orientation in a small, mainly Christian community on balmy Jos Plateau commenced three days after our arrival in Nigeria. Despite little privacy, few communication skills, and no electricity or piped water, we enjoyed this honeymoon introduction into traditional

---

45 *Salla* is the Hausa word referring to each of five daily prayers of Islam. *Sallar Jumma'a* is the Friday prayer. A "salla" also refers to a religious holiday, such as *babbar salla* (Id-el-Kabir) or *karamar salla* (Id-el-Fitr).

rural living. Our bonding with Nigeria positively begun, we returned to Jos for four months of Hausa language training. Then, we ventured far to the northeast, seemingly backwards in time, to toil in the Muslim village of Wulgo on the beach of the Sahara Desert. We arrived in Maiduguri during a sand storm!

Our worksite and church fellowship reminded us of Jos because we associated with Hausa-speaking Christians from Plateau State. Yet, we resided with indigenous Kanuri in another, medieval culture of Arabic prayer calls, Islamic feasts and fasts, multiple young wives kept indoors, and holy men teaching boy disciples (*almajirai*) by firelight after dark to recite the Koran. Strange as these rival societies appeared, they possessed common cultural conventions, which were put aside when we gathered with our English-speaking MCC colleagues. It was a difficult challenge, fitting into each group as we went back and forth between them, but we thanked God for giving us patience and opportunity to try.

Nigerians already respected white people when we entered their country but it behooved us to earn that respect. We realized that sharp differences in upbringing prevented us from becoming Nigerian—even though our daughter, Annora Mairam was born in Maiduguri towards the end of our term—yet we sought to adopt local languages and customs as keys to entering the mainstream of Nigerian life. Nervously alone and illiterate on our first night in Wulgo, we discovered that villagers cared by greeting us, when we returned late from an evening bicycle trip to Jagarawaje. Our task remained to learn from our neighbors of how we might appropriately integrate into their sturdy, time-honored society.

We embarked upon two home-study courses to gain understanding of Kanuris' complex religion and culture. The former examined the Koran through commentaries of a Muslim scholar, to better ascertain thoughts and experiences which directed Muhammad's conveyance of God's message to his fellow Arabs. We studied under tutorage of a Christian professor of Islam, whose monthly reviews in Maiduguri increased our appreciation of what made Muslims tick. We utilized Kanuri language tapes and text purchased from COCIN's Kanuri Bible Translation Project, and invited its translators to make teaching visits to our home in Wulgo. Not only did these guests help break conversational "ice" with our neighbors, but their explanation of Kanuri grammar in English encouraged us to keep on greeting. Although many villagers (especially men) knew Hausa, they preferred to speak in their own language rather than the "market" vernacular historically brought from another tribe, and welcomed our efforts as opportunity to teach us Kanuri.

Language acquisition, patiently and respectfully done, was vital in our cross-cultural experience. Nigeria was a large country, boasting some 460 languages spoken by her 300 million citizens. English may have been the convenient voice of government, news media, and the educated elite, but it was just one of four official languages: Hausa, Yoruba and Igbo being the others, used in the north, southwest and southeast, respectively. Due to twenty major languages spoken, most Nigerians, out of necessity when doing business or daily living in their mobile patterns, conversed through various native tongues across the multi-cultural and sophisticated country. In Bornu State, they heard the Hausa lingua franca used for church or market communication, as well as local languages like Kanuri or Marghi, besides their mother tongue and colonially-imposed English to live in harmony. Nigerians' ability to learn through listening to everyday conversations put us unilingual university graduates from Canada to shame, who still stumbled along in Hausa and Kanuri after months of formal class and conversational sessions.

Living in Hausa and Kanuri allowed us to greet people on the street, converse with neighbors in their homes, conduct market business, work for COCIN, read the Bible, and intimately share in Sunday worship services. Local people—not to mention police and security guards we often dealt with at road checkpoints near our border with Cameroun—were pleasantly surprised that we made special efforts to learn their languages. Aware that most whites residing in Nigeria were unable even to greet in the vernacular, our African friends were eager to teach us more. They recognized our willingness to become vulnerable in Hausa and Kanuri as placing us on an equal footing with themselves, as they shyly strove to improve their English with our help. We helped each other, made the learning process a two-way street.

Valerie and I were amazed at how intimately language associated with culture and religion in the daily life rhythms of Wulgonians. Praises to God filled the simplest conversations. *Bisimilla* was an invitation invoked by the host before commencing a visit or meal. Expressions like "Praise God", "God knows", "May God raise us up well tomorrow", or "May God protect us on our journeys" filled gaps in speech almost by rote, even graced trucks and business signboards in bold praise for the Almighty. Muslims also retained Arabic greetings in deference to that holy language of the Koran. Kanuri greeters attached "*barka*" as a Godly blessing when welcoming or congratulating someone.

Christians coined new words to highlight their spirituality. The church used *Ubangiji* more than *Allah* when referring to God the father, and called Jesus Christ *Yesu Kristi* instead of the prophet *Isa*. Such common Christian terms as *sujada* (church service) and *addu'a* (prayer) seemed unknown to Muslims, for whom *salla* (ritual prayer) encompassed both. We learned to tread softly with our young Hausa vocabulary, however, as we developed friendships with both Christians and Muslims– our conversations should fit the context. Needless to say, the Lord's Prayer written in Arabic script upon a Koranic schoolboy's wooden *allo*[46] by our Hausa teacher (a Christian *bahaushe* who converted from Islam) as a language class graduation gift, became a hot conversation piece for visitors in our home! Both Christians and Muslims have developed special prayers to God, each with unique format and meaning.

Our growing confidence in Hausa speech allowed us to try harder, more often, but our glaring dearth of understanding still excluded us from intimately taking part in community life. How could we grow during those early months on assignment, when our evangelist spoke little English and we grasped but thirty percent of the weekly Hausa church service? Just when we seemed to make progress, somebody

---

46 Hausa name for the wooden writing board used for practicing Arabic script. Also, a scholastic blackboard or slate.

lost us by speeding up dialogue to normal pace or throwing in deeper vocabulary. Though I had to communicate in Hausa to function at work, how did I cope with daily language tests, especially when mockingly labelled by some as "No Hausa" or a child speaker, when I failed? It was even harder for Valerie, who was forced to learn Kanuri if she wished to mingle with the Muslim women of Wulgo, who knew little Hausa, talk less of keeping up her Hausa in order to communicate with fellow Christian women of the *zamunta mata*.[47]

We slipped many times but continued to learn; most Nigerians good-naturedly forgave our cultural clumsiness as typical foreigners' ignorance. Africans did not eat, shake hands, or pass anything with their left hand, as this limb was also reserved for toilet functions. We whites, aptly dubbed "People of the Left Hand" by one cheeky west African author, tended not to show partiality with either hand, and thus unwittingly insulted our hosts during various socials. Used to fast-paced, time-controlled, western society, we often forgot to greet or barter. These ancient African rituals, conducted in many languages, seemed more important than the monetary exchange passed between parties. Hausa and Kanuri greetings set a progression of stock questions and answers in motion, which continued at length before the heart of the matter surfaced, if at all. People initially indicated that all was well, even when not . . . one read between the lines, then patiently waited for bad news to be voiced.

Children and marriage were institutions in rural Nigerian life. Even if one had no children or was single, he/she indicated that the spouse and children were well, when asked during casual conversation. Those, especially women, who lacked either, seemed to be regarded with contempt! Although Valerie and I had enjoyed nearly five years of marriage, we were considered bride and groom by others until our daughter Annora Mairam was born in 1990.

How sweet it was to receive callers when one was ill, in mourning, or just returned from a journey! Like my host would be offended if I

---

47 Hausa name for the Christian Women's Fellowship group within the COCIN church.

refused to sample his fare, how important it was for me to have extra food and drink prepared in case visitors arrived—even unannounced— to partake from my bowl. Men and women ate separately, seated on mats, and preferably used their right hands or a compromise of spoons, to dip maize porridge from a common dish into the hot-sauce pot. We foreigners, who barely cooked enough food to feed our own families and then sat rigidly at table with separate service, needed liberation from our stifling individuality!

Friendships ran deep in Nigerian society and tended to be cemented between persons of similar age and sex. In this male-dominated society, a man must not be seen as coveting another's women or possessions. Sexual relationships were very discrete; being too forward with members of the opposite sex was frowned upon. Any woman who was not properly covered, openly socialized with men, or who lived alone in the village was considered a prostitute! Husbands and wives did not sit together in church, let alone socialize in public; this was initially awkward for us shy newcomers, but freed our personhoods the more we mingled—even held hands or danced—with sexual peers.

Despite all that we observed and learned, living within our village community proved easier said than done. We were odd celebrities, particularly to children, who swarmed around us at village functions, or followed us to and from the market, until some knowing adult drove them off with a stick, like cattle. Children were innocent, so patient and accepting, whereas many adults inwardly considered us as rich, feeble, and ignorant descendants of their cast-off colonial masters. Pretty girls, strong boys, and even grandfathers insisted upon carrying our loads due to our culturally superior status. Villagers flocked to us for money and medicine, believing that we dispensed these cure-alls from some endless treasure house. They expected our van to transport them and their loads where ever they needed to go. We sought to be a caring presence for Christ and MCC, but were we unkind, ungrateful to our hosts by not handing out fancy gifts to salve their many sudden wants?

Did our apparent opulence, inability to barter, and impatient willingness to pay high prices for service target us for those who coveted our privileges? We fought these labels every day when market hawkers expected us to pay twice the going rate for foodstuffs, or we were sought by souvenir dealers, fruit vendors, and beggars outside petrol stations or trendy supermarkets frequented by the rich. These poor street people were initially dumbfounded when I bought oranges for them to eat from a happy curb-side vendor, for they did not realize such odd *turawa* were already tending their gardens and could not feed them all with our lowly development workers' allowances. Yet, they kept coming, aware that we drove our shiny Peugeot sedan even when fuel was scarce or costly, and occasionally shopped in Jos's fancy stores for items not available in the bush.

Jesus said, "The poor will always be us." We could not listen to rumors that all beggars were in league to steal from the rich, for were not we from exploitive western countries that rigged the world market place in our favor, dumped toxic wastes or expired medicines on African shores, and pushed third world countries to quickly pay back expensive loans at high interest? Rather than try to assess each beggar's limitations, determine whether he or she was truly lame or blind, we made everyone a little happier when we passed food rather than money to outstretched hands. As for persistent curio traders, we compromised by purchasing some of their better wares to help the local economy, after briskly engaging them in enthusiastic Hausa bargaining.

I "got it" that Nigeria, although a relatively modern and thriving OPEC[48] nation that led the way for others in sub-Saharan Africa, had millions of poor and under-served people, but what of under-paid customs officers or policemen, who used their judicial power to harass Europeans into paying bribes? We chose to play along in congenial, patient Hausa rather than grease their palms for no reason, but suffered for taking the high road. Checkpoint guards regularly detained us, while locals freely drove through, until we showed that, by speaking Hausa, we were locals ourselves, not tourists. Customs officers delayed our passage back into Nigeria when we visited Burkina Faso for an

---

48 OPEC is the acronym for Organization of Petroleum Exporting Countries.

agricultural conference, even thwarted our attempt to board our jet in final departure from Nigeria, carrying our six-month old baby, until we would "help" them. Thank God, Athanasius was along to steer us through the red tape of *bature* departure when we were so tired and anxious to finally go home to Canada after three hard years abroad. These abuses typically occurred when we were travelling; we lived in relative tranquility in our village.

I was accosted in Jos by a policeman for making a wrong turn at his intersection; he threatened to confiscate my passport and throw me in jail, then forced me to drive to his superior at the barracks for further brow beating. When I still would not pay the subtly requested bribe, even when taken to barter with my MCC country representative, I was told by my superior to return this disappointed traffic signaler to his workplace. I suffered no penalty, but was all shook up with mental trauma and evermore mistrusted Jos policemen, nicknamed "yellow fevers" because of their golden blazers, not to mention their often-fiery tempers!

Our willingness to greet and interact with Nigerians earned us their grudging respect. We were, however, studied all the time by folk who survived with their own ingenuity and resilience in a country that struggled to keep up with mushrooming social needs. Unless we made a positive difference in the lives of our hosts, what good was righteous talk of "service in the name of Christ"? How did we contribute to Christ's work in a strange land? Some Christians back home suggested we hold prayer meetings in our home and promote evangelistic crusades to save Muslims, although local COCIN followers valued more the quiet, "practical" outreach through health and agriculture than winning souls to Christ through provocative blasts in the public square. Our African brethren believed that Valerie and I were more approachable to Muslims than themselves in Wulgo because we were a novelty and naïvely removed from underlying religious tensions. Church leaders who comprised MCC Nigeria's board valued our resilient spirits; they requested that we enlighten young Nigerians, mentor them to continue our good work before we quit the country. Our Nigerian co-workers rated church growth above North American MCCers' idealistic efforts to promote peace, social justice, and appropriate technologies in communities large to small. Religious conflicts could ignite civil war tomorrow but we, who were outsiders, could leave anytime for comfortable North America.

Being a Christian presence in a Nigerian Islamic culture was a full education. We lived for three years in Bornu State, but by the end, had only begun to understand this rich and diverse culture, and to consider what we could do, if anything, to improve things. I, fully spent, so admired the long-term British missionary overseeing COCIN Faith & Farm, who had lived in the land for twenty-five years. I hoped my caring witness showed that North Americans are concerned about Africans yet can learn much from them. We joyfully discovered that we held more in common than difference; I was encouraged at the evidence seen that God was present, shaping cultures which reflected his wisdom and creativity. We grew with the local people and hoped that they would continue to build their community, guided by God's mercy, wisdom and strength.

(Robert and Valerie with COCIN Jagarawaje mission workers 1989)

WHO OWNS THE DESERT'S JEWELS?

BY ROBERT PROUDFOOT

Nigeria's northern Sahel region taught me a stark reality: land and water are life to desert people! Parched land miraculously turned green during the short rainy season and grew guinea corn, beans, and okra, traditional crops that fed millions of folks over ten months of drought. Scrubby, thorny *adoua*[49] trees supplemented the diet with nutritious leaves and fruit. Bush rabbits, squirrels, monitor lizards, various birds, and the occasional impala provided meat when neither chickens nor goats could reach. Water cleansed a dusty world and stemmed its slagging thirst, particularly during the November to March winter, when relentless Harmattan winds, blowing south from the Sahara Desert, obscured the sun with sandy dust. Deep-set boreholes, rain-fed ponds,

---

49 Hausa name for <u>Balanites aegyptiaca</u> (L.) Del., a small to medium-sized, semi-deciduous tree that is thorny and produces elliptical, yellow fruit that are edible. Native to the Lake Chad basin of northeastern Nigeria, *adoua* has been cultivated for thousands of years in desert countries like Egypt as a fruit tree, while its dense but manageable hardwood is used for making bowls, handles of household and agricultural tools, fence posts and barriers, and also as fuel for charcoal.

and reversing waters of immense but shallow Lake Chad, fed by rivers flowing in from greener lands far away, were jewels so rare as to give life-sustaining lustre to the desert.

I managed a small plot of farmland, blessed with a sweet artesian well, near Jagarawaje for the COCIN Faith & Farm program. The farm was fenced and treed with shelterbelts and fruit orchards; within this secure oasis, Mathieu and I raised hardy tree seedlings for sale; grew onions, vegetables, and sorghum; and utilized appropriate technologies designed to curtail the desert's advance. Our high-yielding borehole replenished these lush market gardens, as well as provided water to the adjoining COCIN medical clinic and met the domestic needs of farm and hospital staff living on the church compound. A powerful Christian outreach to the surrounding rural society was COCIN's continuing effort to supply, not only agricultural produce, farm chemicals, improved domestic chickens, and primary health care but also clean drinking water to a nearby girls' boarding school (GG), 500 neighbouring Muslim villagers, and countless nomadic herdsmen. First drilled in 1973 by British engineers, the borehole bequeathed to COCIN—together with its considerably older hospital and agroforestry farm started by white missionaries—still glistened with hope in an otherwise barren landscape when I arrived on-site in 1988.

This hope was severely jolted in 1990 by a significant drop in the water supply. Our dry season cash crops suffered moisture stress from our inability to maintain daily irrigation needs. Efforts to save the market quality of onions, tomatoes, and lettuce by continuing applications throughout the day (as opposed to traditional morning irrigations only) depleted water pressure at public-use taps. Villagers initially showed their displeasure by coming into the farm in twos or threes to demand water. This want surged into a constant, disruptive stream. Rather than grant visitors access to the borehole, Mathieu and I patiently filled their buckets but, in serving the needy, our own work lagged behind schedule . . .. We reduced our irrigation program in return for patience by other users but such patience, although hard-won, was fickle and fleeting. The crops did not complain but then, what voice had they except to wilt on hot, windy days?

This rigorous give and take collapsed as cool, dry winter gave way to April's scorching heat and harsh deprivations of the month-long Ramadan fast. Mathieu and I could no longer bid for patient scheduling of water consumption by others when we continued to daily irrigate our market gardens—which always appeared heavenly lush and burgeoning—to crowds of dusty, thirsty indigents who, armed with jerry cans and basins (and donkeys or wheelbarrows to carry home what borehole water their heads could not), daily migrated into the COCIN compound from outlying taps. They squabbled over trickling water as they bathed, laundered clothing, and washed grain amid the growing rancour of long-suffering church folk upon whose doorstep these hordes camped.

The hospital staff condemned the excessive use of dwindling water by farm staff, for *what*—making vegetables look more juicy, ripe, and firm for market? Where was our faith that God could bring rain in its due season to replenish the earth? Not only was our cosmetic but reckless over-use of a precious, God-given but church-owned resource robbing hospital workers and their families—the *majority* in the COCIN compound—of morning cooking and bathing needs, not to mention water to wash wounds and sterilize medical instruments at the hospital . . .. Mathieu and I also deceived these unwanted and ungrateful bush people massing at their church oasis from the surrounding wilderness with empty promises of water, later on!

Then, the medical workers threw their own curveball: they demanded full access to well-watered farmland inside the fence! Since the hospital was opened years before by white, SUM[50] Christians (like a lady doctor who lived on-site but rode a camel to attend patients at even remoter bush clinics or Doctor Ali Mission, who climbed Gwoza Hills or sailed *Albarka* and *Albashir* hospital ships equipped with operating theatres

---

50 Acronym for Sudan United Mission, a Christian mission group from western Europe, including the UK, who established churches and outreach missions that eventually came under COCIN authority during the 1980s.

on Lake Chad), Christian Africans had farmed the church land for their food. Who was I, a recently arrived foreigner with no concept of local culture, who spoke baby Hausa, to deprive black-skinned people yet brothers and sisters in the Lord, of their nourishment? I forced them to eke out their living on rough and unprotected ground far from home, at the mercy of ravenous livestock and ignorant herders from the Muslim enemy! Aware that the farm had not produced a profit under my bature management, medical staff thwarted me like bandits, cutting the fence and introducing their own sheep to graze on our vegetable gardens.

Initial efforts to solve this land use crisis, like with the water dispute, ended in a noisy, acrimonious impasse. The COCIN Faith & Farm program directors in urban Maiduguri were slow to concede anything, yet expected me, their trustworthy and educated white man on-site, to "patch things up." Strategic options must be considered, rather than prolong the sideshow dispute among local Christians who, after all, worked, lived, and worshipped together and therefore should stand in solidarity. I was sick from dysentery and malaria, while Mathieu's wife Louisa suffered a relapse in mental health from mounting tension. Finding no relief, Mathieu and I resorted to chasing people away using harsh words and locking the farm gate in their faces when they sought not only drinking water but also free vegetables, fruit, and even green leaves to eat. In defiance, they cut locks, broke taps, and invaded the farm in droves, crawling under fences to swarm the almighty borehole. When Mathieu and I, armed with staves, sternly guarded the valve and refused to open it unless they fell back, our desperate customers mocked us as servants of *Iblis* [51] rather than Allah! I dipped water for 40 customers one night in the hope that they might finally realize that I also suffered but my peace was fleeting; next morning, they returned bright and early for more—Aisha among them to be entertained rather than supportive—while *my* aching back was so stiff, I could barely stand!

This grinding charade illustrated our superiors' experienced but jaded reasoning, in the first place, for fencing the borehole and piping

---

51 Hausa name for Satan.

— Enduring Art, Active Faith —

water for school and village to taps safely beyond church property lines. Thirsty people struggling for water regarded this precious resource as God-given for all and would not be denied their drink! I shuddered at my boss's bleak recollection of a broken, ever gushing borehole, where users swam with their livestock in a lake as the *why* behind his refusal to capitulate to groans of heart-wrenching need. He had seen such irresponsible waste, *many times*, during his twenty-five years in the Nigerian mission field. We must protect the borehole for the common good. To open that other floodgate—let medical staff farm church land—he argued further, meant folding our agroforestry tent *gaba daya*[52]!

I reluctantly agreed that we could not surrender land and water and still make a profit for the farm. I also feared losing years of careful investment and vision implementation . . . .. Yet, as a Christian and an emerging DELES[53] worker who promoted community development for the poor, I grieved that our "improved" farming practices unjustly deprived our Muslim neighbours of water, and put us in conflict with anxious fellow Christians also trying to survive in the harsh desert that likewise was not their home. I was emotionally troubled, oppressed with foreboding as I left my smiling white boss at his home within tranquil church headquarters in Maiduguri, and trudged back those long 200 km to the wild frontier . . . ..

I was barely back to work at my post when swirling frustrations on all sides exploded in anger! Some villagers threatened me with violence and curses if Valerie and I did not leave at once for our own place. COCIN's Medical Director, who saw our piddly farming operation as a stumbling block to obtain a legal land title for the entire Jagarawaje

---

52 Hausa expression meaning simultaneously, all together, all at once.
53 Acronym for Development, Education and Leadership Services, a Nigerian Christian effort, which facilitates community development, training workshops to improve economies, education, and social livelihoods of people in rural areas of the country. Their motto is one of balanced spirituality: "Act justly, love tenderly, and walk humbly before God" (Micah 6:8).

complex from the federal government, brusquely offered to buy Faith & Farm out, lock, stock, and barrel and send us "agrics" packing!

If Mathieu and I had any real purpose, it behooved us to rebuild trust and communication within our ailing family. I, the great white agricultural teacher, acknowledged that I did not sufficiently understand the local language and culture (though I lived in them) to solve everything myself. Rather, in reviewing DELES's 3 Cs (Cooperation-Campaign-Confrontation) skill, I saw myself cartoonishly depicted as the fat, cigar-smoking oppressor, against whom little but empowered DELES agents worked for just change. I arranged meetings with village and dispensary leaders, but somebody with more clout and wisdom was needed to facilitate conversation.

Gilman Ruwanzafi, COCIN's regional administrator and a senior Nigerian pastor with regal bearing and years of counselling experience, responded five times to my SOS calls. He brought along Mathieu and I, plus our British Faith & Farm manager Brian and his Nigerian assistant Ishaku, to dialogue with our perceived adversaries. Whether sitting with Jugudum in the shade under the Jagarawaje chief's prized almond trees, greeting the *luwan* in his air-conditioned office in Maiduguri, or eating spicy okra soup and cassava gruel on colourfully woven plastic mats behind the hospital with local medical staff and their director, Pastor Ruwanzafi patiently drew out issues of dispute from various parties but encouraged collaboration towards meeting constructive, mutually beneficial goals. This skilled mediator used DELES's "Big ears, small mouth" approach to generate themes. Under his lead, farm staff explained to Jugudum that recent engineering tests showed that the borehole's underground aquifer was depleting and that an off-stream storage reservoir should be quickly constructed to help conserve water for all users. The village chief responded by offering labour and financial assistance to this joint construction project. Jugudum's concern for a guaranteed water supply for his people and their livestock was further relieved by Faith & Farm's promise to replace the leaky village water line. Medical staff were granted garden plots inside the farm fence. All parties agreed to improve communication and cooperation on quality of life issues.

These promises bore fruit, and we grew to see one another as neighbours in the common struggle for prosperity, rather than as adversaries for control of the desert's jewels. Chief Jugudum's proverb that "ten heads are better than one" in solving problems made sense that parched day in late June when we filled an empty pond so his livestock could drink. With approval and advisory help from Christian farm and medical staff, an assembled crew of Muslim villagers promptly spaded a ditch through which borehole water was conveyed to the stock pond. The chief gratefully granted all COCIN staff additional farmland adjacent to the compound; he vowed that his herders would respectfully keep sheep and goats away from our crops. Prior to the advent of the summer rains, an able crew of Jagarawaje labourers helped me construct the water reservoir and build new water pipelines, with tools, equipment, and wages provided by the church. Thus, we helped one another.

Successful conflict mediation depends upon patient, open-minded discussion and exchange of interests and solutions between parties; study of each other's language and culture, which encourages adaptation in resolving conflict; recognition of existing social structures; and taking time to cool down and objectively review the facts of a dispute. I felt that West Africa's custom of greetings and patience shown in gradually, indirectly approaching problems is wisdom learned over time, which I took home to fast-paced, head-on, individualistic North American society. This time-honoured wisdom helped people survive with less and even enjoy the desert's jewels.

DANGEROUS GAME

BY ROBERT PROUDFOOT

Lions and leopards were wild animals I always feared. They were kings of beasts who hunted their subjects mercilessly for meat: zebra, elephants, wildebeest, and water buffalo who sought water holes and green vegetation across vast African savanna. Stalking the flanks of herds by the cover of darkness or the cool of dawn, watching their dusty and desperate migration from shady bluffs in noon-day heat, these stealthy feline killers selected defenseless babes, the sick, or stray, tired oldsters to feed upon. Lions and leopards crouched in shadows, waiting for the best moment to attack—then suddenly, with ferocity and speed—sprang upon their unsuspecting victim. These savage majesties were called fearless, even of man . . . the most feared by men were the man-eaters! Bwana big-game hunters who hung trophy lion heads on walls, or threw leopard skin rugs on floors of oaken drawing rooms, enhanced their exploits with swashbuckling tales of hunting such ferocious foes.

I learned to dread another type of manhunter while working for MCC in northeastern Nigeria. Bornu State's military governor deployed special forces, code-named Operation Lion in 1989, and Operation Leopard in 1990, to hunt down and execute known criminals at large. Many persons sought were suspected armed robbers, hated by Nigerian society for their vicious attacks on citizens, from Maiduguri's gated mansions to bush taxis plying lonely trails around Lake Chad. Others were petty lawbreakers of various stripes. One butcher in our village was wanted for cheating cattle herders when buying their animals for slaughter. Another villager ran an illegal gambling den. If offenders written on police lists were found, they were shackled and taken forthwith to secret internment camps. Then, upon confirming accusations of two or three witnesses, any unfortunate prisoner could be shot without delay!

I observed these predators in action as they skulked about in the bush near my farm, or roared into unsuspecting villages with armoured cars, hoping to bag some sleeping quarry. One day working at the COCIN farm, I found spent bullet shells in our maize field, which Nigerian staff who lived on the place claimed was litter from target practice done lately by some "lions."

Such wargames seemed like harmless fun for the cops, to break the harsh tension of duty, but I shuddered when my friends or neighbours became prey to these unflinching executioners. Just six months into my MCC farm manager term, all men from nearby Jagarawaje village were arrested and imprisoned in Maiduguri, accused of aiding armed robbers who terrorized the bush trails to Lake Chad. Eventually, most of these small farmers and shepherds were released; only their chief and Idris, the town "enforcer," were tried and sentenced to one-year jail terms with hard labour. Harsh prison conditions aged my friends severely; Idris could not hold a job, and Chief Hassan was forced to relinquish his title to a younger man after their release.

Jugudum, the new chief, gave me Idris as foreman to direct other Jagarawaje men when I sought local labourers to help us construct a clay-lined irrigation reservoir on the farm. Working together daily with this thug tried my patience as Idris continually lobbied for more wages and benefits for his workers; yet, Idris understood how to collaborate with Europeans as well as generate trust, cooperation, and effort from fellow Africans. I resonated with his unvarnished comradery, and was impressed by the skill and work ethic that this mason showed in completing the project before summer rains came, using local materials, community labourers, and appropriate technology, at one-third the cost of a concrete block dam. Idris introduced me to his hard-working farm wife and four daughters—all striving at their parents' urging to achieve the highest Western education possible; he became my friend and window into local Arab culture.

A jaunty delegation gathered to commemorate the reservoir's maiden filling with water from the adjacent artesian borehole: Muslim labourers; Christian farm and hospital staff; our MCC friend John, a civil engineer who had designed the structure; other European or Nigerian church dignitaries who came out from Maiduguri; Abba Mai and Chief Jugudum; Idris and I. Impressed that the berms held, we all cheered when Mathieu opened the steel gate valve and let impounded water run out—like draining a giant bath tub—and flow, with strong head pressure, through irrigation delivery ditches to vegetable gardens in the field beyond. Everyone celebrated our shared achievement by drinking chilled Coca Colas I had purchased from Abba Mai's shop, and feasting on roast chicken and crisp salad tossed with our own garden greens, made by Valerie, Louisa, and other Nigerian women from the rural COCIN compound. Farm and clinic tours showcased our collective work and witness in Christ's name. It was a glorious day, yet it was, sadly, short-lived!

Idris was caught in Operation Leopard's dragnet and imprisoned shortly after the new reservoir was inaugurated. For the next week, Christian and Muslim friends agonized over his uncertain fate. I desperately sought to visit Idris in prison and attest to his good work, in hopes of securing his release, but my closest friends advised me to lay low and wait for a better time. They feared that my public association with a repeat offender would implicate me in his crimes. Did not Christians already suffer within the dominant Islamic culture for following a foreign religion bankrolled by Europeans? Our poor little congregation lived on shaky ground since a local Christian businessman had duped the *luwan* into giving him land outside Wulgo for to build a bakery, which cleverly morphed into a church . . . .. This quaint, mud brick building with a zinc roof would have been destroyed, likely with Christians worshipping inside, by an enraged Muslim mob, had not God placed His guardian angels in the way! Local Christians gained a strong ally with arrival of a *bature* parishioner (me), but then false witness spread among disgruntled Muslims that I had constructed a barbed-wired fence around the farm without duly purchasing the land for commercial crop and fruit production from the Kanuri traditional ruler . . .. If only my COCIN Faith & Farm supervisors in Maiduguri had explained local politics, before ordering me to build that damned fence! They counselled me to do my work quietly but keep my head down; I should not meet the *luwan*, let alone explain to His Highness that the fence was meant to keep others' livestock from damaging our sorghum fields and vegetable gardens, grown on a small plot that his father had bequeathed, years ago, to the church!

Now, *I* had hired Idris—a serial felon! He had been taken away, shackled by powerful lawmen who would decide his miserable fate, once and for all! We could only watch over his family, and pray to Allah for mercy while the authorities passed sentence. Abba Mai who, like many Nigerians, hated armed robbers who violently stole what they did not make or earn, and often killed their victims who lived uprightly, dissuaded me most urgently when I vowed to visit Idris and vouch for his innocence. I should not rush in where angels feared to tread!

"Mr. Robert," Abubakar counselled late one night at our courtyard while his senior brother, Abba Mai, looked sombrely on, nodding in agreement. "Mr. Robert, you must not go to the police, asking for Idris now. He is in Allah's hands and will be dealt with justly. Whether Idris is released or is punished, such is Allah's will. If you try to visit him or even ask about him, you risk trouble on your head, since the police may suspect you as this *Shewa*[54] man's helper—an armed robber like he is. Therefore, you should not seek Idris now, Mr. Robert, only pray to Allah that Idris may receive mercy. Trust Allah, Mr. Robert . . .. That is best—the straight path."

---

54 Kanuri word for a local Arab tribe that lived within their traditional territory.

Although Abubakar and Abba Mai meant well, they failed to comfort me after I dreamed fitfully one night that Idris had been executed for some petty crime never proven: *allegedly* stealing another man's bicycle! What if it had been *my* bicycle or precious *van* that he had grabbed, Abba Mai tried to reason with me? My landlord, a rich shopkeeper who had been violently held up before and now kept a revolver under his robes, wanted me to realize that, even though I was a rich and privileged bature, I had no clout with the police. How well did I really know Idris, that I should care about him? Idris was a thief and bully who hurt others . . . .. He deserved to be punished for his crimes!

Months later, Idris was released from prison; he visited me one day while I flood-irrigated vegetables at the farm. We greeted one another with thankfulness to Allah and for each other's prayers that the merciful and all-knowing creator had kindly answered. Others tied to the farm or clinic who gathered around and greeted Idris were glad to know he was safe. They lauded the reservoir and dispensary *salgas*[55] he had built that still worked so well!

Idris was too feeble to serve me, but I gladdened his heart by showing him how powerfully, yet precisely controlled by man, water flowed about the farm in ditches as it drained from the reservoir. Instead of everyone agonizing over water shortage to the point of fighting and threatening Mathieu and I as borehole's keepers, we all stewardly shared the vital, thirst-quenching liquid. As negotiated by all area users during our recent palaver, Mathieu filled the reservoir at night and irrigated trees and crops during the day with this stored water. Fresh water flowed during the day, with proper pressure, from the borehole through an underground pipe to the clinic's tap; GG's tanker truck could also be filled as needed by its driver from another spigot to supply drinking water to the girls' secondary school. Once a week during the dry season, we filled a dugout constructed between the church property and the Wulgo-to-Ngala highway, to allow passing herders to water their thirsty livestock. Plenty of drinking water was still available, directly from the borehole

---

55 Hausa word for pit latrine.

mouth, when Jagarawaje women or girls cheerily requested Mathieu or I to fill their buckets. Idris, the master builder, was glad he had helped restore peace . . . .

Abba Mai did not share my joy that Idris again walked free on the earth—nor was he impressed with my stupid compassion when another strange friend's fate proved fatal.

❖ ❖ ❖

From the moment we met Yusufu at the Durbar,[56] in Maiduguri, Valerie and I believed him to be the *Shehu*'s learned, world-travelling, teaching nephew. Through him as our personal tour guide, self-proclaimed ambassador of Kanuri culture, history, and royalty, we glimpsed the inner courts of the *Shehu*'s palace. We heard of godly blessings, royal greetings and grants of land, scholarly chronicles of ancient tribal history going back to Kanem-Bornu's kingdom centred at Kukawa, and of Usman dan Fodio, who led the 1804 jihad against Hausa and Kanuri kingdoms he deemed too worldly . . . .. All these tenets were dictated from the Shehu into Yusufu's verbose letters that followed our initial encounter. Then, this jovial prince arrived unannounced at our rural home, to encourage our trust with sound royal advice on ambitious farm and community development projects.

Abba Mai sensed, upon first glimpsing our house guest during evening prayers, that Yusufu was a dangerous imposter—a violent man running from the police. Abba Mai did not kill or even accost this intruder, but came to me privately and required that I put Yusufu into an outward-bound taxi by sunrise, before he robbed us blind, or the authorities caught their quarry in our home, and accused us all of harbouring a criminal. By then, this stranger had slept in our guest room for two nights, eaten with us, played with our baby Mairam, listened

---

56 A traditional Kanuri festival held annually at the *Shehu*'s palace in Maiduguri, where tribal princes assemble on horseback to swear allegiance to the *Shehu*.

as Valerie shared about Jesus's love for all people, toured my farm and community . . . after which he promised to broach his venerable uncle to provide electricity and piped drinking water to all local subjects. Yusufu had prayed five times daily at Abba Mai's mosque . . . where he had been marked as phony by Wulgo's believing Muslims.

How could Yusufu be, as my Kanuri landlord and follower of the *Shehu* harshly suspected, an armed robber hunted by Operation Leopard? Wincing for my astonishment at unvarnished reality, Abba Mai surmised that this thug could, flush with new funds taken from rich but gullible *turawa*, keep running east over the Nigerian border into Cameroun and Chad. Were hotly pursuing police to learn that we had harboured Yusufu in our home, we also could be shot as his collaborators!

When I admonished him for being so suspicious, Abba Mai argued vehemently, "Would the *Shehu* send his nephew to you wearing rags, without fine *kaya*[57], letters of introduction or royal greeting? Mr. Robert, this your stranger has no money or government card to prove that he is a teacher now. He is an imposter and very dangerous. Mr. Robert, put Yusufu out! He must leave Wulgo at once!"

Our friend, when confronted by me early next morning with this judgement, agreed with gentle resignation to return to Maiduguri. Besides, he pled to be ill with malaria, and was uncomfortable with our strange food and harsh living conditions, so the bus ride home—generously paid by me—was a blessing in disguise. Yusufu, looking tired and old, thanked me for my gracious hospitality before joining the bus at Wulgo's marketplace. Our friend did us no harm, but left quietly, almost like a lamb going to his impending slaughter.

I did not see or hear from Yusufu again. Six weeks later, we saw a public execution of some sorry rogue on television while we tried to eat our lunch in an upscale Maiduguri restaurant. My landlord sombrely informed me, upon our return to the village, that Yusufu had been

---

57 Hausa word for loads of goods, tools, ingredients, and/or clothing associated with one's activities.

executed as an armed robber by the Nigerian law court. His death by firing squad had been confirmed by radio broadcast throughout the land—I grieved, having viewed it on television, like I had been present and even pulled a trigger!

This bombshell was relayed with calm self-satisfaction by one who knew everyone, including armed robbers and other criminals in his village, by name, if not by face. Abba Mai, whose workers, clients, goods, and person were always potential targets, was grimly thankful for the tenacious success of government security forces in cleansing Nigeria of such vermin. The country, he claimed, was spoiled by a bad economy, and people were dangerous. Lions and leopards were needed to protect the innocent. My unanswered question was: what about innocent persons who fell under deathly judgement when maliciously or ignorantly, yet falsely accused?

The road was short and straight from Maiduguri's Robbery and Firearms Tribunal office to old borrow pits outside the city where convicts were tied to poles and shot. Those who lived by the sword died by the sword. What about those troopers who killed such violent men under the authority of Operations Lion and Leopard? Had they not also learned to kill without mercy, like savage jungle beasts?

What did Valerie and I learn from these painful experiences? We realized, yet again, that we were naïve strangers in the African culture that flourished around Lake Chad, but our belief was strengthened that God went before us, to prepare for us a space and people with whom we could enjoy community. We understood that God worked in mysterious ways, but why did He take us halfway around the world, and place struggling fringe people like Idris and Yusufu, as well as solid citizens like Abba Mai, into our path? Idris and Yusufu, although labelled by their society as dangerous men, became our friends. Idris built a strong reservoir and useful latrines, and thus helped me solve a water crisis at the COCIN farm. Yusufu sought sanctuary in *our* home when he fled the police, and was grateful for our loving hospitality and witness given—despite great personal risk—during his last, desperate days on earth. God alone understood the hearts and circumstances of everyone that he created. He called Valerie, Abba Mai, and me to be faithful and compassionate in a difficult place, whatever our circumstances, just as he was with us—with all creation.

(Tiger and Eagle Masks 2005)

THE GUARD

BY ROBERT PROUDFOOT

The Greenburghs sat, deep in sober conversation, in the cozy parlour of their rambling stone house. They were a close-knit family, but a bit on the large side among Europeans of Lusaka's expatriate community: a father, mother, and four stair-step children, including two daughters sandwiched between two sons—rambunctious teenagers all. Mr. Hiram Greenburgh, a seasoned diplomat within the British High Commission to newly independent Zambia, had returned—not two hours ago—from a fortnight of high-level talks in UK, deciphering results of the 1972 Pierce Commission's test on acceptability to *all* Rhodesians of the Hone-Smith settlement, proposed by white leaders in London and Salisbury, to assuage the increasingly unsettling business of rebellion since the colony's Unilateral Declaration of Independence seven years ago. Assuming that his loved ones knew how to apply themselves usefully within their various circles, the father had left his plucky family behind in Africa for the first time in two years. He had not forgotten them, but was anxious to know how they had fared during his travels abroad. Now, at home and in the relative safety of their sitting room, the family told him how the other side of the coin lived through turbulent days' past.

Conversation quickly soured when it screeched around this sharp corner of history. A litany of grievances aired—mainly by clambering children while their long-suffering mother sat back on the chesterfield, looking drained yet relieved by her husband's return—centred around one man, tall and dark, who had guarded the compound under Mr. Greenburgh's hire during his absence. This security guard had come into their lives two weeks ago, as an unknown African protector, but had left this grey, rainy morning as a criminal. The family gave Mr. Greenburgh place to pass final judgement, but as he listened to fragments from a seemingly impossible tale of theft and betrayal, he sensed frustration and anger directing the witnesses.

"You say that fellow stole our pet—a *puppy?*" Mr. Greenburgh inquired.

His tanned, middle-aged face was etched with surprise. Perhaps he had been snowed under by bureaucratic paperwork during those hectic weeks before flying to the UK, for he could not remember any cute little animal frolicking about other than Bruno, the austere and seasoned family watch dog.

"He did indeed, sir!" Leroy blustered, the elder son. "That dirty wretch tricked us into believing he was a dedicated night watchman, but then he walked out our gate this very morning with little Ragamuffin tucked under his arm!"

"But!" James piped up. He, despite six years Leroy's junior, was seemingly the more open-minded son. "We didn't *see* Winter take Ragamuffin."

Mr. Greenburgh scrutinized both boys who, on the surface at least, were equally telling the truth . . . albeit at cross-purposes. James jumped in to be heard; Leroy stormed to lead. This angry lad should channel his restless energy hard into academic studies now that the University of Zambia had reopened, nine months after some reckless fellow students had rioted at the French embassy, incensed by France's controversial decision to allow South Africa to manufacture Mirage fighter jets. Rather than enroll in a stable British or South African university, Leroy had diligently stayed the tougher course like a plucky British lad, reading his textbooks, gardening, and running errands for the family while waiting in Lusaka for his local classes to resume. He had bucked his father's solution to hire a guard—insisting that *he* was old enough to protect the home front during his old man's absence. This nineteen-year-old had obviously suffered under the strain of missed academic studies, and now readily displayed emotion that had bunched up during a turbulent fortnight of enforced manhood. *Who* was Winter?

"Winter Banda is a sneaky snake, a disgrace to his people! To think, after all we whites have done to help Zambia, he'd steal from us!" Leroy chafed.

"How do you know that Mr. Banda stole anything. . . er, it's Ragamuffin you say?" Mr. Greenburgh broached. He clarified with unseemly diplomatic fuddy-duddy when the children gazed gloomily at him, although he seemed hesitant to believe such outburst. Compared to Rhodesia's troubles, this domestic tale of woe was embarrassingly trite.

"*We know*," Leroy growled. "That blackguard played tricks on us *every* night."

"His rash conduct betrayed him, Papa—I was afraid," Maryanne added, Leroy's beautiful blonde sister. Her blue eyes glistened with tears.

"Start from the beginning, children," Mrs. Greenburgh suggested.

Hiram gazed incredulously at his wife: she was pale and withdrawn; anxiety wracked every inch of her body! *What* had befallen this bouncy and intelligent socialite of forty years? Indeed, his loved ones were all changed, troubled in ways that the returning diplomat failed to appreciate. He desired peace and quiet . . . . A hot toddy would be nice to relax with beside the glowing hearth fire after his arduous labours to improve Africa, but such luxury he now could not enjoy.

Leroy, pushing to speak for his household, glared at his mother, but a smile finally crinkled his austere, sunburned face. In some ways, pre-ambled this rugby and football champion, secondary school leader, and top-scorer for his Form VI class on Ordinary Level examinations, the guard's antics had actually been quite amusing, but when exposed to them nightly of late, such bizarre entertainment had made for an awful experience!

"When Winter came here the first night, he was immediately Bruno's enemy. We didn't think anything of it then—most expatriates' dogs are trained to go after Africans—but Bruno knew right away that guy was a crook . . . he *behaved* like one! We kept Bruno locked in the house when Banda was here. Although he always arrived well-groomed at sunset, this shady character later skulked around our compound hatless, with uniform unbuttoned. Our guard sometimes brought along his mates: tall, scowling brutes dressed in fragments of uniforms, who smoked cigarettes and carried clubs. They didn't leave until well after dark. Banda invited a different lot every night, like they were casing the joint! They felt to outsmart us, but I could distinguish between such louts—as could Bruno and the neighbouring dogs that always barked at them."

"You mean, including that fine German shepherd belonging to Judge Halpern? Can't be—Halperns no longer live next door."

"Yes, Papa, but the dog stays on with his new owner. I see Toppers every day, sitting regally on the front veranda, when I cycle past to and from the International School. Now the garden stays very neat and trim, since Boswells moved in—not like that old jungle," reported Julia. The pretty face of the younger Greenburgh girl grimaced with disgust.

"The judge deployed prisoners to occasionally clean up his yard, yet it was overgrown as wild bush when his wife got beaten up last summer."

"I remember that terrible night!" Mr. Greenburgh, startled by Leroy's chilling memory, pondered grimly his own. "Halpern was away, presiding over the court on the Copperbelt, when thieves ransacked their house.

"You would think Sir Godfrey knew better, having served down here all these years—since *colonial* times—that it was unsafe to leave white women alone in such a fine house, unprotected. There were too many desperately poor and hungry natives around; they considered rich foreigners like the judge—like *us*—as targets, despite what good we did for their new country. Nobody heard Lady Halpern's screams for help as she fought with those robbers. We knew nothing of her plight, we who lived next door, just behind our lovely red bougainvillea hedge! It was like all our gardens and walls muffled the calamitous sounds, and Africa's dark, silent night swallowed the intruders . . . . Such helplessness caused me to hire a guardian for my chicks."

"Banda and his pals acted like they owned our place; they roamed about the garden, armed, sullen, and silent . . . looked in windows . . . trampled flower beds, harassed our houseboy's kids . . . and generally made a nuisance of themselves."

"They stamped down my mint border, Hiram, just like that rabble did to Edith Halpern's gardens after she and Sir Godfrey pulled out for the UK after the robbery. Those heartless natives stomped out the Judge's memory from their land . . . and we intend to stay on in Lusaka for three more years?"

"Don't take our situation so seriously, Janet!" Mr. Greenburgh implored. "Please, think of our children—they are all the value we brought here, really. The Halperns hoarded vast treasure behind their fortress walls. They were well-known, but despised remnants of an oppressive colonial past, whereas we arrived here unheralded, our reputations clean, to help Great Britain humbly keep the faith with her aspiring young friends in southern Africa."

"Dad!" Leroy grated. He rolled his brilliant blue eyes in exasperation. "What happened, *happened*—just like we are trying to tell you! These security brutes made a damned nuisance of themselves. They terrorized us in our own home."

"Like *we* Europeans did to Africans, Son, not only over a century past but continue to do so . . . even *today*, in Rhodesia, Mozambique, and South Africa! It's *their* country; we're guests here. We come to black Africa with the inherited respect of white missionaries and colonists, but it behooves us to earn that respect," Mr. Greenburgh philosophized. His diplomatic armour was still polished yet showed fatigue and frustration from recent set-tos with the Rhodesian Front[58].

---

58 Rhodesian Front was the conservative political party that governed Rhodesia (now Zimbabwe) after its Unilateral Declaration of Independence in 1965, which illegally elevated the British colony to a sovereign state controlled by the white minority, until escalating African guerilla warfare, international sanctions, and world-wide public displeasure forced transition to black majority rule in 1980. Rhodesian Front, led by Prime Minister Ian Smith, was supported by white colonists who were opposed to immediate change to black majority rule in Southern Rhodesia, after independence of Zambia

Hiram listened, intensely impressed, but the rest of his long-suffering family would not keep quiet long enough to soak in any sage advice. In the face of their mounting opposition, the warily unconvinced diplomat demanded, "What have Banda and his so-called thugs to do with *our* theft?"

"Robbers, yes!" chimed in Julia. Her sapphire eyes gleamed with intrigue, even if Maryanne smirked at her childish report. "Papa, just this morning, Mrs. Johnson—who sold us Ragamuffin—had the rest of his litter taken . . . lifted! Zapped! Mrs. Johnson's own guard was the culprit!"

"Really?"

"Who else could have been inside her compound before sunrise?"

"Our district's night watchmen must have some sort of league going," Janet whispered.

Hiram chuckled wryly, enjoying his family's odd tale of skullduggery.

"Isn't it ironic how security guards are really thieves, who do all sorts of mischief when they go on duty?"

"I still don't believe that Winter did anything wrong!" interrupted James. "Maybe someone else, but *never* Winter. He was a good chap."

When the others looked at him askance, this young, blonde lad—crisply dressed in khaki shorts and collared shirt, his woolen stockings neatly folded below the knee like a proper British schoolboy studying in southern Africa—blushed. Tears welled up in his piercing blue eyes as he blubbered, "Winter read English novels and solved complex mathematical problems to help me with homework. He was my friend . . .."

"Kid's just sticking up for the bloke, Papa," Leroy growled. He feigned a punch towards his little brother, but could not dismiss the little twerp to their father, who seemed surprised by the advancement of young James during his absence. Leroy glared at this thirteen-year-old knave as he continued to campaign hard against the guard, "*Nobody* else was assigned to patrol our property except Banda. Okay, so the

---

(formerly Northern Rhodesia) and Malawi (Nyasaland) marked the end of the British colonial Federation of Rhodesia and Nyasaland in 1963.

guy could read and write—he worked our sympathy by claiming to be enrolled part-time in secondary school—at *his* age?

"It's part of Securicore's drive to create a good reputation within the expatriate community, but that company knows nothing about its staff. When we telephoned this morning to report the theft, the idiot on seat in Securicore's dispatch office didn't even know who Winter Banda was, nor could he recall who *we* were! Mum practically chewed his ears off!"

"I say, Janet," Mr. Greenburgh drawled. He cast his wife a rakish smile.

"Papa, we bet you a thousand pounds that Securicore does nothing to help us," Maryanne and Julia posed collaboratively.

They were not joking as they firmly shook their father's gently clasping hands. Everyone else laughed when Mr. Greenburgh accepted their wager, tenaciously yet with a playful twinkle in his tired eyes, for which the girls were not impressed nor surprised—he typically did not take them seriously unless his cute little pets disobeyed him.

"Those headquarters people are slave drivers," James argued. He seized the momentary lull to vouch further for his mysterious friend. "Did you know that Mr. Banda works a different job by day? He goes on duty at State House every morning. Winter needs money, he told me, to support his wife and five children. How can you expect *any* man to perform like a robot for twenty-four hours per day?"

"As such gave him no right to sleep on our doorstep," Leroy countered. "Banda was quite the electrician, I must say! That security light over our front door blazed for about three hours each evening while he did his homework, and ate the supper we gave him. After the place quieted down, however, that creep removed the light bulb from its socket, and slept the night away. About dawn the next day, he cleverly fixed the light before going home. I don't know how Winter did it; most people would get shocked performing such a trick!"

"Leroy, you've been lounging too much around the public swimming pool, and listening to idle gossip from expatriate sunbathers. I've told you before: don't acquire such hollow intolerance," Mr. Greenburgh chided his older son. "Aren't you taking advantage of free afternoons to catch up at university? We live like kings here, what with Zambian servants doing all yard and household chores that any adolescent back home would normally perform, in addition to school! Why harp on Mr. Banda's conduct?"

"It's scary, being a guard," James added. He was encouraged now to hang in there on Banda's behalf, but this bouncy lad, Leroy noted with annoyance, could hardly keep still, and was just waiting for others to breathe so he could interrupt, spouting poppycock. "How would you guys like to sit up all night, waiting to fight armed robbers? We have a safe compound; at least, Winter could relax here."

"We gave this fellow everything but look how he repaid our favours! Banda behaved in total opposite to his given duties! Bruno and I could have done a far better job," Leroy maintained.

"And *that's* the rub," Mr. Greenburgh ascertained. Recognizing how his older son showed his manhood, amid others' glum sighs, he cautioned, "Though, I don't understand your malice, Leroy; you burn Winter Banda in effigy for allegedly stealing the family puppy, but your little brother loves the man! What did the guard do that truly was so wrong?"

Mr. Greenburgh put up his hand diplomatically, but he was too late in begging clarification! With his two angry sons suddenly rumbling on the floor before him, the returned father demanded a truce, like timeout, *now*! The stalwart referee waded into the donnybrook without breaking a sweat, and pulled out two shouting and flailing boys by the scruffs of their necks. He set them back down firmly on the couch opposite him and sternly interrogated them, determined to get to the bottom of this unseemly guard incident.

"What is this ruckus, boys? If you have become so upset as to fall to fighting, I shan't be going on diplomatic missions abroad in future—I have too much domestic work to settle here in Lusaka. What the deuce happened to you lot during my absence?"

"Our security man let my three chameleons out of their cage, a week ago," Leroy divulged. He glared at his kid brother, daring him to oppose, but this time, James zipped his mouth, and simply nodded as he gazed drolly at his red-faced father. "Banda explained to bro here that lizards were evil spirits, and that his people feared them exceedingly! We've never found our pets since, but now a strange, scurrying sound emanates from the attic. Nobody dares to find out what sort of devil—if any—lives up there!

"Banda did another odd behaviour," Leroy continued. His eyes became wide with excitement as he recalled an unnerving incident from the guard's third night on duty. "I passed through the kitchen on my way to bed, when something caught my attention through the window: the figure of a man—black as ink—stood in the carport, grinning slyly at me. I thought I was dreaming for, when I looked again, the apparition was gone.

"I went to bed, but then the smiling goblin reappeared, and danced outside my bedroom window. This was real—no joke! I panicked when I remembered that the garage was unlocked. A host of handy valuables were stored out there, waiting to be stolen: bicycles, lawn mower, a large canvas tent, two automobiles . . .. I quickly dressed, and called Banda to help me catch the intruder, but then a curious thing happened: the stranger ambled out of the shadows. When he nonchalantly passed me at the screened kitchen door, I realized that here *was* Winter Banda! He shuffled by brazenly, bare-headed, and rolled his eyes at me like some drunken fool—did he think *I* was the idiot? Luckily, nobody got hurt, and nothing was taken."

"I awoke one midnight in a tremble and saw *him* leering through my window at me," Maryanne confessed. She appeared breathlessly distraught, even now, to her fuming father. "I knew this peeping tom was our guard but Winter, flagrantly loafing out of uniform, could have been any intruder. Thank God, he left me alone!"

Maryanne, although a year younger than Leroy, had recently aced her O-Level exams, and would soon be leaving Zambia for boarding school in the UK to do Advanced Levels, then to study medicine at one of her homeland's finest universities. This beautiful and talented daughter was Mr. Greenburgh's pride and joy; like her father, she held wanderlust and a compassion for less-fortunate people. Maryanne might join Britain's far-flung diplomatic service, or return to the tropics someday as a missionary doctor. What could she do with the dodgy likes of Winter Banda?

"He was a hindrance all right," Leroy complained. Not knowing when to quit, the lad was pleased when his father's placid countenance turned hard and surly. "I kept the garden hose on for one hour after dark to water our flower beds; with Winter guarding the compound, I didn't need to shut off the tap. He not only closed the water, but roughly yanked away the hose from the spigot—an unnecessary bit of business, if you ask me . . ..

"He certainly irritated us during his stint here, but I was the first family member to get off my hind end and do something about that strange bloke. Mum became worried too, but she concealed her fears until three days ago, when I overheard her talking to Renfrew about our guard."

"Oh, ho!" Hiram remarked.

He gazed with keen interest upon his deflated, rather nervous little woman. Renfrew was their housekeeper, but the esteemed Madam of the House rarely turned to a servant for advice.

"Renfrew should know what to make of this guard, Hiram," Janet stated, suddenly defensive. "He understands his people better than we do. I believed Renfrew when he insisted that Winter Banda was not a good fellow."

Leroy remembered something odd that had happened only yesterday. Mrs. Wynn, the Barclay's Bank manager's wife, had come over for tea to discuss preparations for a church bazaar the ladies would organize for a fortnight hence. Mrs. Greenburgh had confided her problem to the older, more worldly-wise lady, but as was the usual case, Mrs. Wynn behaved too worldly to ease tensions. As a last resort, her younger host had related Renfrew's version of the guard.

For the first time that evening, the suffering family managed to laugh when shoved by the youth's raw description. "That old bag gave her views loud and clear! Like, 'don't believe the imbecile! Renfrew's no judge of human character!'"

"She said *that*?" Mr. Greenburgh demanded. He searched first Leroy's face and then his wife's, in astonishment.

"She did," the burly white youth asserted.

He exuded an air of satisfaction as his mother nodded drearily.

"Gloria has never really been kind to our houseboy. She fired Renfrew when he was working for them, because the man allegedly stole liquor," Mrs. Greenburgh divulged.

"I believe what Renfrew says about Banda," Leroy insisted, overriding his mother's stumble. "That clod would go back to the *kaya*[59] every evening before making his rounds. I don't know what Banda did then, but I am certain that Renfrew does."

Mr. Greenburgh, disappointment etched upon his red face as the unvarnished bigotry of his *own* people sank in, oathed with iron resolve, "By Jove, I *will* get to the bottom of this! I'll speak to Renfrew tomorrow straight away, and if need be, go to the police, and have Winter Banda arrested for theft and trespassing. Then, we'll get some answers, straight-up!"

Just then, the excited and shrill voice of little James shattered his family's agony. Standing and pointing out the picture window, the lad cheered, "It's *him*! My friend, Winter Banda has come back, and look: he's carrying our little Ragamuffin!"

James ran eagerly outside, followed by his stupefied brother and father. Incredibly, James spoke the truth! Their African visitor was dressed in a dark suit rather than his imposing grey and orange guardian's uniform, but having discretely shut the gate, he walked nervously into the yard. The other Greenburgh males somberly stood by, now washed by setting sun, watching as the newcomer halted and greeted James; the boy, not afraid or even leery, jovially went through with him the ritual of soft handshakes and pleasant salutations. Banda then handed over to grateful James a woolly grey poodle, who gaily barked salutations. When James released this squirming puppy into his home

---

[59] Vernacular slang for backyard, where the servant quarters are typically located.

yard, Ragamuffin gleefully ran about the lawn, checking out familiar flowers and shrubbery. He returned to play loyally at his young master's feet while James and Winter continued to chat amicably about shared topics of interest.

"Banda shows some nerve!" Leroy grumbled to his astonished father as they observed this touching reunion from afar. "Why has he returned?"

"I don't know," his father replied, stiffly advancing, "But I shall find out."

The guard started when he felt Mr. Greenburgh enter, like a fireball, the shade beneath the great jacaranda tree, but he dared not falter—he had come with too important a proposition in hand. Leroy sauntered smugly behind his father, but it was Mr. Greenburgh whom Banda crisply saluted.

"At ease, man, and good evening," Mr. Greenburgh greeted briskly in return. They navigated through a raft of polite formalities by asking each other about the weather, Banda's health, his white family's general condition, the guard's work, the diplomat's travels abroad . . . etcetera, etc. Then, Greenburgh suspiciously demanded, "What can I do for you?"

"Good evening, *Bwana*[60] suh," explained Winter politely. "I come to ask about job, *Bwana* suh."

"Job? Don't you already work?"

"No, *Bwana* suh. I have no job now, since my captain sack me proppa today. He say: I am old man now, *Bwana* suh, too old to guard President KK's house. Suh, I want to be guard at your house."

Banda's horse face was so cast down that flabbergasted Mr. Greenburgh pitied him. Leroy scowled, for he had encountered such clowns before, requesting to borrow his schoolbooks or sturdy Raleigh bicycle from Britain.

"He's lying, Papa, I can tell," Leroy whispered. Then he took old Greenburgh's lead in a powerful, unsympathetic voice. "You stole Ragamuffin, and now you want us to hire you as a full-time guard?"

---

60 Term of respect, meaning mister or sir, used by Bantu Africans when addressing a man of superior social status, including a European man.

"No, young master, Winter did not steal. Winter is a good man. The little dog, he went walking . . . he run away . . .. I find him today, suh, and bring him back."

"Where was he walking?" the father questioned.

The guard pointed to the corner of the house, where an archway straddled the footpath into the back garden. He said in his deep, raspy voice, "I saw him."

"Come again", the father asked. Hiram had trouble following the guard's rapidly pointing hand.

"There, *Bwana* suh," he repeated politely. Banda's ebony hand swept up and down the red laterite driveway.

Leroy, whose eyes were sharp as a whistle, noticed a subtle difference in position. Indeed, the fellow pointed up the driveway on the other end of the house. Leroy broke into laughter when the guard changed his mind.

"I saw him there this morning," Banda insisted. He pointed to a rock pile that lay outside the gates. "That little dog, he walked on the road, going to downtown."

"Papa, it's obvious," James interjected. He looked serious now, having gently released Ragamuffin whom he had been tousling and cooing. "Our adventurous little puppy got loose from the yard too early this morning. Winter Banda found Ragamuffin wandering on the road, recognized him as ours, and returned him here now. This good fellow did his job, and deserves praise and possibly a *dashe*,[61] not a scolding!"

"What about that man staring in our windows at night?" Mr. Greenburgh demanded, sombrely unconvinced. "Was he *you*?"

"Ah . . . no suh, mercy no!" Banda moaned, wounded by such accusation. "He was a thief. I saw him there, Bwana, but I chase him out. He fly away empty."

"Are you certain?" Mr. Greenburgh demanded. He blushed with rage at how his wife and daughters had been terrorized by unscrupulous

---

61 *Dashe* – a colloquial expression for a payment under the table to encourage good service, like a tip or bribe.

men who had not been brought to book for their offence. "Where is the blackguard now? Perhaps he or some of his cronies will return to trouble us another time."

The court-marshalled African guard gazed blankly at the big European, as though he did not understand. He looked completely baffled, about ready to burst with tears. Leroy's smug laughter did not help his morale in the least. Banda's eyes began to roll and look as though they had seen no rest in years. His dissected face gave one the impression he was at least fifty—had seen Abraham, and was going downhill every minute. He silently searched the faces of two European men—strangers in his land yet empowered to seal his fate—with large, beseeching eyes. Truth was in the eye of the beholder. Securicore had, in fact, taken the complaint made by Mrs. Greenburgh seriously, and sacked this sorry bloke even if Winter Banda refused to admit his guilt, for it was disgraceful for the security company to employ guards who were even suspected to be robbers beneath their uniform. Yet, James would argue that it was a shame to force men to slave away for pennies, especially old men with many dependents, who were easily taken advantage of.

"Do you understand my concern?" the white lord demanded.

He emphasized each word harshly to show his profound disappointment with Banda's stubborn refusal to repent of any wrongdoing. Losing patience with this pointless palaver, Mr. Greenburgh grimly considered having Leroy fetch Bruno and Renfrew to help him run this scoundrel off their property. Mr. Greenburgh turned to dispatch the eagerly attentive Leroy, but halted when Banda gruffly cleared his throat.

Gazing curiously at his strange petitioner, the diplomat queried, "I say, Banda, are you all right, man?"

"Armed robbers are not good men, sir. They take too much, and they hurt those they attack."

The dark other remarked in clear but concise English that astonished the white men—all except James, however, who already knew how clever Winter Banda was with the Queen's language, and all the sciences he read that her people had written down in textbooks.

"We agree on that point," Mr. Greenburgh acknowledged, smiling wryly.

"Many young men come to Lusaka from rural areas, looking for work, but when they don't find any jobs, so they become thieves."

"Why can't they find jobs?"

"They do not finish secondary school, *Bwana*. They need jobs to get money—they are poor and hungry yet ambitious to succeed. Zambians go firstly to Ndola or Mufilira, looking to work in the copper mines, but when they can't find a place there, they migrate to the capital city. Too many fellows wander the streets of Lusaka, seeking bread. Young Lusaka men want to wear suit and tie, walk in nice dress shoes, carry a wristwatch by the hand, play the radio, drive a car or a motorcycle . . . . A good-paying job provides such beautiful things. A modern, upbeat fellow may have a wife and children, perhaps elderly parents back in his village to support, but *he* doesn't want to stay in the bush—he desires a vibrant city life. There is not enough work or even place for every young man who searches in Lusaka."

Impressed by Winter Banda's articulately spoken insights, Mr. Greenburgh gazed earnestly upon him and saw intelligence gleaming in the previously hard and unblinking eyes. Enlightenment unfurled across Banda's stern, washboard face . . . . His open hands gestured passionately rather than clenched as fists, ready to strike or grab. The man wore a suit out of respect today to visit his enemy. Facing danger and incrimination, he performed a vital service—stalwartly returned a small, lost puppy he had found to its rightful owner—James, his true friend!

"My son tells me, Mr. Banda, that you are enrolled in an Adult Education program to complete your secondary school program. That is commendable."

"Yes, sir. I take extra-mural classes at the University of Zambia and also follow resident tutors at the Lusaka Adult Education Centre, on seat or by radio. I hope to write my O-levels in June. If successful, I will study to become a teacher," Winter replied, beaming with pride. Just as suddenly, however, he became downcast as he recalled being unceremoniously drummed out of the guard ranks, scant hours ago, "Alas, I can no longer pay for tuition and textbooks; I was sacked from my security job today. Mr. Bwana Greenburgh, I have a wife and five children to support."

"That is a conundrum now, isn't it, sir," Mr. Greenburg concurred. He nodded, sombrely empathetic. "Your situation is difficult but not impossible."

As he weighed everything in the balance, and saw that this well-dressed but hungry black gentleman could not easily leave his property or even step down from his petition empty-handed, Mr. Greenburgh realized that Mr. Banda *had* provided good service. He had returned Ragamuffin in a healthy, loveable state and, other than a few trampled flowers and trembling hearts, the Greenburghs were still shipshape under his watch. Banda sought a higher purpose—more than just eyes watching in the night—but Hiram dared not hire him privately as a night watchman now, after all the malarkey reported to have gone down during his absence. Besides, elder son Leroy was a young man of the *boma*[62] now, eager to prove his valour . . . .

"We no longer require your services to defend *this* property," the sage diplomat intoned to his attentive listeners. He nonetheless hatched a plan worthy for all. "I can help you as follows . . . ."

Firstly, he took 300 kwachas from his billfold, and gave it to the grateful but surprised African. When Banda good-naturedly protested, Mr. Greenburgh insisted, "You earned it—fair and square! This is your reward money for returning Ragamuffin unharmed to us. Son James vouches for you, sir."

"Thank you, *Bwana*," Winter replied jubilantly. He respectfully clasped the Englishman's hand—soft and freckled, though surely it had gripped many hands, white and black, in playing the great diplomatic game for stability in Africa. Winter smiled kindly upon James as he shook his hand and assured the boy, "Thank you, dear friend."

"Thank you, *my* friend," James graciously offered in return. "Winter, I enjoyed discussing Shakespeare with you."

---

62 A *boma* is a traditional, African walled home.

"Hopefully, Mr. Banda, you can in future parlay with many students over our great bard's wonderful plays."

Mr. Greenburgh bestowed his best wishes upon the man. Handing him his business card, written with a flourish, and emblazed with the Union Jack, the able executive assistant to the British High Commissioner to Zambia invited Banda, not only redeemed but also elevated in stature, to visit him the following Thursday afternoon for high tea to discuss his teaching aspirations. Amid a flurry of appreciative handshakes, Greenburgh jovially briefed him, "Dress well—like today—and present my card to the duty clerk, and you should have no trouble being ushered past all the red tape, into my office. Is that fine? Well, then, I look forward to your return visit, Mr. Banda."

"Thank you, *Bwana*, sir. I will meet you then," Winter promised, taking Mr. Greenburgh's noble hand in both of his calloused mitts, and bowing low with the utmost respect and gratitude. Having made progress that each could feel good about, he informed his odd benefactor, "I go now."

Banda then bade each white *bwana* farewell, and strode purposefully out of their lofty abode. The three British staunchly watched him go, but soon lost sight as he melted into a tiny silhouette, walking with many others, along the upward road awash in the red glow of the setting African sun.

PART II
WHAT IF?

(Winter Sunrise near Conklin, Alberta, 2010)

THE PRICE OF BELONGING

BY NORMA PROUDFOOT

A one-room schoolhouse is a community. All grades, from one to eleven, are or can be represented. The children of that community come from different homes and lifestyles. Several nationalities are usually included. Moral, ethical, and religious codes are a veritable parade. A whole slate board of languages could be named, yet each family comes to terms to a greater or lesser degree with English as the spoken language. Cultural dress, fashions, manners, customs, games . . . all become integrated into a common question such as, "What shall it be this recess?" In the chase to be first to "kick the can" over the snowfield trodden hard and slippery by the passage of many feet, external differences absolve themselves in a common goal. Marybelle MacDonald was once a member of such a community in northern Alberta. The whole concept of her community had its counterparts in other provinces in the Dominion of Canada. It survived because it operated within the best tenets of a democratic society.

The largest group of settlers in the surrounding homelands was of the pioneer families. Marybelle's father and mother were members of this group, and like everyone else in the area, they had come from "away" sometime during the previous twenty years. They had both been born on Prince Edward Island, and had come west on different dates, finally meeting in Edmonton. Her mother was a school teacher when they met, her father a constable with the Edmonton Police Service. The outbreak of World War I interrupted their romance as her father joined the army, ending up in France, a sergeant in charge of machine guns and the men required to operate them. As a returned man, he married his sweetheart, and the young couple, along with many other returned men, went farming within the terms of the Soldiers' Settlement Board, and under the government's new policies for opening up the Peace River Country.

The MacDonald children walked 2.5 miles to school, with other children who joined them along the way. They carried their lunch in lard pails, their sandwiches frozen solid in winter, and warmed to almost soggy 'neath summer's sun. Bundled up as they were with layers of clothes and moccasin-clad feet, they seldom missed a day. It was universal knowledge that the school would be closed at minus forty degrees. On the coldest mornings, warm-up exercises were the best way to get the blood circulating. The air-tight heater in the middle of the room was fine for warming one side or the other, but a body had to keep turning like a chicken on a spit in order to approach total warmth. Cold and heat, body sensations, laughter, and fun were the same in any language. It was at times like these that the children learned the idiomatic English language, and the homogeneity of their community was approaching its best reality.

It must be acknowledged that the one-room schoolhouse had its learning limitations. Some grades, like grade nines who had to write departmental examinations, required more teacher time than the other grades. Some scholars demanded more than their share of the teacher's time. Marybelle started off to school with the special eagerness with which she approached most things. She could read words, but could hardly wait to delve into all those books her brother read to her before bedtime. How wonderful it would be to open up the storybook world for herself. Tom Munro was the only other grade one student. Where she was good at reading, he was good at arithmetic, but neither was cognizant about spelling. Marybelle had to stay after school one night, full of worry about walking the long road home alone, until she learned how to spell sleigh. If s-l-a-y did not work, how could she find out? Finally, Clara spelt this odd word into her ear as she stood by Marybelle's desk in the waiting line to get her own words corrected. That was an unbelievable word, but when Marybelle read it to the teacher, it worked! Of course, the kids waited for her, but she never again allowed herself the disadvantage of having to "stay in." She came to school to learn.

Marybelle was bothered by some of the big boys who wasted their own time, as well as that of the teacher and the other students, by doing no work and always causing trouble. Annoyances, like the spitball craze, and the collecting of sun rays in mirrors that could then be slanted to reflect on the bald head of the teacher as he stood writing important truths on the blackboard, were certainly fun for older kids who knew everything already. The grade ones seemed to depend more on a kind of osmosis, which worked well enough to boost them into grade three during their second year. That was how it worked in a one-room school. If you wanted to learn, there was really very little to stop the process.

Enter the Galicians: the "sheepskin people" of Clifford Sifton's era. They originated as Professor Oleskow's hand-picked farmers from over-populated, mountainous slopes in eastern Europe to begin the great emigration to Canada, as many as 150,000 Poles and Ukrainians from war-defeated Austria-Hungary. Some 40,000 of these new Canadians settled in and around Vegreville; a crowd of them also ventured into the Peace River Country to take up the challenge of farming. Of course, the children had to come to the school. They were poor. Marybelle's father was at the station the day they detrained. He saw their beautiful sheepskin coats, but he also saw their confusion, lostness, and need for understanding. As the chairman of the School Board, he was quick to give the schoolchildren their first lesson in acceptance of something very new. It was Marybelle's brother who stood before the class, and used his own words to cover the embarrassment of Mary who, not knowing how to be excused, had wet her pants, her desk, the floor . . . . . It was Marybelle's brother who asked Marybelle that very day to take as her friend this same Mary, who was bigger and older, but who so needed such a friend to help her with the same frightening process of assimilation which she herself had faced on her first day of school.

Mary acquired another friend who could spend after-school time with her. He was a bachelor named Eli, who had often been in and out of trouble with the law because of his penchant for moonshining. Eli, however, liked homemade bread, and could smell it baking at Mary's house; he was there one day when Mary came home from school, crying with the frustrations of learning to read the English language. Eli took her in hand. Eli loved to read. One wall of his cabin was lined with books. These were not "children's" literature but they did the trick. Mary learned to read, and Eli earned his regular fresh loaf of bread. Many of those adult heroes stayed in Mary's memory so well that, when she found them again in later years, she recognized them as old friends. Through reading about them with Eli, Mary gained her certain sense of belonging in a classroom full of readers . . .. Had the school children been more aware of such things, they would surely have been surprised at how quickly this assimilation took place—not only with Mary, but with many of the others. They would also have become aware that, during the process, the new children did not lose their dignity, their cultural heritage, their own language, their souls.

This unique community known as the one-room schoolhouse could not remain as it was. The west was opening up. Marquis wheat came west and north because it had the right qualities to thrive in the Peace River Country: early maturing and head-resistant to strong winds. This improved wheat variety opened a whole new dream to farmers. The Peace River Country gave up its aspen forests. Place names like Grizzly Bear Prairie and Little Prairie were lost in the expanding farmlands. Schools grew, were added to, rebuilt, amalgamated. A whole new set of names was heard in the hallways. The graduates of one-room schools were pioneers of the new high schools, and continued on to higher education. Some of them—some of those very ones who, although clever, had not applied themselves to learning what the classroom had to offer—stayed at home, but became some of the best area farmers the future could afford.

— Enduring Art, Active Faith —

As churches were built to group people together in the name of religion, some farming communities began to be recognized as Mennonite, Hutterite, and other such ilk. Marybelle learned, again more from osmosis than any other means, that many people had come to Canada—to the Peace River Country—to escape tyranny, religious oppression, and gain the freedom to live and worship as they chose. Marybelle's family attended the Presbyterian Church, which in this setting was no particular ethnic group as much as it was a place for people to meet God on their own terms. It seemed to suit all the people who did not fit any other particular persuasion, but felt at home in this simple expression of faith.

Mrs. Pickard, Marybelle's friend, came to the Presbyterian Church. She liked to sit in the big black rocker at the MacDonald's house to do her sewing. One day, she had taken Marybelle up into her big lap to show her how to make knots at the end of her thread: knots that would keep the thread where you wanted it to stay. Every time Mrs. Pickard saw Marybelle at the church, she had some special words that were just for her. Marybelle knew Mrs. Pickard had darker skin than any of her other friends, as did her son the blacksmith, one of the men who had helped get the logs from the bush for building the church. One day when Marybelle asked her father about that, he just said that Mrs. Pickard was an Indian lady, as if that explained everything. All she knew about Indians was what she had read in the books at school: how they lived in tents, wore skin clothing, rode bareback on spotted horses, and gave their daughters wonderful, magical names like Running Deer and Laughing Water . . .. Mrs. Pickard and her son did not do any of these things!

Years later, when the surrounding districts became part of her life, Marybelle discovered that Mrs. Pickard had daughters, even granddaughters, whose skin were almost as white as her own, and whose names were very similar to hers. Mrs. Pickard, in fact, had been the widow of a white man. Marybelle would discover that such marriages had taken place in other districts where she taught school, and that the history books were right about one thing: the Scotsmen who had come to Canada with the fur brigade were lonesome for home, and did marry Indian women. Finally, she met a girl her own age who was a granddaughter of an Indian lady, whose last name was MacDonald.

During her career as a school teacher, Marybelle formed an opinion about the government's system of reserves, land areas upon which Indian people could live, ideally to carry on their own way of life. It would occur to her then that, for them, there never was and could never be a sense of belonging to the settler society. Although much was taken away—in a takeover of someone else's land there is always a sense of loss never to be fully regained—there was also much given in return. The Indian people could not have remained so peacefully on their reserves had this not been so. Yet, educators like Marybelle surely recognized that the education system did not serve the Indians well. Why would anyone impose upon a culture so removed from the concept, learning to read, write, ideate, and create from a setting of the white man's culture? In spite of these discrepancies, some Indian children and their parents wanted more out of life. They continued on through the channels of higher learning to change things for themselves, and to gain a way of life that better fit their expectations in the world of today.

So, what is the price of belonging? There are many kinds of prices, and many different ways of belonging. Some people have a problem belonging in their own family. Some people never learn how to belong anywhere to anyone or anything. The first price for belonging one must pay is that of *wanting* to belong—wanting to belong so strongly that the price becomes secondary. That need to belong must come from within so that self-motivation, even self-preservation, plays a part. A price is paid to move, yes to relocate, to reinstate . . . a monetary price that is anticipated, but there is an aspect of belonging that cannot be bought or sold. It involves acceptance on the part of both he who would belong and the welcomer, the other component in the partnership or fellowship. It includes a sense of responsibility on both sides to balance the equation, and make it hold true.

Marybelle's father paid a price common to all those who went to war "for God, King, and country" and for a "peace that would end all wars." Her parents met challenges in going to farm on a frontier that would allow them a way of life for the children they hoped to have. The frontier farmers worked hard to build farms out of the wilderness, a new community where people of many nationalities, cultures, and faiths could live together in a sharing, caring way. Marybelle paid her own dues by walking to school through weather that compares today's standards as very cold; of leaving home at an early age to be educated beyond junior high school; and of taking up residence in unfamiliar surroundings of the big city in order to pursue her life-long dream of becoming a schoolteacher.

The Galicians left everything they knew, faced exploitation on shipboard by the very persons they trusted, to arrive in a brand-new land, penniless except for the sheepskin coats they had on their backs. In Canada, they could gain land for the exchange of a relatively small monetary price, but worked very hard to build homes, have families, make a new way of life in which they could still preserve their own heritage and self-worth, yet also gain a sense of belonging to mainstream society. So good a job did they do, in fact, that Canadians soon dropped the group name of Galician and singled them out to fit their true nationalities or ethnic origins.

It seems that we have to think separately about the Indian people, the people of First Nations, because they were already well-established here when European immigrants arrived. Were indigenous Canadians ever one nation? Were they not always what they claim to be today, a group of tribes/nations who separated themselves into pockets all over this vast land? Perhaps "pocket" is too stabilizing a concept to describe the nomadic way of life led by these people . . . .. They sought out their livelihood, and became specialists in bartering with the white man, who came first as the explorer, then as the trader seeking out special commodities such as beaver pelts and gold ore, and ultimately, as the two rival fur trading companies that would vie with each other not only for goods but for supremacy on Canadian soil. When the British won the war against France, the strife and turmoil among Europeans brought to Canada interrupted the various ways of life of the indigenous peoples, but were *they* ever really a conquered nation? It was then expected that they would curb their nomadic tendencies and agree to live on reserved lands set aside for their use. The marvel is that Indians remained in their "situation" for so long; they did not "break out" sooner and become more responsible for their own future. Maybe they lived so long as takers that they became too comfortable with it. Maybe, they never did plan to "belong" in Canada, at least not within the present colonial model.

In essence, all who belong pay a price for the belonging, a membership if you will. It has a lot to do with how we interact within the family circle, as neighbours in a community, as students in the halls of learning, in our professions as employees and employers. Responsibility and commitment go hand in hand, but if self-motivation and preservation are involved with a community spirit of goodwill towards our fellow man, the price is right.

ESSAY ON FARMING

BY NORMA PROUDFOOT

The east road no longer began at the school corner but swung instead on a curve at the base of the hill. Eve would go up that hill to the school so as not to confuse herself with landmarks. She thought she could distinguish Richard Johnston's place, but the fields had extended themselves beyond their bounds. All the landmarks—like Eli Barrit's log house and Mazelenko's unplowed hill where the crocuses, buttercups, and even shy little purple violets announced each spring with gay abandon—were gone. Ole Tamsen's slough had been drained, and standing in the midst of it was a nice new house built by the Wells family. Eve thought she recognized the house Mollie and Clifford had lived in, so this must be the lane that led to her old home. She turned in. Rumours had been laid that big-time farmers had bought up miles of farmland and worked them all with big machinery. There was a patch of scarred grass where the picket gate had swung on its squeaky hinges; a few bare roots and scrawny branches were all that was left of the caragana hedges and maple windbreak. Turning slowly, 180 degrees, Eve saw sky and field meet in a nothingness that only the still-familiar line of dear old Birch Hills could thwart.

Then she saw it! Five rocks edged one side of the gumbo-bowl of water; the other side was gradually filling in with black dirt from off the fields. A pole had been dropped into the hole, announcing it to the unwary . . . five rocks were the sole remains of the dam that Dad and Russell had worked so hard to constrain. Quietly, Eve stooped to touch those rocks, as if to gain some sense of endurance. Swiftly, a swallow swooped to the gumbo mud at her feet, to grasp in its beak the dab so urgently needed to complete the hanging nest in which her young could be laid.

"But there is no barn on which to secure your nest!" Eve called after the swallow. Her eyes followed its flight to some unknown destiny, but the swallow heeded her not, so intent was she to be about her own business. "Little winged creature, your message comes clearly to me. Only you of all the creatures who once lived here have adapted to change. Only you have remained to continue the last resources of a dam that Dad struggled to maintain."

❖ ❖ ❖

Babies come whether wanted or not, expected that day or another, healthy and strong or weak and sensitive. Eve had come instead of the threshers in the midst of a Sunday morning snow storm. Daddy had ridden horseback, leading an empty horse, to fetch the District Nurse who knew midwifery from the British system under which she had been trained. The round trip was six miles, but the nurse arrived in time to deliver a healthy baby "born with a caul."

Throughout her lifetime, Eve had tried to make some connection with the meaning for a "caul." From Farley Mowat[63], for instance, she

---

63 Farley Mowat (1921 to 2014), a Canadian author and environmentalist, achieved fame with publication of his books set in the Arctic, including: *People of the Deer* (1952), *Lost in the Barrens* (1956), *Never Cry Wolf* (1963), and *The Snow Walker* (1976, 2014). Mowat won numerous literary awards, including the Stephen Leacock Memorial Medal for Humour for *The Boat that Wouldn't Float*, as well as the Vicky Metcalfe Award for Children's Literature, both in 1970. His writings also advocated for protection and understanding of wolves in North America and mountain

had learned that he had been born with a caul which, to him, meant that he would have safety on the sea, and so began his life-long addiction to boats and the waters upon which they float. Yet, Eve did not have need of that kind of security because water was a scarcity in her life. It was her Mom and Dad who had come west from "The Island"—Prince Edward Island, that is—each at his or her own time in their teenage years. Wells, even witched-for-wells, had been dug on Dad's farm with expense of time and money . . . but to no avail! A rapidly flowing stream burst down from the Birch Hills every spring, cutting along a draw that was dry enough at seeding time to be cultivated but only after the run-off forced its way through the dam so labouriously rebuilt the previous year, taking the precious water through the pig yard, to lose itself in parts unknown. It was Aunt Gertie who finally defined "caul" to her satisfaction: "It means you are special," she had said.

Special? Born during the Depression, fourth child into a family where other siblings were already six, five, and four years old? Her dad practiced mixed farming, and nobody went hungry, even in the midst of lean times. Eve heard people talking about "depression"; some said it was here, some said it was coming, but if one did not know what to look for, how could one tell if it came? She did feel kind of special, and that is really all that mattered. Looking back on her life on that mixed farm gave Eve no doubt that she had enjoyed a special childhood.

There were always cows on the farm . . . a herd that seemed to replenish by itself every spring . . . cows that were primarily Hereford, Shorthorn or a mixture of both . . . cows mostly red, with adorable white faces holding large, dreamy eyes within their curls. Even Johnny Bull had those eyes that made you feel he could be gentle as a lamb. There were red and white bodies, oddly speckled bodies and red roans.

---

gorillas in Rwanda. In 1987, Mowat published biographies of Dian Fossey (*Virunga: The Passion of Dian Fossey*; and *Woman of the Mists: The Story of Dian Fossey and the Mountain Gorillas of Africa*), an American ethologist who studied and advocated for these gorillas, but was murdered in 1985.

Some cows were for milking, some for fattening up to be shipped to market and some to be kept to mother next year's calves, thus building up the herd. A blue roan and a scrawny little Holstein came into this herd as payment to Dad for services rendered to other farmers. The former became the best milker his farm ever knew; the latter, without announcing the fact to anyone, was in calf when she came. When the unexpected did announce itself, Dad was wary of just how the Holstein could accomplish this feat, being such a young, skittery little thing herself. The morning the little Holstein was missing from the herd, Dad knew why; his daughter went with him on his knowledgeable search. In a little thicket, they found her, even more skittish and very confused. On the grass beside her lay the cutest little calf. He was snow white except for very black patches that looked like they had been sewn in place. As soon as Daddy had determined both animals were healthy, he talked to the new mother in his most calming voice.

Nellie had been bought from Uncle Rob Webster to make a hay team with Jess. They were reliable horses that pulled the big wagon into town during summer trips; yet, they were not equals as Nellie was big with heavy feet, while Jess could pull her own weight with Nellie any day. Maybe that was why Nellie was always used as the anchor horse when training colts. It took a lot to unnerve steady Nellie, whom Dad often said was worth her weight in gold. They were mothers of "The Blacks," a pretty little pair of good pullers used with the fresno to dig the dam deeper. The Blacks were sold during some hard times to a man who needed a team as much as Daddy needed some money.

The sorrels, however, were special: Topsy, Jiggs, and Chief made excellent workhorses that could team up in any arrangement required of them. When winter came, and the cutter Dad built for fast sleighing over the snow was used for trips into town, Judy and Punch did the job with pride. She was foaled by Jess, while he, that staunch partner of the steady trot, came out of Nellie. With long flowing tail and mane of lighter colour, Punch was the perfect background for Judy's beautifully bowed neck and prancing feet. Men offered to buy them, but when, at the height of the Depression, Dad gave in, it was not Judy who went to

Fox Creek with Punch, but her brother Jiggs, stall-mate for Topsy. It was difficult for Dad to see them go, but the $300 sale price filled a hole in his pocket.

It was not quite two years later, on a sunny April Fools' Sunday morning, that his daughters had heard the dog bark and seen the sorrels standing at the gate half a mile away, waiting to be let through. Dad, nonplused to see them there, walked down to open the gate. After a familiar greeting of nose rubs and soft whinnies, the happy pair galloped up to the house, skittered past a still growling dog, and waited at the barnyard gate. Dad opened that too and the barn door, which was their next stop. It was unsettling to see them take their own familiar places in separate stalls where they had previously stood beside Judy and Topsy. Dad was saddened again, two days later, when their new owner came to pick them up. He told Dad that these sorrels, Punch and Jiggs, had tried to leave once before, but he had caught them halfway "home." That was why he knew where to find them.

Farm families need a good dog, too. Everybody loved old Mike, the sheepdog that at first the kids thought had no eyes, so covered up they were with hair. He was already old when she first found him lying around by the door. Mike quickly became Eve's first friend and babysitter while she, in turn, used Mike for a pillow when they were both tired, and told him all the words she knew. Every other dog that followed in Mike's wake was also loved, from border collie to mongrel. Tip was probably the most mongrel of them all yet was the best cattle dog that ever-obeyed Dad's whistled commands. To have a dog is to love him, and there is no more faithful friend through life.

Cats, too, were the farmer's friends, faithful at keeping down the rodent population. Eve learned all about farm mothers and their babies from cats who were little and unthreatening and let her close to their kittens—but *pigs*, on the other hand, were an enigma! Dad struck it lucky with pigs by "going into them" when the price was right. He really did it in a big way, finding out how as he went along. Dad built farrowing pens, cute little houses, all over the pig yard for the sows to have their litters in private, but Dad had not counted on them starting the process in the early hours of the coldest night in January! Those little piglets were so cold that Dad kept bringing boxes full of them into the house to be warmed up in the oven. As soon as his youngest daughter had awakened to what was happening, she helped her Mom all that day with wrapping up wee piglets in pieces of Dad's old underwear, so to add more warmth as they lay in their boxes in the oven. Eve watched them turn from cold, stiff little things into lively squealers wanting something more than warmth. Eve loved those little piglets, and heaped all the questions she would ever have to know upon them as she helped her Mom and very cold Daddy, who kept taking the boxes back and forth. Where did piglets come from? Why didn't they have warm fur coats like the kittens? Why couldn't they grow long hair for winter like the horses did? Didn't God like piglets, and where was Daddy taking them?

Perhaps the strangest summation of all was, "I knew that cows had milk for calves, and cats had milk for kittens but *pigs*? I didn't know that mother pigs had milk bottles too!"

That was how it was on a mixed farm; kids found out how it worked by a kind of osmosis. When Rod, Dad's beautiful dappled grey gelding, cut his leg on a barbed-wire fence, Eve did not see the offending cut, but watched Dad pour the potent liquid out of a big green bottle into pans full of boiling hot water and take them into the barn to bathe that cut. She knew Dad had to make two trips into town before he could contact the veterinarian by telephone, and get him to come to Rod. She knew the vet's trip came too late, and that Rod's carcass was now lying on the old manure pile in the pasture.

One night, when the family time for hot cocoa and crackers had been interrupted by a cacophony of high-pitched yelping, Eve heard Dad explain that the coyotes were "at the carcass." What she had to take in by osmosis way was the meaning of the next morning's maneuvers. Dad brought old Mike to the house and asked in quiet tones that he be kept inside for a while, because there was a big black bear eating the dead horse. Was her Dad protecting Mike from something too big for him to handle? How did the gun, silently taken from the closet and that small box on the topmost shelf above the wood box, enter the mystery of

Mike's protection? It was not until that cold day in December one year later, when Dad went for the freight, and picked up the kids to bring them home from school, that the solutions came to her. The "freight" was the biggest parcel she had ever seen, which had to have layer after layer of wrappings peeled away from it before the contents tumbled out before her amazed eyes. There, on the hardwood floor that was stained chocolate brown, was a beautiful, black bearskin rug! All that mattered afterwards was the many ways the family used and enjoyed its soft, thick fur.

Guns continued to be a mystery to her, stored as they were in what was always known as "the gun closet." Eve knew it was thanks to guns there was deer and moose meat to eat—moose steak smothered in rich brown gravy and onions was a most welcome meal to come home to on a cold winter day, during which the round trip of five miles to school had been made. One sunny, winter Saturday, however, when she and Daddy were walking in the north quarter to check on the horses pastured there, and they came quietly upon two beautiful deer standing in the thicket, she saw it happen. One deer sprang away to freedom; the other lay dead in the snow. He was warm to her touch, and his big, limpid eyes looked at her. Eve cried. It was not a time for words, but Daddy's gun was returned to the gun closet, never again to take the life of a deer.

The kids also had their part of the farm work to do on weekends and after school. Eve's brother helped Dad with chores, while her oldest sister worked with Mom. During the days that she was too young for school, Eve helped her Mom feed the chickens and gather their eggs. When they had returned from school, she helped her brother and second sister get loads of wood to fill the wood box, loads of snow chunks to melt in the big barrel by the stove, and fetch the load of coal that would keep cinders in the fire at night.

It was on one last trip for coal that they shared and tried to solve Eve's next mystery. The smallest pieces of coal seemed different in the light of the full moon and kind of netted over with something that seemed to glow with a greenish-yellow light. They looked around in the snow by the door and found this funny, little, weaving path trodden hard into the snow. Eve and Gordon followed it into the hay-yard at the back of the barn, by the feed alley door, under the log fence of the pig yard, and beyond the pig house to the farrowing pens. Nothing seemed amiss. There was only one litter of small piglets left by then. They were born much later than the others and not big enough to go to market in the fall. They were snuggled down together in the straw, sleeping quite soundly. Only the old sows stirred and grunted, but they were used to kids, and did not move from where they lay. Mystery unsolved, the clue-seekers returned home. It became part of the supper table discussion, but Mom and Dad only smiled, assuring them that, as tomorrow was Saturday, they could look for more clues in the morning.

It was the funniest joke they had ever had, to look out the kitchen window next morning and see little pigs following the path to the coal bin, one so close behind the other that the path seemed to be moving. Her brother noticed that their noses were quite black, and their faces were half covered with black soot. After the family had enjoyed the joke, Daddy explained that pigs had been known to crunch small pieces of coal to make up for some chemical deficiency in their genes or diets. Pigs certainly were an enigma!

Other mysteries took care of themselves in much the same way: you had to be in the right place at the right time to find out the answers for yourself. Eve was with Daddy and Gordon as much as possible, helping to feed cattle and horses, pigs, and chickens. When the dam broke, and the water escaped, Eve went with Dad to haul water in a big tank pulled by Topsy and Brownie from the neighbour's farm four miles away on the round trip. All winter long they had to keep the snow melter filled with wood and snow so the many farm animals could drink. The newborn calves and colts were the cutest of all the animals. Eve went with Daddy to find them in the early mornings of spring, in the hidden, private sorts of places the mothers chose but, although Eve was curious to see it happen, she never saw any of them being born. Of course, nobody could tell you things like that in a way you could understand. When they found cute little Brownie lying beside Jess, Eve marveled at how four long legs could have been inside Jess in the first place.

Her Grandma MacDonald said, "Ach! Tic a mir-racle that only the gud Lor-rd himsel' cud ever ha' per-rfected!"

Gordon told Eve that there was a little secret door that opened when the baby wanted to come out, then shut up again behind it. A funny little cat she had called Peter showed her exactly what happens. When she went in to get socks from her sock-drawer, there was Peter in the midst of them, giving birth to five small, wet kittens! Gordon and Grandma were both right. If anyone had bothered to tell her the whole truth, she would not have believed it, but Peter had done it just for her—and she loved Peter and those five little kittens.

Eve learned early how babies got inside the mother in the first place. Johnny Bull showed her that as she walked with Daddy to get the milk cows. She could tell the difference between the male and female pigs and she deduced why the "Government boar" had a place of his own on their farm, to which other farmers could bring their sows for a visit . . .. Yet, on those days when the huge, rampant stallion came, led behind the Bennett buggy, shaking the ground with every step, she was happy enough to do as was told and stay away from the barnyard. There were other days too when Eve was told that, like when Daddy unwrapped his shiny set of instruments on the kitchen table and sterilized them in boiling water. Hired men gathered to help him do things she did not even want to watch—but, by deduction and observation, she knew that little bulls had become steers and colts were made into geldings.

It was important to know these words and their meanings because one might be asked someday on a Grade Nine exam, like Gordon was. "What is a heifer . . . a gelding . . . an ewe?" A farm kid, of all people, should know such words, even if he did not understand their meanings! Dad had done veterinarian tasks for farmers in the early days, but as those jobs became too frequent and time-consuming, he had given them up to attend to his own interests.

Dad was also a grain farmer. He grew wheat, mostly to sell, and oats and barley to make chop for the animals to eat. The horses ate oats as grain to be ground by their long jawbone. Some of the barley was sold. Oat bundles made green feed, which Eve helped to feed to the milk cows and working horses. These bundles were brought into the barn through the feed alley, where the binder twine was clipped with a knife and the feed was then spread into mangers.

Two of the best sounds inside the barn were the "purring" of the horses as they were fed, and the grinding of their teeth as they ate. The sound of milking was also neat. First, the tinkling of two streams hitting an empty pail, then splats and splashes and, finally, the throaty sound of milk foaming and rising up the sides of the pail to its very top. Daddy and the hired men milked the cows, but it was satisfying to sit quietly on the extra three-legged stool beside the barn cats, who sat waiting for their share of the warm milk. A barn has many smells: warm breath smells, warm milk smells, the sweet smell of hay, and the not so sweet odour of a fresh cow pie often dropped at milking time. Eve watched for the cud to roll itself up those long bovine throats and get chewed once it reached the mouth. She watched for the wary wee mice who took advantage of the waiting cats to slip by and go about their business unnoticed. If you were very quiet, you could hear the twitter of sparrows in the hayloft as they tucked their babies in for the night. Like mice, they would also be taking advantage of the pre-occupied barn cats.

Early in May, as soon as the ground temperature was warm enough to encourage seed germination, the field work began. The grain had to be cleaned and treated with formaldehyde in the fight against wheat diseases like rust and smut. Kids could work the fanning mill, but were not allowed near the seed treating process; masks had to be worn by those who worked.

Eve did not really trust those workhorses until they were harnessed and hitched up to machinery, but once Daddy had the reins in his hands and could control four horses at once, she could leave her safe vantage point and join him. The fields were all fenced and named. They had been hewn out of poplar groves, with a few spruce and jack pine scattered throughout. Daddy had done the early work alone, but when help became available and affordable, hired men worked with him. Brush was piled and burned, a good strategy to ward off the hordes of mosquitoes that plagued man and beast. Each year, there was more land to first plough, then disk. Mother did not want Eve riding the implements with those sharp blades following along behind, but the drill was safe; there was even a board on which she could stand beside Daddy.

The four horses varied with availability; sometimes Jess, Judy, and Nellie had little colts to care for. The year Brownie was born, Jess worked, and he followed along. When he wandered too far away, Jess would whinny, and he would come galloping, his tiny, cookie-cutter hooves beating the ground and his little tail flapping like curly brown wool held high in the air. The sky was usually blue over them as they worked the fields, seeding the grain. Yet, there were a few soft, fluffy clouds, and enough breeze to scatter their dust and to lessen the sun's heat as it shone down upon them.

Eve liked best the field south of the dam. It stretched as far south as the "line fence" and along it to the draw, back to the dam to run parallel to it so as to join up with the east fence. You had to leave an undisturbed, grassy area around the field so the horses could have room to turn the machines. The east side followed the pasture fence where trees still grew. Eve could watch the birds and find out from Daddy their names and where they built their nests. Bluebirds nested in the hollow tree where the round hole indicated their nest; they were as blue as the sky, with a bit of rosy red on the chest. Along that side, too, Dad often stopped to rest the horses. Then Eve could walk in the grass where the buttercups and violets grew. Daddy showed her bluebeard's tongue: a vivid blue puff of petals, in the midst of which were tiny pink ones resembling an open mouth, wherein grew another tuft of blue to form the tongue. A ground bird flew up as they walked in the grass that surprised her and the resting horses. Daddy showed Eve how to carefully search out the nest; it was safely tucked under a very small rosebush, the neatest wee thing holding tiny speckled eggs. They moved quietly away so the worried bird would return.

❖ ❖ ❖

Eve shook her head and blinked her tear-filled eyes. Her memories washed away as if in the flood of spring water escaping from the dam. Where had it all gone? All her special places where she was want to sit and read her favourite books: the hayloft with its door open just enough for a splash of sunlight to touch her as she lay on the sweet-smelling hay; or in the smokehouse during its off-season, when the long ladder reached almost to the smoke hole, where sunlight and fresh breezes could enter. On the ladder's highest rung, Eve had read without interruption, totally absorbed in the antics of *Anne of Green Gables*, the fantasies of the *Girl of the Limberloss*, and adventures of *Rebecca of Sunnybrook Farm*. She also enjoyed the mushroom-shaped straw stack in the pig yard, where she lay on her back with her friend Helen, seeing only the treetops and the sky above, taking turns reading aloud from *Forest Babies* and those wonderful books of poetry and fairy stories that came out of Ireland. Everything was gone! The mixed farm she grew up on had become one huge, impersonal field with no distinguishing features except the sky above, the distant, tree-clad Birch Hills, and the highway running along its northern edge.

Farm and farmer had become specialized. A grain farmer, good at his job, purchased manufactured chemical fertilizers, and exercised crop rotation to keep his land healthy. No horse ever trod on his soil; his tractor was bigger than the biggest stallion that had ever pranced up the lane behind the Bennett buggy. It had a dust-free, air-conditioned cab, complete with AM/FM radio, remote control telephone, hydraulic controls to operate machinery following in its wake, and hot coffee and eats in hand. Perched on his cushy tractor seat high above the ground, the farmer had a panoramic view, was master of all he surveyed. Headlights allowed for the night shift. Cultivators and swathers were the machinery of specialists. Fields that could reach as far as two miles square had to be big to accommodate large-scale cash crops; yields and prices had to be high enough to buy and maintain such huge farming operations.

Where had all the horses gone? Eve hated to think! Riding stables and racetracks accepted only the best; heritage and pioneer farms could accommodate only a few....

Cattle fared better in the scheme of things. They were popular, saleable commodities. Range cattle still roamed the hills and well-watered valleys but grass, no longer considered the best food for cows, was replaced by prepared silage that contained all the ingredients needed to induce high milk production and make strong calves. Highly specialized dairy farms had come into existence: computer-run operations where cows wore number tags rather than names, and seldom left their barns. They were not allowed to roam the fields seeking sheltered places in which to calve. Their exercise circle was called a "cow parlour." The dairy farmer fed and watered his cows, removed their wastes, pumped and delivered milk, all by the flick of a switch. The calf production process was computerized. Johnny Bull had become such a valuable specimen that artificial insemination was practiced to protect his pedigree as well as his progeny.

. . . And pigs? That enigma of her childhood days was now raised in very modern piggeries. There were industrial-scale chicken and poultry hatchery ranches that led directly to egg plants or slaughterhouses, the better to bring the impatient and hungry consumer a drumstick or omelettes to satisfy his busy schedule!

The swallow twice returned, catching on the wing dabs of gumbo from the remains of the dam. Now it was thrice, and a tired little bird landed on the silt slide of the hole, dipped her muddy beak into the water, held her head at a rakish angle, and let its coolness run down her parched throat. Loaded with yet another beakful of the sticky tuft, she flew away, leaving the daintiest of footprints in the silt.

Eve stood to her full height, one foot secure on a protruding rock, and wistfully mused, "Little winged creature, your message comes clearly to me. Only you of all the creatures that once lived here have adapted to change. Life must go on, because out of life comes life. The thread must weave its length. We must build our security upon the one from which we came."

A DAY OF SUMMER SUPPLY AT THE OFFICE WHILE THE SECRETARY TAKES A HOLIDAY

BY NORMA PROUDFOOT

"I saw your church on TV one day not so long ago." The hungry customer conversed with a lady who helped him find suitable leftovers in hampers that remained on one of the four tables onto which the delivery man from the food bank had made his Tuesday delivery. "Are churches really in that kind of trouble? Somehow, a person always expects the church to be there, even when everything else fails."

"Ya." Her depletive came softly, accompanied by a sort of apologetic little giggle. "Well, that may be just the trouble in a nutshell. People expect the church to help in time of need . . . and, most of the time, the church is there. One big problem is that each person comes to the door loaded with his or her own needs, but sometimes the span is too broad to cover it all."

"Oh, look at this!" he interrupted her. "Turnips! Nice, home-grown turnips! I haven't seen any of these little guys for a while. May I take two?"

Her mind raced back to the visitor who had come about a half hour before. He too had come for leftovers. He was Ken, a frequenter, who had been there at other times as a customer by telephone.

"Ma'am," Ken had addressed her, a bit too politely. "I know I should have come on food bank day yesterday, but I got held up. When that happens, your regular fellow just lets me come in to help myself."

"You are welcome. We happen to have some food that hasn't been picked up, and we're happy to see it used."

Ken was already thumbing through the boxes, knowingly lifting something here, tossing something else aside there. He brushed the "little turnips" aside as being of no consequence, flaring his nostrils in such a way that you knew he hated turnips.

"Now, look at this, Ma'am." Ken spoke a little less politely as he held forth a box of Kraft Dinner too close to her face, and pointed at the print with a grubby finger. There was the smell of booze on his breath, but she had smelled worse. "It says right on the box that you mix this with margarine and milk, but I don't have either one of them things."

"Well, the margarine and milk are extra, as a suggestion but you don't have to use them," she explained patiently. "You can cook the macaroni and just stir in the cheese to make a healthy meal. Here is a package of vegetables all nicely chopped up, ready to eat with it."

His laugh was not as much an apology as a guffaw. "Ya know, Ma'am, you're a nice lady, and I sure do appreciate what'cha tryin' to do but see here . . . . I've tried cooking this macaroni stuff, and you really need to watch it so it don't boil all over your stove. I just don't have the patience to stand around, watching it cook. As far as that veggie stuff goes, you can take the cabbage and give it to someone who has teeth to chew it."

The office phone was ringing. She was reluctant to leave Ken alone while she went to answer it, but there was no other receptionist around. It was someone she knew, telephoning to inquire after a mutual friend who had undergone a medical operation the day before.

"I'll have to put you on hold for the moment. I'm busy with someone looking for food from the food bank."

"Was not yesterday the day for the food bank?"

"Yes! I'll explain in a moment."

Leaving the receiver to rest on the desk, she returned to find Ken juggling a tin in hand. He bantered, "You see what it says on this here can, Ma'am? It says: pork and beans. I've never seen any pork in this stuff. I like eggs!"

Whilst explaining that there probably had been some eggs available yesterday, she spotted a small package of margarine and was putting it together with a package of Kraft Dinner when he interrupted her. "I'd rather put the margarine together with some of that nice brad over there. That's good brad and, by the way, there are some eggs in this box, but they're all loose!"

Rescuing an open, half-empty carton from the box and filling it with those loose eggs, she carefully placed it into his bag, explaining that the carton should be put into its place with the uncut side downwards, so that the eggs would not get loose again.

"I sure do love you, Ma'am," Ken said. He grinned from ear to ear and, this time, with compassion softening his voice. "You remind me of my mother. I had a nice mother once, but she died—choked to death from drinking too much."

Edging Ken, who actually had found enough likeable stuff to fill two bags, towards the door, and saying with considerable compassion in her own voice that too much drinking was not good for anybody, she managed to open the door just as he thought of one last need. He would like to have one of those nice little crosses that churches were forever giving out to hang around his neck.

She was about to try explaining to Ken that hers was not the kind of church that gave out crosses, when she remembered how he had explained earlier the keys on a shoelace wrapped around his neck: one key for his own room, and another for the front door of the apartment house. He had lost his first key, and someone had stolen things from him.

She said to him, "Tell you what Ken. When you are sure that you can keep your key safe, you come back again, and someone here will give you a little cross to hang with the key around your neck."

He went outside as she swung the door shut on his last words, "Thank you, Ma'am. you *are* a kind lady."

Returning to the office, making a mental note to buy such a "nice little cross" in case Ken remembered her words of advice on his next visit, she suddenly remembered why the phone was off the hook. It was no surprise to find that her friend had hung up on her.

Her next visitor was quite a contrast. Coming all too soon after Ken, she held the door open only wide enough to inquire if he might be the man who had phoned her earlier, to say he was coming today to pick up his food hamper. He had missed yesterday because he was on medication that put him to sleep; he did not wake up in time to come. The nicely dressed man at the door gave his full name, explaining that he had a church card for a food bank box, but he was moving into a new lodging, and had the card hiding somewhere inside his backpack. His cowboy boots were made of real leather.

"Come in," she encouraged him through the door. "We do have some food for you to look at."

As he bent to unload his large-sized backpack, she noticed its quality. As he raised his face to her, she noticed his sunken eye sockets and sweating face. His enthusiasm over turnips was just the beginning; the broccoli came next . . . then, the boxes of Kraft Dinner. He seemed to deem it a pleasure to eat macaroni, to have to wait for while it boiled. One of the bags at his feet was his own: it held a lot of strawberries in various stages from soft and mushy to a firm red. She gave the bag a puzzled look, knowing she had not seen it before. With a slightly embarrassed smile, he explained that he had stopped at the Salvation Army on his way here. He was choosing pork with beans . . . and Chinese noodles with shrimp! A few over-ripe bananas came next, which he handed to her with a broad smile.

"These would make good bread if you want to take them home," he quipped. They laughed together.

"How is it that a nice, clean-cut young man like you is so down and out?" she asked. "Are jobs that difficult to come by?"

"I've been ill," he replied without hesitation. "I'm on medication, though. I am almost recovered and ready to try for a job I should handle, until I can return to the hard work I'm used to . . . in the oil patch!" He instinctively knew the second question she knew she had no right to ask.

"That TV presentation you saw, involving our church, was the media's own way of dealing with statements made by the government, in response to public criticism of recent cuts that hurt those who are already in the low-income brackets."

"Yes, I realize that. Klein[64] thinks the churches should move in to pick up the slack left by those cuts, but the media are trying to point out that churches are also losing ground in this sagging economy and shouldn't be expected to do so."

"I think," and, in her mind, she was holding this discussion with a peer, "that the church might be better served by media coverage saying that they have *always* been in the business of helping those in greatest need, and have made a noticeable contribution in this area. We continue to help when the government's strategy to save up a fund for a rainy day gets sidelined because of recent disorganized cuts—it's surely raining now; people's *need* has too suddenly become a deluge!"

"Well, I for one would be willing to give Klein credit for making cuts. He must do so in order to get the economy back on track, but why doesn't our Premier trim the *fat*? If Pocklington's[65] big, million-dollar loans were put into circulation where they could do some good, fellows like me wouldn't be begging off churches. We might even be able to

---

64 Ralph Klein was premier of Alberta and leader of the Progressive Conservative Party during 1992 to 2006, when social services budgets were drastically cut to help reduce the provincial debt.

65 Peter Pocklington was a high-profile but controversial entrepreneur in Edmonton during the 1970s to 1990s, former owner of the Edmonton Oilers hockey team (1976 to 1998), and two meat packing plants (Gainers and Swift Canadian) in the city.

make contributions to the collection plate. I could do quite a lot of good with a piece of the big loss caused by mismanagement at NovaTel."[66]

Two more bags stood on the floor beside his strawberries.

"I hate to see all this good food pass me by," he continued. This bright but suffering customer sounded so much like one of her own young and hungry sons. "But, with my backpack, I can only carry so much. Would you consider holding some for me until tomorrow when a friend could offer me some transportation?"

"I'll tell you what I can do. You fill a box and label it, and I'll leave a note in the office explaining what we've done."

His appreciation was straightforward, his "thank you" genuine. They shook hands, she expressing her hope that things would soon improve for him. They said good-bye and Walter Cox carried his three bags onto the busy street.

---

66 NovaTel, a communications company specializing in manufacture of cellphones, then a new innovation, was operated as a joint venture between Nova Corp and Alberta Government Telephones during the 1980s. NovaTel went out of business in 1992, with total losses of up to $615 million.

LEARNING THE ROPES

BY ROBERT PROUDFOOT

That turbulent summer of 1975, I wistfully regarded as my debut into manhood. Clutching my hard-won university degree like a sword of truth, I hit the pavement of the rigorous working world, a zealot determined to cleanse all ignorance with new wave knowledge and technology. I was a young crusader crying out for justice and love, a New Order soldier coming of age with my country.

I promised God I would move mountains in his honour, but he seemed to have more education of the rigorously realistic kind ordered for me. His omnipotent mind saw fit to eject me into the mosquito-infested wilderness of Alberta's northern boreal forest and dull my boiling soapbox rhetoric on the shovel end of a workaholic soil survey team. I blistered sorely to netherworld bush life of rugged men labouring against the elements on oil rigs and in coal mines or sawmills, eating at greasy, smoky coffee shops, playing pool in rowdy bars, and sleeping in crowded bush camps—at the end of the Technicolor world.

My baleful supervisor, himself a despised lackey of intellectual dirt doctors dreaming up new soil series on maps in urban headquarters far away, reduced me to slave status in boot camp. A "real" man with morbid outlook and raw tastes, sandpaper-rough from grueling desert wars with the French Foreign Legion, Olaf found little affinity for my flowery poetry or social justice rants. Olaf scoffed at my naïve pretension of honourable manhood and presumed to teach me the "real" life during my summer's sentence within his iron grasp. Our first night on the road, he made a pass at me! I staked my right to life by stubbornly refusing his sexual advances, but I had already lost my freedom from Olaf's foul companionship when this one job opportunity for my impractical skills drifted me into his time warp for the next four months, far from home.

Having implored Olaf then that I was a man, I toughened determinedly beneath his vindictive lash. We marched long hours through the unchartered wilderness, battling clawing thickets and ferocious legions of vampire insects; I craved safe drinking water while slogging waist-deep in muskeg swamps. Olaf dragged me into bars during our rare nights in some frontier oil town, where he chased and fought over hard-bitten barfly women and drank me under the table while regaling about his grisly war stories. He boasted of racking "points" by killing enemy soldiers and fashioning crude lamps with their severed heads! I relived with Olaf many gruesome desert battles through outpourings of his surreal imagination; I believed that he only found peace when he was too drunk to acknowledge their lingering horrors. Olaf carried a loaded rifle in the bush like he was still in uniform . . . to safeguard against attacking bears, he claimed. I dutifully obeyed his barking commands on all fronts, lest I become his next moving target if ever I failed to please him!

Olaf hated women as fiercely as he despised non-Christians or people of colour, though he professed no Christly qualities as he lusted after Elsie Desjarlais, our plucky native landlady, and her teenaged daughters whenever they ventured into view. He played my young man's courting game like he was twenty instead of forty. What had he to lose when his wife of honourable Catholic upbringing had plied many eager suitors on the home front during his patriotic wars to keep far-flung African colonies for the glory of France? That she and many jaded mistresses had fled Olaf I could readily understand; he was an immoral, unwashed animal who smoked acrid cigars, and took pride in belching his daily diet of sardines, rye bread, raw onions, and garlic. Olaf's heroes were bull-headed warriors of the Third Reich, with whom he amused himself during our drudgeries by detailing how these tough "real" men honed their fighting skills. Olaf was a holdout from a previous era that existed on a strange wavelength, where women had no rights, and man's life was primitive, harsh, and ruled by fear.

Insulted by his vulgar language . . . threatened by his harsh edicts, I could barely relate to this oaf with whom I must eat, breathe, and have my being. He was obviously wrong and not long for this world in my righteous eyes, yet I was the one who made childish mistakes that hampered our work. Olaf berated me mercilessly when my forgetting the simple task of filling our water thermos caused us to labour all day in nagging thirst. I languished in his doghouse another day, hating myself when I broke the motor propeller, then lost an oar to our powerboat during a routine voyage between camp and our work area across Calling Lake. Olaf rebuked me again for being hard on machinery when I nearly rolled our truck in vigilant effort to miss a bear that had ambled onto the road. Reduced to buffoon status of carrying Olaf's pen or briefcase into the headquarters office when we finally returned to Edmonton after a month of brushwork, I was laughed down by him and his coffee-drinking cronies when told to wash the truck during a Friday afternoon cloudburst.

I grit my teeth and decided to grow up fast or quit in acknowledgement of this thug's unreal mastery over me. I saved my job by cultivating a working relationship with Olaf: read the newspaper more and played less with the radio; and, coming out of my shell of brooding prose, entered mealtime conversations with my rugged field partner. By humouring Olaf in co-screenwriting victorious dramas for our fictitious war heroes—General Killinger, Admiral Shootofsky, Colonel Strike, and Captain Otto Blast—I learned to understand the troubled past of this defeat-haunted warrior. His loneliness was vividly portrayed to me one evening as I approached the lakeshore, driving our motorboat to collect Olaf, and barely deciphered him frantically waving at me against the immense backdrop of forest and sunset sky.

I suffered to appreciate the rugged adventures of our regal fighting men as a buffer against drudgery, isolation, and mosquitoes of our bush existence. The more we jawed and fantasized about the brutal Nazi era, my fascination grew for researching that dark war history. My readings confirmed general rumours that Adolf Hitler had been a ruthless dictator, driven by delusions of military conquest and establishment of a new world order ruled by an Aryan master race. Olaf zealously countered that, prior to World War II, Der Führer had brought hope and stability to Germany's chaotic Depression economy, and fostered such new technologies as the *Autobahn* highway system. Had not brilliant military strategies and iron might of the Wehrmacht and Luftwaffe brought the world to her knees? We relived harsh Eastern Front warfare between Germany and Russia, debated its great human waste against staving off the greater evil of communism. Although Olaf doubted published numbers of six million Jews exterminated, he could not deny that concentration camps and SS atrocities had been evil realities. He rebuked today's glib hate mongers who now taught that the Holocaust was a hoax, and cursed neo-Nazi "skinheads"—springing up even in Bible-Belt Alberta as totally useless—good only for picking up broken glass!

At least Josef Mengele and Klaus Barbie[67], wanted as notorious war criminals, had believed and sacrificed all for their cause! Discredited and

---

67 Dr. Josef Mengele (1911 to 1979) and Klaus Barbie (1913 to 1991) were two high-profile and actively hunted, Nazi war criminals from the Second War who were still at large in 1975. Mengele, dubbed "The Angel of Death", was a German SS officer and physician in Auschwitz concentration camp who performed deadly "medical" experiments for genetic research on prisoners, many of them children or twins, and was a member of the team of doctors who determined which arriving prisoners would be saved for slave labor or killed in the gas chambers. He was deemed responsible for the deaths of some 400,000 people. Mengele fled to South America after the war.

Klaus Barbie, dubbed "Butcher of Lyon", was an SS officer and Gestapo functionary accused of personally torturing and sexually abusing prisoners in Lyon, France. Barbie was directly responsible for the deaths of up to defeated in war, they had spent the rest of their harrowing lives hiding from justice demanded by a supposedly new and more just world galloping past them into the space age. Was there no mercy or forgiveness for these now decrepit old men, a lifetime after they had committed their dastardly crimes against humanity's weak and vulnerable? The Angel of Death suffered more by living on the lam and seeing his fiercely proud, Nazi ideals wither away over the past thirty years, than in facing swift court justice meted out upon many of his colleagues at Nuremberg Trials shortly after Germany's surrender.

Mengele may have escaped, but Canada was prepared to continue reopening old wounds by judiciously moving against other war criminals who stayed too long in her good graces. Was this justice—at last? What about Olaf, I inwardly worried? Was he just venting bravado, telling me old war stories? If any of his gruesome jokes were true about Legionnaires making "posters" from splattered blood or "lamps" from the chopped heads of captured Arab enemies, shot as they were forced to "run to the wall," was Olaf not a war criminal flying under the radar, albeit from a more recent conflict? Was I an idiot to stay with him, a fool to humour him? Should I report Olaf to the police? Why was he reaching out to me?

◆ ◆ ◆

Olaf and I finally seemed to be cobbling together a friendship when I committed another stupid mistake on the job that brought everything crashing down. Olaf trusted me enough one bright August morn to fetch a fresh tank of boat fuel and haul it aboard for our run across the lake.

14,000 people, including 44 Jewish orphaned children, whom he deported to Auschwitz in 1944. After World War II ended in 1945, but before his capture and conviction in France for crimes against humanity in 1983, Barbie worked for the US (1947) and West German intelligence services (1965) and, as a Bolivian army officer, was suspected to have helped Luis Garcia Meza Tejada gain power in Bolivia through a *coup d'état*. Barbie died in a French prison.

Getting the fuel from Elsie was easy, but my trouble began when I lazily drove the tank down by truck instead of toting it from the gravel road's end to where our boat was moored at the shoreline. I was rocking to the blaring radio and admiring whitecaps rolling into shore when the truck suddenly powered out, and I buried its wheels in moist, soft sand on the beach!

Olaf, who was contentedly loading our boat with tackle in anticipation of some heavy fishing to offset a little work on this Friday before a big weekend furlough in Edmonton, suddenly stood up shouting and waving his hammer fists at me. Terrified that he was running at me, shovel club raised in ready to kill me, I vainly tried to barrel out my snared vehicle in reverse to freedom.

"Brent, you goddam idiot!" Olaf bellowed. He threw me from the cab, and killed the engine of my churning truck in one irate motion. "What the hell you doing, drilling for oil?"

I hit the ground hard, and lay there dazed as Olaf stamped around the truck, muttering oaths mixed with death threats in his rough-hewn French as he grimly surveyed my damaging handiwork. He took a few mighty swings at the sand hugging the wheels, then hurled his shovel into the truck box with disgust. I swallowed hard as I mourned the sudden death of tomorrow's plans to go trapshooting, made during a mellow campfire conversation with Olaf last evening.

I, desperate to redeem myself in his glowering eyes, picked myself up and began digging out the truck with the shovel Olaf had discarded, but my apparently brazen attempt to complete what he could not infuriated my overseer anew. Like some high school bully, he rapidly went from cajoling me on the sidelines to yanking the shovel from my hands and throwing it deep into the forest.

"You think you are somebody, Brent!" Olaf growled. He ridiculed my tears of chagrin. "You think your education makes you better than me?

"You are *nothing*, Brent! You talk good with me about General Killinger and Wehrmacht, but you are only trouble for this job! Don't come back next summer to work for me, Brent. I no want your trouble!

Maybe better you stay in university and write poetry than play like fool in man's world!"

"Olaf, it's my fault the truck got stuck, and I'm gonna get it out if it takes me all day!" I vowed, putting everything on the line.

"*Mon Dieu! Voila, l'homme qui arrive!*" oathed this brute. He mocked my tenacious will to clean up my bad act, but when I failed to respond, Olaf declared, "Okay, Brent, I go to the cabin for to sleep —maybe screw the girl! Bring the truck when you will come. *À bientôt, mon ami!*"

He stormed up the gravel road, abandoning me to sink or swim in my plight. I angrily marveled at the speed of his distancing gait, then set myself defiantly into my seemingly hopeless task—that I might persevere and prove to Olaf that I was as good a man as him. Driven by his ridiculing sneer, I dug and tossed sand until I had unearthed the pick-up's tires all around. Then, I jumped into the cab and tried to drive out of my hole backwards . . . frontward, even sideways but this trap—however weakened—held firm and my vehicle crazily buried itself again. I tried jacking up the wheels and making a road underneath with scrounged rocks and branches but "Plan B" failed when the truck refused to stay in harness.

"What shall I do now, God?" I begged the cloudless sky as I surveyed the damage I had done. Fatigued and sweat-soaked from pointless labours, I slumped onto the beach and watched the placid lake for a while. Then, getting nowhere, I lashed myself like Olaf had so often done in three long months, "Think, Brent, *think*! What you can do now?"

Suddenly remembering that Elsie owned a tractor, I locked my truck, placed all tools in the box, and sprinted up to the rustic resort office that she had carved from the bush. Striding boldly into her yard, I spied my potential saviour hanging out laundry.

Her wolfish watch dogs alerted Mrs. Desjarlais to my intrusion with vicious howls as they charged me, but this attractive Métis woods woman playfully called off the pack before it could move in for the kill.

"Just doin' their jobs, sonny," Elsie giggled from behind growling canine protection. "A single mom like me needs a little help, y'know, though these huskies are really just pups. You ain't afraid now?"

When I hung back and failed to share her humour, this wild beauty tossed her dark mane and knowingly pegged my purpose. "You're a gentleman, eh, unlike your droolin' boss! Brent, you never come around here to talk unless you're payin' the rent or need somethin' fixed . . .. So, what's up?"

"Our truck's stuck on the beach, and I was hoping I could borrow your tractor to pull it out," I blurted. I was embarrassed to come begging for help for my foolish mistakes from such a smugly amused object of our bunkhouse male fantasies.

My reeling male ego could not suffer this woman to drive a tractor, let alone know that I never had, but my mistress gave me an unexpected out by apologetically informing me that her tractor was presently out of commission. She wryly motioned towards the barn, where her hulking, grease monkey son had the machine up on blocks for major engine repairs.

"Ambrose could try to pull ya with the school bus," she offered brightly. Reviving my sinking hopes with a mischievous wink, Elsie ordered her two daughters to fall out from kitchen duty. "Take a break from peelin' spuds, you gals; we've got more important work at hand! Antoinette, fetch your brother and tell him to fire up the bus. Get my tow chains from the barn, Georgina. We're gonna help Mr. Williams here get his truck pulled off the beach."

"The *beach*?" Georgina wowed. She gave me an odd smirk as she plaited her raven hair with freshly polished nails. "Who'd be so dumb as get stuck down there?"

"You're lookin' at him!" Antoinette jeered. Hers was a teasing bid to see if I could actually speak. "Mr. Beachboy himself! He's from the city, eh!"

"Hush now and get on with your work!" scolded mother hen. Elsie shooed her primping daughters into action. This was a big event in her family's life that day, and she wanted them all to catch hold of the excitement. "Where's Grandma?"

"She's in the biffy," Antoinette shouted back from across the barnyard. "I saw Granny goin' there with a fresh roll of toilet paper."

"Well, then, knock on her sliver moon door on your way by. Grandma shouldn't miss the fun."

This "fun" became a circus as Ambrose loaded me and his rollicking family into the bus, and chugged us a kilometre down to the beach. With the dogs furiously biting the tires, Georgina blaring her radio in back, Antoinette singing camp songs to lull to sleep her baby, who was cradled in Grandma's doting arms, and Elsie asking me a million questions about my own people, we assembled the first beach party for the future park.

We arrived to find another party humming, with several would-be rescue artists crawling about the stranded truck, eager to improve upon my own abandoned efforts. Two leather-jacketed hoods had lassoed the beast behind a crew cab, and were trying to hotwire its engine to life, while others laboured to free the front tires. Already pumped to red alert, my friends, and I swarmed from the bus and reclaimed the disputed goods.

Embroiled in chewing out Leather Jacket Number One as he grudgingly removed his lariat from my truck's bumper, I stiffened to a vice-like hand suddenly locked upon my shoulder. Whirling around, I stared into Olaf's menacing face.

"What goddam hell is going here, Brent?" he demanded, primed to deck me. "I seen this parade of guys going past my window, and thought I better check on you."

"I tried my best to dig out the truck myself, but finally sought Elsie's help," I stammered. I grinned sheepishly by bringing our beaming landlady into the rugged conversation.

My courage returned when Olaf was rendered blushingly speechless by the real woman whom he had pillaged countless times in his vulgar imagination. I left him at her mercy as I helped Ambrose heave my truck to the safety of higher ground. That night, we celebrated with a scrumptious roast beef dinner around Elsie's table. It was our first meal out with caring female company in many moons, a time of warm fellowship that we would never forget.

The rest of summer passed in a flash. There had been many hardships of learning the ropes of life, but these were softened by better times: frolicking on silver beaches or fishing in the shallows for northern pike and walleye during the loon's haunting twilight. God protected one stormy night when Ambrose bravely piloted us across the lake in his jet boat through lightning and tumultuous, rain-lashed waves; we three men huddled in a storm-tossed tub became manly adventurers then. We made it safely to shore, and enjoyed the comforts of home—supper before Elsie's welcoming hearth—before turning in to sleep peacefully in our beds.

I felt encouraged, even healed to develop mutual friendships with indigenous people who, thriving on their own turf, were willing to engage and share with me, a son of Canadian settlers and Olaf, an old warrior who struggled to survive in a new land. He and I also worked with less-accepting natives in the Rocky Mountains that summer, where we planted trees and seeded grass together on steep, alpine slopes being reclaimed after coal had been mined for export to Japanese steel firms. I thought I worked pleasantly with Russell, a young Indian fellow about my own age, yet he bitterly chewed me out, and told me to "get the hell out of *his* country" when we met by chance in a Grande Cache store on our Saturday off. Feeling hurt and rejected, I left the store alone, never to see Russell again. I thought, naively perhaps, as one whose Canadian roots grew deep through many generations of family nurturing the land, that I belonged in my home. While Russell and his jeering friends from the nearby reservation had shattered such a notion, the Desjarlais family proved respectful and generous when Olaf and I behaved truthfully well, offered to learn from them, and gratefully accepted their hospitality. We were different, yet equal, but I had more listening to do, in order to learn from indigenous peoples to understand their deep troubles experienced daily through 500 years of colonization by Europeans like me.

I sadly bid farewell to our down-home hosts and the hills, lakes, forests, and skies of northern Alberta when our survey work finally ended, and Olaf and I left the boreal solitudes for Edmonton's noise and bright lights. Olaf and I good-naturedly shook hands when we parted; I earned his grudging respect as both a helper and friend. Elsie also had positively impacted my colleague's troubled life; I hope to witness that day when he is not so lonely anymore.

NIGHT TRAINS

BY ROBERT PROUDFOOT

The telephone clanged one hot, summer Sunday afternoon, awakening John rudely from his nap. Not that he slumbered peacefully, for John stumbled off the living room couch, threw away his blanket of scattered newspapers, and slipped on the hardwood floor as he scurried to find, then silence, the incessant ringer. He was bathed in sweat and felt lethargic, as he struggled in the humid Pennsylvania air that permeated every nook and cranny of the crowded landscape. That his wife Louise was gone five days now, visiting her younger sister Jean in faraway Kansas City and he, left baching, showed itself by scattered clothing awaiting a trip to the laundromat and dirty dishes stacked in the kitchen sink. Despite looming thunderstorms, all the windows were propped open in a vain effort to create cross breezes. Shiny cars droned past incessantly, but he also heard the clip-clop of horses pulling covered Amish or Mennonite buggies on the street below. Which plain folk rode in black buggies . . . or grey? John stretched his racing mind to recall.

John heard jocular male banter and repeated pinging sounds through the open front door, and noted with annoyance that, just a few yards beyond his porch, a couple of batters were hitting baseballs to several athletic lads fielding on his front lawn. Okay, John gnashed: while he and Louise waited for visas that would let them do MCC development work in West Africa, they squatted in this old farmhouse perched on a grassy knoll at the edge of town—morbidly known by staff at the MCC thrift store next door as the Grey Owl because it stared at you like some predator bird when evening lamps were lit—but what gave locals the right to disturb his peace, especially on the Sabbath?

Finally reaching the telephone after its sixth ring, John grabbed the receiver and breathlessly inquired, "Hello? Can I help you?"

"John, this is Dan," the caller informed him, "Like, in your brother-in-law . . . *only* one?" Dan sounded irritated, but not just because John fumbled to recognize his deep, twangy voice. Dan cut to the chase, "When're you coming out west to collect your wife?"

John babbled, embarrassed for skipping his in-laws' baby celebration, "We are leaving for Nigeria in two weeks and need to save our money, so I didn't accompany Louise to visit you guys *this* time, Dan . . . . Nonetheless, I heartily congratulate you from afar, as Louise and I are ecstatic over the birth of your son Nathan: a new brother for your two daughters; that makes three kids to zip for our younger couple! Wow!"

"What's wrong with your wife?" Dan interrupted. He was unimpressed with John's lame song and dance routine.

"Sorry, I don't get your drift."

"Louise suffered a meltdown and was admitted last night into a psychiatric hospital here in KC. She ain't fit to travel to Africa any time soon," Dan toned forbiddingly. "You better come quick now, and deal with her!"

"Say what?"

"Louise is a nut case, man—very serious. She argued with us all the time since arrival, but her behaviour got scary worse! Louise claimed we were all possessed with demons, and tried to cast them out. She hurt Jean and frightened our children with wild accusations about idol worship and devils running amok. We are devout Christians, John—maybe not your do-gooder Mennonite brand but Godly believers nonetheless. Louise locked herself in her attic bedroom, where she loudly read scriptures, and prayed for hours on end, with candles burning. I invited our pastor over to the house to reason with Louise but she, afraid that he wanted to kill her, jumped out the attic window when we busted down her door. Jean, almost delirious herself, and fearing that Louise would harm our children, called the police. The boys in blue tackled and cuffed Louise, then hauled your wild, swearing, threatening woman away.

"My girls won't settle, and Nathan cries all the time. Jean is stressed to her breaking point," Dan railed. He sounded at the end of his tether, yet gloated at Louise's bizarre behaviour, so sideshow in his family's successful and reasonable, white middle-class circle. He demanded apologies as well as answers, "John, what's happening with you guys? Can't you keep your wife under control? We can't stand any more craziness—if Louise won't listen, she's no longer our relative or our problem.

"She can't stay here, man—we're totally done. You gotta deal with her, John—*fix* her! Louise is no good for Africa or here; take her home to Canada, back with her weird parents where she belongs."

"Dan, I am *so sorry!*" John cried. His despair erupting, he smacked the wall with his fist to stop ripping apart the telephone. "Louise, Jean's only sibling, just wanted to celebrate her new baby, and say goodbye to our special nieces before we disappear for the next three years. I encouraged Louise to visit you folks—share good news of finally receiving the green light for Africa, after months of gathering dust on the shelf here at headquarters. I didn't foresee *this* gong show, Dan, honestly."

"*I* saw it coming from *miles* away," Dan gnashed. He sounded triumphantly clever across thousands of miles of crackling telephone wires. "I know the drill, John; having been married to Jean for ten years, I understand how Louise suffers mentally."

"You probably drove her into a rage, being a hard-assed smart-aleck," John retorted. His limited first impression of Dan as an anti-social bully darkly dismissed any help from his American brother-in-law.

"You don't know your wife very well, huh."

"I have no idea," John chafed. Angry and confused, he hated Dan but, before slamming down the receiver on this bearer of bad tidings, he promised to catch the next flight out west.

Racing against time, John refused to crash on his bed. He spent the rest of the afternoon feverishly slapping together, implementing, failing, and revising plans to save Louise. Quoting his seldom-used credit card, the desperate young man-on-mission purchased an American Airlines ticket one-way from Philadelphia to KC. Tomorrow would start before sunrise, taking him across the country from Grey Owl to some Midwestern looney bin where Louise languished like a criminal.

This hurtful vision lashed John to telephone long-distance, home to Alberta. He had spoken with his own parents in Edmonton just the previous week, when John was overjoyed to learn that, despite living in the river valley east of downtown, they had been spared by a huge tornado that had demolished several nearby businesses and a trailer court, killing thirty people. Until Black Friday in July 1987, Albertans had vaguely understood tornadoes as whirling funnel storms that scourged the hot-dry *Kansas* plains—where Dorothy had been scooped inside her farmhouse, and transported to the mythical Land of Oz—therefore could never hurt *them*! Talk about a wake-up call! John had gaily relayed his own news: he and Louise were finally cleared for Nigeria after six months' wait, and would head there as soon as she returned from visiting her sister. Today's bizarre switcheroo made blubbering John feel foolish and broken, weaknesses that his strong but silent father (a competent professional engineer who had built his own house, not to mention created technical schools across Africa) could not solve.

Informing Louise's parents brought expected condemnation from her mother, who tongue-lashed John as some fox who dared steal her daughter away, to the burning sands and teeming heathens of darkest Africa. Their travels were rightly judged because the couple disobeyed God's will by leaving family and commitments to the Christian community in Alberta. *Why* did he force her to go? What calling could they find in Africa that was more important than becoming pastors to their own people in Edmonton? If John was not so stiff-necked in pushing to return to the wilds where he had spent his youth, they would likely have their own happy, bouncy child now instead of Louise suffering a miscarriage last year!

John, blown away by such venomous spite, demanded to know why Mrs. Poettcher had not told him prior to marriage that her daughter was mentally ill. Though he had vowed to love his bride in sickness or health, John bitterly chafed now that he was stuck with a lunatic!

Mrs. Poettcher insisted that Louise was not sick, and demanded that John repent of such sinful thoughts . . .. Bring her daughter home immediately, where she could be helped by people who loved her! Rev. Poettcher, who had worked in prisons and many churches across North America, came onto the line to smooth things over. Perhaps thinking his wife's demands were too harsh, he admitted that Louise had suffered bouts of "sadness" in the past, but had managed to rally, with God's help. He solemnly promised to pray for her healing, but also that John, whom he loved, would find peace despite present difficulties. With God, all things were possible.

"Yeah, right, thanks for nothing!" John muttered. Wretchedly, he quit the searing line.

Feeling down and out, he flung himself dejectedly on his bed. He sought insights as he stared at wildflowers blooming on the beige wallpaper, but soon was bathed anew with sweat. A fly kept bugging him. Raucous laughter and incessant whacking of baseballs continued outside his house. He loved baseball; why the hell couldn't those jaunty boys of summer invite him to join their fun? When he heard a loud thud on the wall, precariously close to a window, John stuck his red face out the front door and screamed foul, but the ballplayers were long gone. Only a couple of horses in the neighbouring pasture regarded him as they dully looked up from browsing sorrel over a shared fence line. It was still humid and sticky in the brilliant sunlight when John clambered to the bank to cash all his money, but storm clouds poured down rain as he dashed back to Grey Owl, his wallet stuffed with 200 greenbacks. John was quickly soaked but he had no time to feel sorry for himself when Louise needed help . . ... Really, his time to act was fleeting fast!

Since MCC offices were closed on Sundays, John telephoned Rod, august chair of the Africa desk and Bill, the Canadian vice president at home but, finding nobody on-seat, left anxious voicemails. Both gentlemen, affable yet not to be treated as friends, were unavailable when needed most to advise, lend money, or provide a vehicle to their addled pawn. They were likely enjoying idyllic Sunday afternoon pursuits with their families, blissfully unaware of his debacle!

John and Louise were not yet working overseas, but they volunteered at MCC headquarters doing odd jobs while waiting to ship out. Both washed dishes, cleaned tables, and mopped floors in the kitchen. When not shingling roofs, cutting grass, or laying sod for office staff, John prepared for his overseas assignment by studying the Hausa language or reading novels by Nigerian authors Achebe, Ekwensi, and Nwapa. Louise helped present MCC to the public and church constituency, host activities for new or returning workers, drive elderly to medical appointments, or teach English to immigrants. The plucky, flexible couple was active in a local Mennonite church, attended social justice rallies against KKK or military arms sales, and volunteered whenever farms or villages needed clean-up after floods or tornados. They shopped locally, cooked their own meals, and visited points of interest within walking distance: farmers' markets and craft fairs; the historical Ephrata Cloister with its warren of mud walls and communal room; and a shadowy religious sect that met in a mansion across the road. John and Louise eagerly snapped up opportunities to drive MCC dignitaries or workers between headquarters and airports in New York, Philadelphia, or Harrisburg, as such outings allowed them to explore the bustling cities and idyllic countryside of New England. Yet, it bugged John that their passengers went jet-setting on paid assignment, while he and his wife remained stuck on the ground—now, maybe forever.

❖ ❖ ❖

Everything was working well, John marveled as, drinking coffee from his window seat of a jumbo jet streaking ahead of the sun, he gazed out at wispy clouds floating like guardian angels over the vast Midwestern plains far below. Travel arrangements frantically cobbled together twenty hours previously came together like clock-work: he woke up at 5:00 a.m.; met the taxi behind Grey Owl at 5:30 a.m.; zoomed via Amtrak passenger train eastward, past corn fields and dairies where Amish farmed with draft horses and Mennonites attended brick churches with white trim and spires or drove black cars without chrome bumpers. He rode into William Penn's great "City of Brotherly Love" by 8:00 a.m. A black taxi driver took him through teaming, row house neighbourhoods and past ship docks, outlet malls, and smoky factories, eventually plying Roosevelt Boulevard to Northeast Philadelphia Airport, from where his jet took off by 9:00 a.m. No time for breakfast on the ground but perky AA stewardesses served him adequately with coffee, orange juice, and a hot ham and egg sandwich while crossing over the Appalachian Mountains. His small suitcase was secure in the rack overhead, and he still had plenty of money in the wallet plunked snugly inside his blue jeans pocket.

John could finally relax—maybe read his *Time* magazine and *USA Today* newspaper en route—but these rags were proudly American, and focused on issues that he, a polite foreigner flying under the radar, could not solve. He leaned back slightly when fatigue hit him, but could not sleep, as anguish over Louise hurt his heart, and he stewed instead over how to find her, and what he would say to Dan and Jean when finally, they should meet. He must look affright, as his beefy bench mates dared not look at, let alone chat with him. He carried heavy burdens as he travelled towards a terrible fate, a stranger sojourning in a strange land.

A stewardess, noting John's distress, smiled sympathetically at him as she refilled his coffee cup, and gave him more pepper-roasted peanuts. Reaching adroitly over the other two passengers—one who was asleep and the other, engrossed in pulp fiction—she asked, "Are you enjoying our flight, sir?"

"Trying to," replied John. Although gloomy, he was thankful for her service. When the stewardess brightened, genuinely appreciative of his accolade, John shared, "I've enjoyed watching the various landscapes unfold below. The Appalachians were green and round, but I think we already followed the Ohio River to where it confluences with the big, broad Mississippi. Going west, it's been farmland, farmland, and *more* farmland, ripening towards golden."

"That's our mid-west corn belt for you—corn, soybeans, oats, and winter wheat, as far as the eye can see," she concurred wryly. She noted how he tentatively sipped coffee from the mug, gripped in his trembling hands, and silently wondered at anxious wrinkles and unshaven stubble on his otherwise ruddy face of healthy youth. "Soon, we'll be flying over St. Louis, but won't stop there. Pity, it's an exciting city—they've got that big arch you can travel on and see the whole downtown—the skyline is beautiful at night! Are you getting off at KC, or do you go farther to somewhere more exciting, like LA or 'Frisco, perhaps?"

"I'm just travelling to Kansas City. That's where I need to go, not so much want to, but it's as far as my money can take me," John quipped. He sponged his dour look with a touch of humour.

"Then, you must visit Crown Centre, a fabulous shopping mall with all these chic stores, fountains, Lego Land, even a hamburger joint where the waitresses bring food to your table via a toy train. Kansas City is famous for barbecued fare, so make sure you check out some of those sizzling eateries! It's also the home of jazz—like in American Jazz Museum—if such is your favourite music."

"Like Satchmo playing trumpet? Oh yeah!" John, liking the banter with this pretty, chatty girl, dug deep to flip out what little he knew about all that jazz!

"You could take in a Royals baseball game," she suggested, while attentively topping up his coffee cup the moment he set it down in the hole on his tray. "They won the World Series just two seasons ago and are still a powerhouse, American League team. You've heard of George Brett?"

"Yes," John acknowledged. He had watched the all-star, clutch-hitting infielder way more on Canadian TV than the perennially strong Montreal Expos or up-and-coming Toronto Blue Jays. He proudly shared, to the astonishment of the stewardess and other passengers who listened in as they impatiently waited for her to serve them, "I'm an Expos fan, first and foremost."

"They're National League, right?" queried his server. She gingerly stepped back into the aisle when a disgruntled traveler behind her tapped more coffee. When John nodded appreciatively, she surmised, "You're Canadian, huh?"

"Hundred percent, born and raised," chuckled John, "'Crazy Canuck,'[68] from eh to zed!"

They laughed at his idiosyncrasies tossed out apologetically from the Great White North, but the dark circles under his bloodshot eyes, and his suddenly edgy voice made her wonder at how happy and stable AA passenger John Brightwood really was.

She moved on quickly now, to serve passengers ahead, but John savoured their own pleasant exchange as a good omen. Was it true that apples were in season—or crabapples—he wondered as he nodded off to sleep? After the jet taxied into port, enlivened passengers arose, jostled to grab their belongings, and filed purposefully out of the jet; some thanked the stewardesses where they stood near the exit door, and wished everyone pleasant days in Kansas City. John assumed it was her job to be polite and useful when the friendly stewardess smiled and thanked him for flying American Airlines but he, in his sudden stress, embraced her when she gave him a meaningful gaze and wished him all the best. This blonde and blue-eyed angel reminded him of Louise, helpful and caring yet so bubbly and free-spirited, before the miscarriages or stress of waiting for Africa had dragged them down . . . .

John, lugging his suddenly heavy and battered little suitcase, trudged up twisting tunnel ramps, through hallways, and down escalators, following other passengers like a sheep through the airport. John was about to grab a taxi into the city and find a cheap hotel, when he ran smack-dab into Dan Briggs, who was sombrely waiting for him to set foot on the wooden floor inside the busy, horseshoe-shaped arrivals terminal.

---

68 The "Crazy Canucks" were on the Canadian national ski team, featuring five young men (Jungle Jim Hunter, Ken Read, Steve Podborski, Dave Irwin, and Dave Murray) during the 1970s and 1980s, who powerfully, courageously, and successfully represented Canada in alpine downhill skiing events at the Winter Olympics and world skiing championships. They had a reputation for fast and seemingly reckless skiing.

"Howdy, John!" Dan greeted. Boisterously corralling his startled in-law, Briggs gave his feebly extended hand a bone-jarring shake. Dan looked like a cowboy, yet was all scrubbed clean and looking sharp, as if come into the city to meet some soft eastern lawyer or dance hall woman. Dan must own a dude ranch or was a Hollywood western actor—a stuntman, perhaps? Who in this busy, mid-west airport knew the difference? Under his white Stetson hat, Dan was crisply decked in his white and navy checkered shirt, string tie, brown leather cowboy boots, and tight denim jeans neatly etched by white lariats. He drawled, "I hope you had a good flight. Got more luggage to fetch before we head out?"

"This is it," replied John. Chagrinned, he lifted his compact little suitcase for notice.

"I thought that was Louise's make-up bag," Dan scoffed. As they traipsed around the horseshoe towards glassy exits that gleamed in the afternoon sunlight, he gave John a hard gaze, despite tossing him glib remarks a bystander might find humorous. "You travel light . . . planning on a short stay in KC, like getting outta Dodge before sunset?"

"I'm here for the duration—whatever it takes to help Louise get mobile."

"MCC's training you for backpacking around Nigeria, huh? Like I told you on the phone yesterday, John, your wife is one sick woman. She ain't going to Nigeria or anywhere else soon. Since you don't believe me, let's go to the hospital now, so you can see Louise for yourself."

"Okay, let's visit Louise," agreed John. Had he said the wrong thing now as he, struggling to carry his own load in the sweltering heat, panted and stumbled to keep up with Dan? His dour in-law donned his mirror sunglasses, and strode briskly across a vast parking lot full of glistening vehicles to where only he knew his car was waiting.

At length, they arrived at Dan's gleaming new Cadillac, which was really only a stone's throw from the terminal. Dan clicked open the doors with his remote, and smoothly stepped into the plush, leather-covered driver's seat like he was mounting a horse. When John stood nervously, seemingly stuck to melting asphalt, Dan skimmed down his passenger window and impatiently yelled, "Hey man, put your bag on the back seat, and then climb in beside me! Let's roll—I took time off work to fetch you, and don't have all day to play chauffeur!"

"'S a'right," John saluted. He jumped aboard for whatever lay ahead.

Within seconds, they pulled up to the gang of ticket booths, where Dan paid for parking with some shiny American coins, engaged the spunky female attendant with debonair small talk, and then passed through the wicket with a wave and smile. They entered the roadway, and soon encountered a bustling octopus of concrete interchange; fearlessly in charge, however, Dan ramped onto Interstate 435, and joined the flow of traffic zooming towards distant skyscrapers arrayed like sentinels over downtown Kansas City.

John understood from previous visits that Kansas City was a vibrant metropolis of over 2 million people—bigger than any Canadian city except Toronto and Montreal—which made Edmonton look like some backwoods hick town! John morbidly looked forward to seeing what a two million city looked like, and hoped to check out all the fantastic sights his witty stewardess friend had suggested, hopefully with Louise gaily skipping at his side. Yet, as they motored southward through wheat fields and sprawling residential subdivisions under construction, the glassy towers watching him got no closer, just moved strategically along his eastern flank. The two men, hardly jovial or even related, crossed the wide Missouri River, and then skirted Kansas City, Kansas, a bustling urban centre in its own right but apparently junior sister to the amazon crowned farther east. Signs pointing to Lakeside Speedway, Wyandotte County Lake Park, and The Woodlands Race Tracks blurred past, but Dan showed no interest in such frivolous entertainments. They crossed the Kansas River, and continued south through suburban Shawnee and Lenexa, bedroom communities both yet full of strip malls, golf courses, and parks, that offered a green look for John's intensely observant eyes.

Dan kept the shaded eyes of his grim face glaring straight ahead like flint. He watched traffic and read signs like he knew his mission well, but tenderfoot John, who nervously clung to his seat, and recorded every detail as vital, finally blurted out, "How did you know where and when to meet me? I gave you no travel details yesterday . . . didn't expect to see you at the airport . . . and thought, after our chilly phone talk, I'd best be drifting into town like an outlaw."

"I took a hunch you'd be arriving today; American had the most realistic schedule," Dan explained dryly. He was not amused by his unwanted passenger's joke. "We're almost there."

Soon after this austere posting, Dan left the busy ring road at I-35, and wheeled down many nondescript streets that led into the leafy grounds of some liberal arts college. Parked cars lined the roads, and students migrated like sheep between academic buildings, chatted in chummy knots under shady elm trees, or casually played football on the manicured lawns. They seemed at peace with the world . . . that they had by the tail, John chafed bitterly. Dan moved purposefully forward until he found a parking stall in front of a sprawling, glassy building at the end of the lane.

"Here we are, John, Louise's fancy country club," Dan informed his gloomy passenger. "It's the best resort in KC."

The driver smiled menacingly like the Cheshire Cat as he stepped off his stallion. John rubbed his bloodshot eyes in disbelief at the modern, officious complex that arose benignly to greet him from among brilliant flower gardens and emerald lawns, dotted with shade trees that seemed contiguous with the rest of these tranquil campus grounds. This sublime haven seemed totally bogus, however, given his terrible vision of what a mental hospital should be: a forbidding, dark castle with turrets, baleful guards, and small, barred windows that stared at you like would any lunatic or needle-toting nurse. Where were the patients who, dressed in bedroom robes and slippers, should sit dazed in wheelchairs or shuffle about the grounds, attended by nurses in white uniforms?

Like he remembered while playing with his brothers and sisters as children on the grounds of Oliver Mental Hospital near Edmonton some sunny Saturdays, while their father inspected lighting and plumbing he had designed inside the ancient facility. Other Saturdays, Mr. Brightwood gave John's mother a break and took their six children further down Fort Road to the Fort Saskatchewan Jail, where the kids played tag or catch on the lawn beneath the forbidding beige walls of this fortress, while their father inspected the jail's utilities. John remembered seeing prisoners working in the gardens under the watchful eyes of armed guards; his father crustily remarked that having inmates raise their own food was more useful than making license plates! Had his old man, during his engineering rounds inside these dark, gloomy castles, ever seen somebody get hung, wear a straitjacket, or be shocked into reality while strapped down in a padded room? Mr. Rochester's mad wife Bertha languished in the attic of his gothic home, under Grace Poole's care, where she was treated better than most lunatics could expect in an asylum; yet, Bertha freely wandered the halls at night, setting fires, attacking people, laughing hysterically . . .. At both austere facilities, six Brightwood children and inmates alike had gazed wistfully when a train whistle suddenly tooted; had they not pined to climb aboard and fly away to freedom, as the passing train engineer waved back, friendly like, in plying his rumbling locomotive and clattering string of freight cars further down the tracks? The engineer could not stop, for he had a schedule to keep but knew his destination . . .. John laughed now at his bizarre notions, earning a harsh glare from his baleful relative.

"Wow," John whistled, "Are we in Disneyland or what?"

"This is Johnson Gardens Hospital, man, a well-rounded medical facility that has top-notch psychiatric services," Dan assured this dolt. "Louise is in good hands here."

"This I gotta see. Let's go in then and visit her," John suggested. He breathed deeply to cover his mounting nervousness.

"You go ahead," Dan encouraged dourly, almost ordering his older but less confident in-law. They had each married a Poettcher woman; were they not teammates, John gnashed, suddenly realizing he was being dumped in this strange place? Dan, protesting his dismay, explained edgily, "I need to get back to work now. After all that's come down lately with Louise, I can't visit her with you today. You sort it out with your wife and her doctor. I'm leaving now, John."

For emphasis, Dan tossed his suitcase out of the caddy before jumping inside and firing up the quietly powerful car.

"Just like that?" John cried.

Dan determinedly backed away, but offered no words of assurance through the open window as he passed, glowering, beside this useless, cry-baby Canadian who nearly got himself run over in a reckless bid to grab his dumb luggage from beneath the car's screeching tires.

"Yeah, John that's how it is, at least for *now*!" Dan sombrely laid down the law. "Jean and our kids are too fragile for a visit, so there's no fricking way we can give you room and board. Maybe I'll check up on you in a few days, but don't call our home meanwhile. Understand?"

"Whatever," muttered John.

He turned away, bewildered and bitter, and strode up the sidewalk towards the hospital without looking back. They had torn themselves apart, each angry man going his own way, to his own fate. As he ground his teeth, and stamped across Johnson Gardens' wide entryway, John vowed to sort out this horrible mess!

He was about to yank open the front door when the huge glass sections glided apart. John gingerly stepped through one yawning opening, and paused but momentarily, as inner glass gladly spread open, granting him entry into a huge and comfortable lobby that welcomed the weary visitor like a first-class guest to a luxurious hotel. His strained eyes blinked in disbelief as they beheld soft carpets and marble floors, upon which plush couches and blooming potted plants clustered about oak coffee tables and softly lit lamps. Beautiful paintings of snow-capped mountains or playing children hung in carved frames upon oak-paneled walls. Exquisite alabaster sculptures of young women carrying fruit baskets or Jesus finding his lost lamb observed John from the alcoves as he traipsed through the lobby to a broad reception desk at the far end.

"Good afternoon, sir. How can I help you?" inquired a pleasant desk clerk with stylish blonde hair. She acknowledged John with a wide smile and brilliant blue eyes, while her cohorts kindly looked on.

"I'm here to visit Louise Brightwood, who I understand is a new patient in your psychiatric ward?" John disclosed. He exuded breezy calm, belying his jitters, but when the attending trio seemed unfamiliar with the name, he quickly became defensive and emotionally divulged,

"I'm her husband, John Brightwood. Our relative, who resides nearby, told me that the police brought Louise here, two nights ago. I just arrived from Philadelphia, so did not commit my wife."

"Mr. Brightwood, I understand." The blonde attendant looked up from her busy but rapidly scrolling computer screen to assure him. "I'm just checking our records of recent arrivals."

Having connected with John by gently clasping his arm, she resumed her intense work of scanning lists. At length, she smiled again and notified, "Yes, here is Louise, all booked into Room 325, in East Wing on the Third Floor. She is under medical observation. Do you wish to visit her?"

"Of course," John declared. He chuckled feistily at what, in his suffering mind, was a no-brainer. "Does somebody need to escort me, or can I just head to her room?"

"You are free to go up," the attendant agreed pleasantly. "Just check in first with the duty nurse at Station 3C; she can help you find Louise. Straightforward, like at any good hospital, huh."

"You've got that right." John gave a positive, thumbs-up salute. "Thanks for your help."

"Any time," she purred. "You can access the third floor by one of those elevators in the hallway beyond our desk. Have a good day now, Mr. Brightwood."

"It's way better than five minutes ago," John promised. He gave the smiling blonde attendant a meaningful grin before he rounded her desk, and headed for the elevators. She was Louise III!

He boarded the first lift that opened, and ascended smoothly to the top floor. Stepping out, he followed signed instructions down a clean, well-lit corridor to Nursing Station 3C. John went through two sets of swinging doors, followed by a heavier door he had to pull open by a knob, and then entered a large room containing several clusters of easy chairs and couches, most of which were occupied by visitors chatting with patients and staff. Small consultation rooms ringed the outside, beyond which were reinforced plexiglass windows that allowed some of the bright, mid-afternoon sun to filter through. A few people sat in one shady nook where the blinds were drawn, watching the soap opera *All My Children*; even the TV actors spoke in hushed tones! The floors were polished tile while the walls and ceiling, an antiseptic beige, but among the fluorescent lights John noted a security camera—apparently watching him! The duty nurses' cubical was prominently positioned in the centre of the rear wall—all in all, this seemed relatively normal—for a *hospital*, John wryly surmised, having visited friends and relatives convalescing inside various medical facilities in the past. Striding up to meet the inquisitive monitor standing behind the counter, however, John noted that heavy doors embedded with thick glass windows provided restricted entry into patient wards to her right or left.

"How are you today, sir? How can we help you?" the duty nurse inquired. She was cordial, although dressed in a starched white uniform and decidedly more sombre than the perky young things who had greeted him in the frilly lobby downstairs.

"I'd like to visit my wife, Louise Brightwood. I understand she is a patient here."

"We have an L. Brightwood in Room 325," the nurse acknowledged dourly. Scrutinizing John with hard, knowing eyes as if he was breaking the rules, perhaps an escaped patient himself or possibly the cause of Louise's debacle, she requested briskly, "Can I see some photo ID please?"

"Of course," John replied breathlessly. He was almost over the goal line.

He fished into his blue jeans pockets, one after the other but could not catch his wallet. Blushing with embarrassment, John suddenly remembered the security pack he had strapped to his chest. The nurse may have thought him odd to begin with, seeing this scowling, red-faced galute clattering into her domain, but now she frowned with disapproval as John pulled up his shirt, exposing his bare waist, and then pulled down his pouch low enough so he could rip open the Velcro clasp to retrieve his papers from inside. He produced his passport and driver's license for her austere review. She looked several times between the character fidgeting before her and his grey mug shots as John scrambled to unclasp his pack altogether before dressing himself.

"Okay, you look the part," the nurse wryly concluded. A hint of a smile pursed her stiff lips. "Canadian, huh. Louise sounds like a typical Kansas gal."

"She went to high school in Wichita, where her dad pastored a Mennonite church. Louise's younger sister is married to an American; Jean and her tots have the local accent down pat."

"You don't say. Can you speak both French and English, like your passport suggests?"

"Yes, like our government wants," John boasted. "I learned French starting in junior high school and hope to use it when my wife and I travel to West Africa in the near future."

Failing to understand that she was joking, just doing small talk while she waited for the men in white suits to come and drag him away, John rolled his eyes in recall of all those bilingual cereal boxes, federal edicts, and airport signs that he had left behind in the Great White North since coming to America six long months ago. Her country was a breath of fresh air, for sure. Too late, he realized he offered too much information about his great expectations.

"You are cleared to visit Louise now, Mr. Brightwood," the nurse declared, albeit with a cautionary rider. "You will, however, require an escort today, and the length of your visit may be brief, depending upon how your wife is feeling. Louise is quite fragile. Take a seat momentarily, while I page one of my colleagues to lead you into Ward A."

John had barely sat with the TV crowd before another nurse came to guide him into Ward A. He needed a wise escort, as the hospital's psychiatric area was to John a shadowy world of grey hallways and spartan rooms, where patients and attendants whispered, and drifted about like dull-eyed ghosts. While everyone seemed polite, he felt a gloomy cloud hanging over the place, and thus dared not look anyone in the eye, or speak unless spoken to. Glancing into rooms in search of Louise, John noted that some patients were awake and interacting with visitors or attenders in white suits, or were reading, watching or just present, hovering, pacing, or sitting beside their windows, but many slept on low, narrow beds. In passing, John saw patients watching television or reading magazines in a lounge, while still others were enjoying an energetic volleyball game in the gymnasium—yet, Louise was not among such lucid folk.

"Here is Louise's room," Nurse Jane announced. She stopped in front of a beige door with number 325 blackened onto it. She noted a figure curled up on her bed, covered by a grey woolen blanket except for her face, which even in sleep looked gloomy and tormented despite her golden hair. Jane allowed John to peer through the embedded window upon his wife, but she gently cautioned him from rushing in, "Louise is asleep—she seems weary today, despite all the hubbub of medical assessments and a fitness stint in the gym. Should I wake her, or would you like to come back later to visit, at supper time perhaps?"

"I'd like to visit with her *now*, ma'am . . . . I don't have anywhere else to go," John parlayed. "I think Louise will be okay with me."

"Sounds good, Mr. Brightwood. Louise has been asking for you. Let's check in with her," Nurse Jane concurred. With kindly acumen, she opened the door, and led John inside. Gently touching him to wait, she moved over to Louise's bedside, bent over the sleeping patient, and softly called to her, "Louise, wake up. You have a special visitor."

With a start and a gasp, Louise opened her blue eyes, and regarded the nurse with concern. Where had she come from, Louise wondered? What was Louise dreaming, the nurse and John wondered in response? When the nurse gently touched Louise's quivering shoulder, and told her that her husband had come, the patient whirled her sapphire eyes wildly around the room, anxiously calling for John. When she noted a remote figure hovering timidly in the corner, yet gazing with loving concern upon her, Louise threw off her blankets and ran, half-naked but squealing thankfully, to embrace John. Nurse Jane, spooked by this outburst, pressed the red emergency button calling for back-up, but it didn't matter to either spouse as they hugged, wept, and festooned each other with kisses.

"You are really here, John, not just in my dreams. I've waited so long for you!" Louise, breathlessly crying and desperately clinging to him, admonished her sombre husband with gleaming eyes, "Get me out of this awful place. Take me home, John—I don't belong here! I don't know why or how I even got here. Please . . . help me."

"I *am* here . . . to help you, Louise . . . . I love *you* and . . . will do whatever I can . . . to bring healing," John promised, repeatedly but haltingly. Yet, he was unable to appease his distraught wife.

"I am not insane! You moron, stop looking at me like that!"

Angry and anguished, Louise gripped John with amazon strength, and threw him down onto her bed when he could not do her bidding. Climbing astride, she shouted at him, profanity lacing her harsh demands that he repent of his oppression, his lack of faith. John, stunned by such wild behaviour, stayed prone, but submissively promised, over and over again, to stand by Louise . . . help her get better . . . . Soon two burly orderlies smocked in white burst in and restrained Louise from behind, while Nurse Jane, standing face to face with the patient, sternly talked her into a subdued state. Back in the bad old days, Louise would have been strapped into a straitjacket and tranquilized, but Nurse Jane and one bodyguard were able to use calming directives to lead Louise, whimpering with shame and despair, into a safe corner where she stood, neutralized, while the other orderly helped worried John regain his rubbery feet.

"You should go now, Mr. Brightwood," Nurse Jane counselled. She smiled grimly as she stood beside Louise, her hand gently stroking the patient's disheveled stack of golden hair. "You two have had enough excitement for one day. You can always come again to visit your wife, but should likely phone ahead to make sure she can receive you."

"Okay," sighed John as he shuffled past the two women towards the door, accompanied by one of the orderlies. He smiled at his wife, who watched his every movement like a hungry lioness, as he promised. "I'll return tomorrow to visit with you, Louise . . . . I love you."

"Don't be late," she muttered, her frown creasing into a strangely wicked grin.

After they exited, the accompanying orderly locked the door to Louise's room. As the two men walked down the hallway towards the nursing station, John gloomily asked that staff be patient and understanding with his wife, since she was obviously *not* herself.

"Of course, Mr. Brightwood, totally understood," Orderly Bob promised. Congenial and intelligent, John thought wryly for a madhouse guard, Bob shared, "Your wife, recently arrived, has not been put on any treatment other than bed rest as yet, but she is still under strict observation. Doctor Jones will prescribe an appropriate program, including exercises, therapy, and medications, when next he comes to visit Louise, in a day or two."

"In a couple of days? I need answers *now*!" John growled, totally frustrated. "Who is Dr. Jones? Where is he?"

"Please, Mr. Brightwood, be patient and let healing work. Dr. Jones is one of America's leading psychiatrists—very sound, caring and innovative," the orderly soothed. He invited a fuming John to follow him quietly out, rather than make a useless scene. Shouting and belligerence just agitated the patients in what should be a calm and healing environment for all. "Dr. Jones met Louise yesterday. Having made notes and contemplated his initial observations, he will return later this week to prescribe a course of action for Louise, as he does with all his patients. Monitoring will follow, with tweaks to the program made where warranted.

"Each patient, while unique, benefits from the good doctor's guidance. Johnson Gardens is a leading psychiatric facility, Mr. Brightwood; your wife is well cared for here."

"So, what will Nurse Jane do with Louise now, spank and put her to bed without supper for being naughty?" asked John, unconvinced. He dared push the envelope, despite his morbid notion that Orderly Bob, a hulking Igoresque brute, could easily break him in two if *he* was bad.

"Oh, never like *that* nursery rhyme. How scary!" thought Bob. He chuckled politely without telling John anything. "She might be given a magazine to read, or crayons and paper to draw something in her room. Louise could opt to watch television in the patient's lounge, as long as some attendant sits with her. She's pretty fragile; we don't want her mixing with other patients yet. A stroll about our spacious grounds might do her good next week, but is definitely out of the question today. Doctor Jones will give the green light when she is ready to step out. Louise could be given a sedative now, and placed on bed rest until supper time, but that's pretty soon. I wouldn't want to spoil the lady's nighttime repose."

"I just saw another patient punching the heck out of his own pillow. What's that for?"

"It helps them get rid of the rage and aggression built up inside. Louise, as you saw, is pretty angry."

"Yes, I see," John gnashed, wondering *why?* "Better she pounds on a pillow instead of me."

"She will act better in a day or so—you'll notice a difference," Bob assured as they parted.

John was not certain—about *anything*—as he left Johnson Gardens under a dark cloud, and aimlessly wandered through the adjoining campus, looking for a bus or taxi that could carry him into the city. He could not find the streets Dan had sped over nor remember any landmarks they had whizzed past to get to the hospital. Students seemed too engrossed in their paper chase to take time to understand this older, sweaty, and red-faced stranger who carried a battered suitcase like some bag lady, and seemed to be mumbling to himself like an escaped patient from yonder psych ward . . . .. All John needed was a tip or two about public transportation—better yet, someone who might give him a lift. John finally stuck out his thumb and, after waiting on some curb for a few minutes, hitchhiked down Quivera Road with a preppy young man sporting a toothpaste smile and fashionable clothing. This handy lad dropped him at Oak Park Mall before speeding off in his snazzy Mustang convertible to some gated high-brow neighbourhood in Olathe, farther out. John, not finding a hotel nearby, kept walking, and eventually found himself trekking northeast on I-35, with the downtown skyscrapers, windows ablaze by setting sun, in his sight. Where was he going, what was he doing? John knew not . . . nor did he really care. The horrible encounter with his once sweet wife left him dazed.

Automobiles roared past on the busy interstate; some motorists rudely honked or chattered provocative insults—some idiot tossed John a fresh apple core in passing—but the wrangly Canadian, self-absorbed by his own frustrations, ignored such chaff as he strode fiercely down the grassed allowance. He failed to notice a police car, its red cherry lights flashing ominously, moving stealthily along the road shoulder beside him. He vaguely felt under surveillance, but did not respond until a window glided down, and a policeman bellowed at him through a bull-horn. "Hey, Mister. Get over here! You're trespassing on public property."

John, feeling foolish, sprinted out of the ditch towards the idling police car. A beefy, uniformed state trooper, wearing reflector shades beneath his Mountie hat, but toting a revolver and nightstick strapped to his belt, stepped out and grimly directed the obviously disoriented lad to take his place in the front seat. The smokie, muttering profanities as he wondered what the hell was wrong with this kid, slammed the door behind John and then sat, cross-armed in the back seat beside another cop, while their driver droned into their constantly muttering radio that they now had secured the "suspect" in custody.

"What were you doing, wandering in the highway allowance? Picking bottles? Planning to derail a train? What ya got in the suitcase—a bomb . . . a stash of money?" the two troopers demanded in turn behind John's burning neck. The middle-aged driver, a senior officer with a hard, sunburned face, went from scrutinizing John to comparing his red, sweaty face against mugshots of known felons scrolling down his computer screens.

"I was walking back to my hotel from the hospital," John explained.

"That's *all*?" demanded one of the hulking twin smokies in back. "Numerous passers-by reported seeing a thug—who looked like you—wandering drunkenly on the road, occasionally threatening motorists with a firearm. You got a sawed-off shotgun in your possession, boy?"

"No! I don't carry guns. I was minding my own business, but I probably look weird—I just left off visiting my wife in Johnson Gardens psychiatric hospital, where she's a patient."

"You're not from around here, huh?" the older cop surmised. When John nodded sheepishly, he wryly pointed out, "That hospital is ten miles away—you've been walking all that distance? You're headed downtown now, but you're going the wrong way and need to get off the interstate if you want a hotel room near Johnson Gardens. You even know where you're going, boy?"

"I'm trying to get back to that Holiday Inn, you know, with the swimming pool and patio restaurant? I must have missed a turn and got lost," John admitted. He giggled sheepishly as he pointed skyward.

"Must have," agreed one younger cop in back. He grinned sardonically; most KC hotels provided such perks.

"Can I see some papers, boy—you got any ID?" the older cop required. He was not impressed when John fumbled in his blue jean pockets, before digging his passport out of the body pouch inside his shirt. At gruff request, he then handed over his suitcase for inspection by the driver's young sidekicks.

The sergeant frowned at the crisp blue booklet boldly stamped on the cover by a fancy emblem of lions, lilies, maple leaves, and a harp, anchored by lion and unicorn holding the British Union Jack or French fleur-de-lis, all capped by the British crown—symbols of a colonial European past far removed from the mighty American Eagle's republic. He flipped it open to view John's most recent photo, taken nearly a year ago when he still had a red beard and moustache. "Canadian! You're a clean-shaven youth now. Is this Grizzly Adams in the photo really you?"

"Yes, I swear to God," John oathed. He felt totally embarrassed when all three policemen glowered at him, as though he had insulted both their country and its entrusted deity.

"Sarge, he's just got a change of clothes and toiletries inside this sack. New blades are separately stored in their case," one of the suitcase inspectors reported. His mate confirmed these blasé findings, "Yeah Sarge, roger that . . . nothing contraband here."

"Okay, I guess we're done here," the lead trooper concluded. Nodding to John, he informed him, "You're free to go, Mr. Brightwood but we can't leave you out here, walking the interstate. Such ain't legal or safe here in the State of Kansas. That said, it looks like you need to be driven somewhere other than police headquarters. How about your Holiday Inn?"

"That would be awesome," John cheered. "I arrived only three hours ago from Philly[69] and have not checked in yet."

The sergeant radioed his dispatcher that Unit 55 had completed its investigation, and was returning to headquarters . . .. All was clear, there was no incident or situation to control. Crisply hanging up the CB microphone, he pulled his squad car into the lane and motored to the nearest cross-over bridge. Returning to the southbound lanes of I-35, they zoomed back to the Holiday Inn, where John was chivalrously dropped off at the lobby door. His strange chauffeurs tipped their Mountie hats, and wished him well, before they disappeared into the twilight.

John secured a fine, air-conditioned hotel room with an inviting view of an outdoor swimming pool, surrounded by manicured lawns and pampered shrubbery. He brewed a coffee, then stepped onto the balcony to leisurely sip his java fix and breathe in the attractive grounds. This sanctuary was idyllic for being surrounded by restless urban sprawl. John appreciated hearing a train whistle toot nearby, as it gave him peace, though he saw no train anywhere across urbanity that stretched far beyond his perch, towards the downtown skyscrapers, now securely lit at dusk.

Feeling famished yet weirdly free, he sourced out the dining room, where he ate a delicious slab of barbecued steak with all the trimmings: sautéed mushrooms; baked potato smothered with sour cream, green onions, and real bacon bits; Caesar salad, and a chilled rye-and-coke, his first alcohol and red meat since arriving at MCC headquarters six months ago. John would have swum in the pool during the cool of evening but had not brought his swimsuit, as he did not expect a long

---

69 Shortened nickname of Philadelphia, Pennsylvania.

stay. He settled for a lukewarm bath indoors to wash off the day's grime and soothe his aching body. While he soaked luxuriously in his massive tub, John heard another train as it rumbled through the darkness, somewhere outside. It was a melancholy sound, like a foghorn warning him of jagged rocks ahead: take heed and be careful. Why? Did he not already know that his life sucked? John wished to telephone a friend whom he could to talk to without being judged but, not knowing anyone then who cared, he succumbed to his fatigue, and went to bed.

❖ ❖ ❖

John liked trains . . . and nature . . . . These interests gave him peace. As a child, his father had delighted him by drawing smoke-belching steam locomotives or sleek diesel engines that powered into view, effortlessly pulling long lines of oil tanks, box cars, wagons piled high with coal or flat decks carrying lumber or pipes, out from misty hills. John had seen many a freight or passenger train gliding across the parklands by day, when his family travelled to visit relatives down on the farm; he was comforted that the engineer knew where he was going and followed a sure schedule. Night trains worried him, however, because he could not see them when they mournfully tooted his name; only a headlight shining in his face warned him of oncoming danger.

John had grown from boy into teenager on his father's riverbank acreage in east Edmonton where, seemingly far from the city's acrid roar, white-blossomed chokecherries and saskatoons promised juicy wild fruits; tall poplars laughed as they danced in river-cooled breezes; robins twittered lovely songs; and pheasants walked peacefully beside him in the shade. At age fifteen—on a hot summer day when youthful Progressive Conservatives defeated Alberta's outdated Bible Belt Social Credit government of thirty-six years—John's parents carried away their brood to southern Africa, where John fell in love with tropical plants. After completing his British O-level exams at the end of secondary school, he studied agriculture at the new University of Zambia.

Despite enjoying a four-year Zambian safari, John returned to Edmonton to complete his agriculture degree. He had a soft heart for Africans, however, and vowed to return someday to the Dark Continent. When doors to travel overseas did not open after university, he embarked upon a secure government job, working for farmers across Alberta. John met Louise, a special woman: witty, beautiful, good like him at table tennis and skiing, willing to share each other's friends . . . .. Elder daughter of a Mennonite pastor, Louise was chaste and well-mannered. She desired to help God's poor, and was willing to go to the ends of the earth to serve him, particularly if John journeyed beside her.

John was thirty years old when he married Louise, four years his junior. They settled in Edmonton, rented a modest bungalow with apple trees and pretty flowers in the spacious yard, thirty minutes' drive away from their parents' homes. The young couple thrived at church, flourished in their chosen professions of agriculture and health care, and enjoyed friends and family, yet kept stepping towards realizing their shared dream of working overseas for the Lord. In 1986, John and Louise wrapped things up at home after they were successfully interviewed by MCC Alberta in response to their application for African work. Louise was also pregnant but, three months along, she suffered a miscarriage; John was called in from some distant field to comfort his wife during her recovery. Loss of a beautiful new life harshly signaled that their comfortably settled lives were about to change . . . .

So why had they failed and were being punished, John railed at God as he waited outside the hotel for a taxi to take him to visit Louise again at Johnson Gardens? It was a sunny morning, and he had a base from which to operate, yet John felt pressed down by heavy foreboding as he arrived in front of the placidly inviting hospital. He morbidly glimpsed Louise leering at him from some shadowy window . . . or was that her crouching, ready to jump, instead of an air conditioner on the roof? With the cabbie watching him askance, John scanned the porch and grounds for kooks. Was *he* the mad one, John inwardly rebuked himself? He must get a grip, shape up for Louise's sake! Rather than flee, he paid his fare and dismissed the taxi. He did not enter the hospital immediately, but found a bench under a nearby tree and silently prayed to God for strength, patience and understanding.

John needed his creator's help big time but could not find it during today's . . . or even tomorrow's twilight zone visits with his crazy wife, rightly locked in her looney bin! Today, he hardly recognized the trembling, bizarre creature whose rubbery, uncontrollably curling and flipping tongue made her mumble, incoherently but incessantly, to him about strange ideas only she and her closely watching nurse understood. Louise laughed or shrieked at him harshly when John, totally flustered, asked her for an explanation. Finally, he put his own shaky index finger to his own quivering lips, and signaled for Louise to stop striving and keep quiet. John held his wife's hand and stroked her hair in yeoman bid to soothe her as they sat side by side on her bed, under Nurse Jane's eagle eye. Louise, her sapphire eyes streaming tears, smiled brokenly as John sang "Everlasting Arms", a favourite inspirational hymn. Though they connected, how he wished the songwriter's beautiful words were true—for him and Louise. John inwardly grieved when, after thirty minutes of suffering with her, he must leave, to protect his own fragile mental health.

Next morning, John was escorted to the gymnasium to meet Louise, where he found her chattering and laughing in the midst of a feisty game of ping-pong with another patient. Louise, cheering to see that her husband returned, dropped her paddle and ran to embrace him, shouting, "John! My beloved, you *are* here! I'm so glad to see you!"

Louise fervently hugged and kissed her husband, stupefying him that she could now speak so clearly! Yet, she terrified John with her immense strength, wild spirit, and blazing eyes. He suggested that they go somewhere quiet to talk, like in her bedroom or the TV lounge, but Louise verbosely dismissed his chicken ideas. Shooing Janelle, her last opponent off the table, she insisted that John play table tennis with her. After all, Louise enthusiastically recalled, they both enjoyed the game and used to attend church and city-wide tournaments together in years past!

"I played table tennis in the 1985 Alberta Winter Games!" Louise boasted to staff and other patients. They watched with interest as she whipped John's butt with hard smashes, curving loops, and insurmountable spins. Enjoying John's doggedly competitive spirit even as she toyed with his valiant efforts to keep the match close, Louise smugly cajoled as she returned his best serve down his throat, "John, nice try but you can do better . . . for a *lady*! You used to win all the games we played back home. Come on, bucko, up your game!"

John tried his best, but he was no match for this wonder woman fighting him from across the table. Janelle, a coloured woman about her own age, whistled from the sidelines, "My God, that girl is *good*! Ain't nobody gonna stop her!"

"Hey, Brightwood, your wife is cleaning your clock, man!" Orderly Bob heckled. "You gotta at least show up for your bros!"

John, recognizing he could not win this day, gave up after losing three straight matches, and good-naturedly shook hands with Louise. She glowed with energy, but despite her triumphant smile, glared at John with fiery rage in her brilliant blue eyes. Unnerved, he broached, "Can we talk now, perchance sitting down . . . over a glass of iced tea, my dear?"

"I am not your dear or doll, my lad!" Louise chastised him before the ogling crowd. She slammed down her racket on the table and strode haughtily out of the room. When John gazed after her, totally confused, Louise turned in the doorway and smiled, dangerously beckoning, "You comin' John? Let's get those cold drinks you promised!"

"All right!" John uttered. He tried to be happy, at least to show these gawking spectators that everything was cool between him and Louise.

He hopefully followed his wife out of the gymnasium, but nearly ran into her where she stood, arguing with her nurse. When John shrugged his shoulders to ask what was up, Nurse Rose sombrely turned to explain, while Louise fumed at her side. "Louise needs to shower and change attire before she meets with you in the cafeteria. Why don't you wait in the TV lounge, Mr. Brightwood, and we'll join you in a few minutes?"

"Okay, see you in a jiffy," collaborated John. He smiled encouragingly at his pouting wife before heading into the side room that her nurse had pointed to.

A women's talk show was already playing on TV for a couple of grey folks, wearing slippers and housecoats, who were camped in front of it. They seemed asleep or stuffed when John tiptoed past to find something more interesting to follow, like a *Time* or *Sports Illustrated* magazine to read from the "library" rack. The best John found was a dog-eared *People* magazine, featuring the latest fashions, party exploits, and romantic flings of Hollywood celebrities, definitely more interesting to fussy John than crayons and colouring books left as an option.

One patient flopped back his head, and began to snore, but his mate coughed loudly and flicked open his eyes when John quietly padded past. He, glaring at the newcomer, grouched, "You're not supposed to change the channel. Only the nurses are allowed to touch the TV. Why did you change the channel?"

"I didn't do anything to the TV," John protested. He dared not look at the old codger with rheumy, bloodshot eyes, but raised his magazine apologetically. "I just want to read."

"Okay," the patient noted. He then muttered for emphasis, "Just don't play with the tube."

"Right," John agreed. He sat back down in a corner seat. When the oldster drifted back into his stupor, John muttered to himself, "Thank you, Lord."

Flipping through *People*'s flotsam, John read a breathless, edgy article about former Senator Gary Hart, who was making waves from a self-imposed writing sabbatical in Ireland that he would re-enter the election campaign to become the Democratic Party nomination for President of the United States. Initially the clear front-runner, Hart had withdrawn his bid in May, after the press exposed his penchant for extramarital affairs, most recently with model Donna Rice, as well as his mounting campaign debts—allegations that Hart continued to righteously refute. Hart, a handsome and telegenic warrior, vowed that he would let American voters decide his fate.

"Why are you reading that rag of drivel, instead of your Bible?" queried a large, bearded man who suddenly loomed in front of John, blotting out the fluorescent ceiling lights.

Startled, John glanced up from his interesting read to peer into the face of a young man in a coarse brown tunic who looked like Jesus. John, struggling to find a pious response to this potentially holy intruder of his space, confessed, "Sorry, sir, but I was simply reading this magazine while I waited for my wife to arrive, who is a patient here. I don't have a Bible."

"You should," the rough-hewn stranger admonished as he emphatically pointed to leather-bound scriptures that suddenly appeared on the seat beside John, "And now you do have. You should read the Beatitudes that I taught during my 'Sermon on the Mount'—summarized in Matthew Chapter 5 by my erstwhile disciple, Matthew—of course!"

"Are you claiming to be Jesus Christ, risen Son of God?" John asked. Nervously, his eyes darted from the fellow's piercing blues to the Bible that he piously handed him, crisply opened to Matthew 5.

"Verily, man, I say unto you, I am he," Jesus vowed. He reached down to bless John.

"That being the case, I will read the Beatitudes of course, but can I do that later? There is so much I need to ask you first, Jesus, about my wife Louise . . . concerning Nigeria . . . . What should I do next?" blubbered John.

Totally flummoxed, he desired to get down on his knees instantly, and touch the hem of his master's garment, kiss his hands, cry out repentance for his multitude of sins . . . but was this particular Bible not placed by the Gideons? True enough, he had not *seen* them place it, but neither had he noticed Jesus call down the scriptures from Heaven just now, for his mercy. Where were the dove or helping angels?

"There you are, Gotlieb," Nurse Jane interrupted. She charged ox-like to the prophet's side, followed by another patient, who concentrated on his fingers as he mumbled through solving complex mathematical problems.

Nurse Jane looked harried from many duties today as, holding Gotlieb by the hand, she steered him out of harm's way. Yet, the big woman, sporting a watch pinned to the collar of her starched, white uniform like a medal, cracked a smile as she looked over her shoulder and sympathized with John, still fidgeting on the chair.

"Gotlieb is a harmless case, actually, Mr. Brightwood. He sensed you were down, and tried to help you, like he does with every hurting person who comes here. Thank you for humouring Gotlieb a bit. Come along, Solomon."

Nurse Jane then calmly directed the much bigger but gentle Gotlieb out of the lounge, followed by Solomon, her mathematical genius, who seemed totally dependent upon her, despite being absorbed in muttering myriads of useless calculations. John, composing himself, took up Gotlieb's suggestion, and read not only Christ's venerable Sermon on the Mount but the entire gospel of Matthew during the next half hour while he waited patiently for his wife to show.

Yet, when she did not arrive, and he grew weary of reading, John placed the Bible back on its chair and got up, stretched his stiff frame, and went to look for Louise in her room. He reached Room 325 just as Nurse Rose left, locking the door behind her.

"What gives, ma'am? My wife wanted to meet me for a drink after she freshened up."

"L. Brightwood is presently sleeping, sir. Maybe, she can see you after lunch," she suggested dourly. When John, not believing this jailer, rushed past her and peered in the window, he groaned to see Louise lethargically punching a pillow on her bed. Nurse Rose, cautioning the distraught man to step away from the window, took pains to explain the situation. "Mr. Brightwood, when you visited yesterday, Louise was struggling under a medication called Haldol, that Dr. Jones initially prescribed her, to help stabilize her psychotic mood swings. Her body did not cooperate, so the doctor administered lithium carbonate, a different medication, last night that appears to work better, at least for Louise. We are trying our best to get it right, but psychiatric programs take time to succeed for individual patients. Unfortunately, these drugs tend to have side effects on the patient, like drowsiness or temporary memory loss. Louise is already tired, not only from the drug. All that exercise she did in the gym, particularly playing ping-pong with you, is a total whammy."

"I thought she was really glad to see me. She really enjoyed our game!" John groused.

"She did, Mr. Brightwood, honestly!" Nurse Rose assured when John, against the rules, looked into Louise again, and bawled as he saw his wife, totally bagged, curl up dejectedly in bed. "Louise kept telling me, laughing and beaming, how much fun she had playing ping-pong with you . . . while I helped her undress . . . shower . . . towel off . . . and dress again. She knows you love her and your wife really loves you, Mr. Brightwood."

"That's nice," John replied. Smiling tightly, he acted more like Caliga, the wooden cigar store Indian, than Louise's effervescently praised husband.

Nurse Rose touched him comfortingly upon his shoulder, and softly offered to accompany him out of the ward. John nodded, and followed the buxom nurse towards daylight. He shook his head when Rose and Jane asked if he would be coming back later this afternoon.

"See you tomorrow, then?"

"Uh, huh," John muttered vaguely as he trudged away.

John was fatigued and sad himself as he exited through the sumptuous main floor lobby. He was marching down the sidewalk towards the parking lot when he slapped himself upside the head, suddenly realizing that there was no waiting taxi—because he had *not* hailed one to convey him back to the hotel. John remembered that the hospital lobby was flush with white telephones for express use by a departing person to call a cab. A VIP could then wait in a comfortable easy chair, chatting with friends or reading his newspaper—even enjoy a cigar—until the big boat moored at the dock to take aboard its first-class passenger. John, tossing out these freaky images, stamped back into the lobby, and dialed the nearest taxi line.

"Mr. Brightwood? Hi," the blonde front desk clerk broached once John got off the telephone. She smiled at his recognition, however stressed, for he had chatted with her on day one and they had greeted each other every time since, when he went to and from Louise.

"Yes? How is going today, Sylvia," John queried. He gazed up with a cautious smile from where he sat in a plush leather chair, seeking peace among ornamental statues and potted plants.

"I am doing well, thanks," Sylvia assured him. When he continued to gaze, questioning with his haunted brown eyes, she shared her business, "A gentleman called at the hospital this morning while you were upstairs, asking for you."

"Who was he, a rude cowpuncher named Dan Briggs, perhaps?" John surmised drolly.

"He would not say but gave me this telephone number, and suggested you call him, as soon as possible," Sylvia divulged. She mysteriously smiled, even as she handed John a yellow sticky note. "It is in our local calling area, Mr. Brightwood—costs only a quarter to dial by pay phone."

"Okay, I'll give this dude a ring," John promised. He jauntily tucked her note into the breast pocket of his golf shirt. "Meantime, if he calls here again, tell him I stay at the Holiday Inn, Pflumm Road and 87 Street, near Lenexa City Hall. You copy, Sylvia?"

"Sure do," chuckled the desk clerk.

"Okay, there's my taxi—I better go. I'll be back sometime tomorrow, God willing."

"See you then, Mr. Brightwood. Have a good rest of the day."

John rode high going back to his hotel, but seemed to falter at the end when he emptied his wallet paying fare for the hard-knowing cabbie. Cloistering himself in his room, he recounted his remaining funds, and anxiously concluded that he barely had enough left to pay his lodging bill—that is, if he checked out today! Louise looked like long-term hospital care but, for him to stay around KC much longer, he must tighten his belt: find a no-frills motel, preferably with free continental breakfasts, eat in fast food restaurants, ride the bus or walk to and from hospital, plead with Dan and Jean to take him in . . . as *if*! Maybe, he could find a local dishwashing or gas jockey job, at least generate enough money to buy two tickets on Amtrak back to PA. What would Rod and Bill—their parents for that matter—think of these kids now if they disappeared off the face of the earth? Who the hell wanted to find him, anyway?

John entered the patio lounge to have lunch, his last good meal on this tough journey. He would order a cheap garden salad and coffee, ice water of course—because it was free and would quench his burning thirst—maybe throw in a barbecued hot dog from the kids' menu. He'd answer the waitress's question with his own—wasn't *he* a kid, for all his immature antics during this crisis, when Louise desperately needed a man to uphold her? John wore dark shades to remain anonymous, and focused on the menu to avoid eye contact with the sassy waitress as she scribbled down his weird order. She joshed him into exchanging the salad for today's awesome onion soup special, enriched with sautéed spicy oysters—the "prairie" variety, like from castrated bull calves—she chirped to this gobsmacked tenderfoot! John would try it, having eaten such rich fare before, on cattle ranches of southern Alberta, he assured her, but no, the adventurous lad would not start off with a martini or plate of appetizer ribs—he would stick with the healthy diet option.

"Okay sir," the waitress chuckled. She concluded that John was a funny clown.

She went around the patio, pouring coffee and taking more orders, before disappearing behind the counter to apprise the cook. She was young and worked efficiently but wanted tips, so returned several times to attend her customers.

"Hey, John," somebody call his name. "How's it going?"

The weary lad glanced up from his soup bowl but saw nobody seated opposite or even looking at him. Dan was not there to harass him. Blinking hard through his shades, he searched the happy luncheon crowd in vain for anyone familiar. Surely, there were none. He expected to be left alone, stay on the fringe, fly under the radar; was he not a stranger in this busy Midwestern American crowd? Why should anyone want to hear about his woes, let alone know him?

"John, you are in good hands," the same gentle, reassuring voice promised.

John gazed frantically around the patio for his wannabe friend, but everyone seemed stuck, gregariously chowing down, oblivious to his bewilderment. A young couple to his right was chatting amicably about wedding plans, now that the beaming young man had gifted his beloved with a diamond so brilliant John needed to cover his tired, bloodshot eyes. Three nattily attired gentlemen sat with beautiful ladies at another table, who nodded attentively and nibbled salad while the men boasted of their golfing exploits and business deals over wine and platters of barbecued beef. Behind him, a bald, middle-aged guy read the newspaper while his wife clucked to three restless children dressed in cowboy suits to keep still—their grilled cheese sandwiches and fries would soon arrive, and if they ate nicely, after lunch they would all go to "Worlds and Oceans of Fun."

Life went on but not for John. He prayed to God that it was not all in his head, even if he was living a nightmare! It was bad enough that an anonymous caller wanted a piece of him. Now, he was hearing voices—in broad daylight, someone had spoken kindly, directly to him by name. Why? What was up?

The waitress, standing ahead with her back to him, suddenly moved and John found himself gazing into the kind brown eyes of a middle-aged black American, jauntily seated at the next table. John swore he had never seen this guy before, though he was certainly one of a kind: wore soft white clothes, like a toga, which contrasted brilliantly with his dark, congenial face. A gleaming watch adorned his left wrist, while a golden band shone on his manicured right ring finger.

"God loves you, John," the elegant stranger promised. He flashed the startled lad a pearly smile. "Our Heavenly Father is watching over you; he knows your needs before you ask."

"What does God know? He doesn't care a hoot about me—or my crazy wife!" John gnashed. This accoster's fiercely fervent eyes unnerved him.

"Don't worry, he *is* helping you, even now."

"Really?"

"Your wife Louise has taken ill, yet now is being treated in a fine local hospital. God has brought good doctors and nurses there to help her until she is ready to accompany you back to Pennsylvania," the odd fellow shared. He smiled assuringly, testified realities that he could not know . . . unless *somebody*—certainly *not* John—had told him.

Who was he actually . . . some creepy con artist who spied on him . . . a shrink or fortune teller . . . an *angel*, perhaps? The latter concept worried John. Although claiming to be a born-again Christian, he must be one arrogant dude to think he could preach the gospel to Africans, when his own faith was in tatters. If this black angel really stood in the presence of God, what bad report would he take back to Heaven, to so enrage the Lord that he should strike John Brightwood down after breaking his mind—like *he* had already done to Louise! They were obviously not fit to serve God, not even close to this brilliant messenger who now beguiled him with hope!

"How do you know these things?" John demanded. "You've been following me!"

"Yes," the black visitor admitted. Without losing his lustre, he patiently explained. "God sent me to look after Louise and you because our Father cares about both of you, your families and friends. Although things are presently grim and uncertain, you are *not* alone. God holds you securely in the palms of his mighty hands."

"I emptied my bank account to fly out here. My money is gone now, and I've maxed out my credit card, paying room and board, riding taxis. I walked one day to save nickels and dimes, but then I got arrested for trespassing! How will I cover Louise's medical bills? Canadian Medicare doesn't work a damn down here. Our in-laws hate us and MCC doesn't care, let alone know where we are," John complained bitterly to his intent listener. "We're broke, man, helpless."

"John, you and Louise are safe with God," the messenger promised. "Do not give up hope."

"Were you the dude looking for me today at Johnson Gardens?"

"No, but I know who is," the other revealed. "You two will come together soon."

"Okay, bring it on," John shot back, grinning, though his innards churned with anguish.

The fancy black stranger arose from his empty plate and approached John, towering over him, but he offered lovingkindness rather than fisticuffs for the lad's impertinence. Before taking leave of this nervous mortal, the angel touched him with his huge, six-fingered but softly reassuring hand and instilled in John the promise that God walked, ever present, with his beloved creation.

❖ ❖ ❖

Early the next morning, John was awakened by a sharp knock on his hotel room door. Found lying fully clothed on his bed, he looked wildly around and was shocked to see that sunlight was streaming through his wide-open balcony windows. When the knocking continued, he struggled out of his hovel and hit the floor running. Quickly adjusting his collar and slapping down his flying hair, John opened the door, only to be confronted by a sombre, middle-aged man he had never met.

"Yes," John croaked. He, scowling against the brazen sun, could hardly see. "Can I help you?"

"Are you John Brightwood?"

"Yes, what of it?"

The stranger smiled and extended his hand in friendly greeting. "John, my name is Orville Metzler, the MCC representative here in KC. I was asked by Rod Friesen at MCC Headquarters to look you up. You work for MCC out east, no?"

"I'm *trying* to work," John qualified. He gnashed with frustration as he spilt beans of woe. "My wife Louise and I were recruited six months ago to fill three-year positions in Nigeria, but our visas have been held up since April. We're stuck at headquarters, but then Louise got hospitalized while visiting her sister here in KC. Do you perchance know Dan and Jean Briggs?"

"Can't say that I do . . . . Are they Mennonites?"

"No!" John replied emphatically. Shaking his woolly head, he gloomily recalled how Dan loudly dissed the traditional faith of Jean's family, and required that she get re-baptized to attend his own fundamental, evangelical brand of Christianity. When Metzler gazed at him dourly with owlish, bespectacled eyes, John admitted, "They're Baptist, I think."

"My business is with you, son," the MCC rep declared. "I'm here to offer you support during your difficult time in our city. I'm inviting you to stay at my home, and will help you with food, transportation, and funds until you can see your way clearly as to what's to be done."

"That is wonderfully helpful," John acknowledged. He floundered on the verge of tears as he hugged his strange deliverer. Refusing to doubt the fellow's generosity or look for catches, John recognized his need for a hand up as he humbly stammered, "How should we go about this?"

"Why don't you pack up your things and check out of this hotel. I'll foot the cost," Orville suggested kindly. "We can chat over breakfast and figure out a plan."

"Okay, sounds swell to me," John cheered. He not only shook hands but embraced this fellow believer in gratitude. Embarrassed to let Orville see his disheveled room, John promised to quickly grab his things, and meet him at the hotel office.

"Will do," Orville agreed wryly to the shut door. "See you soon."

After checking out and enjoying a scrumptious breakfast of bacon and eggs, John and Orville drove across the city to a leafy suburban neighbourhood dotted by lakes and golf courses, where Metzlers resided in a comfortable, upscale home. They were met at the front door by Orville's wife Gladys, who hospitably welcomed John and provided him with a pleasant guest bedroom already made up, complete with fresh towels and an adjoining washroom, which she indicated was often used by travelers who valued their bed and breakfast home through *Mennonite Your Way*. The home was presently a quiet abode, as other guests were not booked and their own children were all grown up and had left the nest for Bible School, marriage, or overseas missions.

"We are nonetheless a busy household, what with us both working, but you can come and go as you please, Mr. Brightwood. I understand that you are attending to your wife, who is in hospital over in Lenexa," Gladys assured. She sat with her husband and John in the comfortable, shady living room, sipping coffee after the house tour. A grandfather clock, standing as tall and wide as John, chimed ten bells as she laid out simple rules, "We eat breakfast here starting at 7:00 a.m.; lunch follows at 12 noon and supper, at 6:00 p.m. You are welcome to join us at meals, as your schedule permits."

"Driving over here, you seemed worried about finding bus routes back to Johnson Gardens," Orville observed balefully. Suddenly laughing and waving his hand against such formality, he divulged, "John, you can use one of our cars to run your errands as needed. Rod told me you have a valid driver's license, and have driven numerous dignitaries around Pennsylvania—even gone to the Big Apple using MCC cars without a hitch, so no worries, man—we trust you! Gladys or I can also drive you places, but as we both have regular jobs, we give you freedom to make your own travels. It sounds like you'll be here a while, so feel at home."

"Wow, thanks," John gushed.

Orville and Gladys briefly checked in with each other, before Orville set down his mug, crisply arose, and explained to their attentively watching guest, "I need to get back to work at the Sprint office, John, you know where they make fibre optics for telecommunications? I'm an engineer there—no, I don't drive trains—but I still move fast across the USA. My workplace is not really in the same direction as the hospital, so that's why I've given you keys to our Impala. I will see you tonight for supper?"

"Sure," John promised, albeit vaguely. He had his own worries but was already tired.

"I need to run some household errands myself before lunch," Gladys said. Kindly regarding John, she inquired, "What are your plans, son? Are you heading to the hospital, or would you rather rest here for a while?"

"I think I'll crash this morning, but will likely visit my wife after eating lunch here," John responded. Overwhelmed by Metzlers' kindness, and content with the safety net MCC had arranged for him, he responded as legibly as his fatigue would permit him, while hoping his choice was suitable to his busy hosts.

John rested well for two hours and, after a consuming tasty soup and sandwiches with his pleasant hostess, drove to Johnson Gardens to visit Louise. Their hour together was sweet: they chatted about various light and sundry topics over iced tea (sun-brewed without sugar, American style) and apple pie in the ward cafeteria, watched over from a distance by Nurse Rose. Encouraged by his wife's generally upbeat spirits and helpful care, John returned the next afternoon and enjoyed a walk about the tranquil, sun-dappled grounds with Louise and Nurse Jane. John went out for supper that evening with Orville to Ponderosa Steak House; they did some much-needed male bonding over beers and hearty platters of barbecued steak. Metzlers took John to church on Sunday, where he met supportive fellow Christians who promised to pray for him and Louise. They read instructive Bible passages on Joseph's odyssey in Egypt, as well as the Beatitudes, and absorbed a compelling sermon from the pastor that encouraged all adherents to wait patiently upon the Lord. John wept gratefully as the huge, well-heeled congregation invoked worship to God through vibrant singing of his favourite, old-time gospel hymns: "Rifted Rock", "He Leadeth Me", "What a Friend We Have in Jesus", and fittingly, "They That Wait Upon the Lord Will Renew Their Strength".

What was *he* being strengthened by the Lord for, John wondered, as he left the church after Sunday service? *What* was God teaching him and Louise through their struggles? He learned patience, even as he enjoyed *faspa*[70] with his new Christian brothers and sisters at the

---

70 *Faspa* is a low German word for a Sunday afternoon social gathering, where participants visit at church or in a host family's home and eat a light meal together. Food can include bread, buns, cold meat cuts, pickles, cheese, fruit, and beverages that generally do not need to be cooked in advance.

Metzlers' home that sunny afternoon. He got to know them better, but several parishioners, intrigued to have a live MCC worker managing quietly in their midst rather than begging for money through deputation or heart-rending letters of need written from remote corners of the earth, also probed John about his background. *Brightwood* was certainly not German, Swiss or Dutch and therefore, in the opinion of some, John was *not* a Mennonite. They seemed frustrated that he would not play the Mennonite "Game" with them, where players guessed how their ancestors were related. Why was he, an English outsider whose grandfather and uncles had fought in wars—against *Germany* no less, interested in joining their pacifist organization? Had John undertaken believer's baptism as a Christ-confessing adult? Could he justify how his Protestant ancestors had martyred Anabaptists for their divergent but true faith?

John solemnly answered all these hostile questions by professing that he had duly been baptized as an infant and confirmed by choice and calling as a teenager into his home congregation of the Presbyterian Church in Canada, as legitimate a part of the same Christian body as the Mennonites. He had, however, joined First Mennonite (General Conference) Church in Edmonton (not *Edmountain,* as somebody quizzed him) when he married Louise Poettcher, who had grown up in that congregation, was baptized there, and whose father was the Alberta conference pastor. Reverend Poettcher gladly accepted John as a fellow believer and son-in-law, without requiring that he re-baptize. No, he did not believe that his present debacle was the result of his "checkered" religious background. John had already lived cross-culturally four years in Zambia and both he and Louise were delighted with the prospect of serving God among Africans. He respected MCC's "presence" philosophy to work alongside locals for seeking social justice, bringing peace, and improving quality of life in their shared community, in the Name of Christ. He respected his neighbour's religion, even if it was different from his own. John believed that all the world's great religions—Christianity, Judaism, Islam, Hinduism, and Buddhism, to name just a few—were viable pathways to Heaven because they acknowledged higher powers, and practiced Godly teachings of honesty, peace, and human dignity. He honoured Christ's assertion that he had many sheepfolds, and professed that the poor, who were rich in faith, would inherit the Kingdom of Heaven.

By now, some of his sombre listeners tagged John as a misguided radical but Orville, listening with interest, sensed that John needed a break. He jovially rescued him by inviting all his guests to partake in the afternoon fare of cold cuts, pickles, and freshly baked *zwieback* (traditional, two-lobed buns) laid out on the Metzlers' spacious dining room table. Did anyone wish fresh-squeezed lemonade . . . coffee or tea, just brewed? He chuckled that everyone should answer to their hearty appetites now, worked up by discussing the complex affairs of the world. Let John Brightwood rest his voice and replenish his strength—he needed both to work for the Lord in MCC, where ever God placed him. Orville was impressed at how John's articulate vitality shone through his adversity.

Later on, the seasoned MCC officer gave John and other interested fellows a tour around his sprawling acreage. They noted his trout pond and prize roses, but Orville took special pleasure in leading them through his walnut grove, where trees now supplied nuts for grocery stores and his own table, but were also selectively harvested for their even more valuable furniture or cabinet wood. Orville custom-sawed his own boards for dining room table sets; bedroom headboards, dressers, and night tables; kitchen cupboards; office desks and cabinets; or various chimes clocks that he crafted in his backyard woodshop as Christmas gifts or donation items to MCC fundraising auctions. He opened his spacious, clean workshop to his intrigued visitors, who marveled over his array of chisels, files, power saws, and lathes. Inviting them in, everyone crowded around the craftsman's workbench as Orville showed the intricate movements of precise works recently installed into the unfinished walnut box of his latest grandfather clock. John noted farther down the brass pendulum and wind chains meticulously hung inside leaded glass doors, not to mention the vivid depictions of day (golden sun beaming on a blue sky among puffy white clouds) and night (full moon and stars glimmering upon a black sky) that progressively slid on plates beneath the ornate clock face. This partially constructed appliance would precisely emulate, yet receive its own unique character from the creator, the masterpiece already keeping time in Metzlers' inviting living room.

Orville provided John with a positive role model of a confident, secure man, thriving on top of his game, embracing the niche that God had given him. How John, who had no material assets, made nothing of value, and received no inkling as to what tomorrow would bring, wished even a small portion of Metzler's success would rub onto him! *Au contraire*, his happy host claimed to envy John and Louise, for their important story yet to be penned and their determined faith to keep seeking God's will in their lives. They were willing to serve, whatever their circumstances, wherever he sent them—the makings of an exciting adventure!

John, provided with a sanctuary where he could become physically and emotionally grounded, continued to visit Louise daily over the ensuing week, encouraged by her generally upbeat spirits and helpful care. She seemed to have stabilized, as had he, but they sought patience to wait upon the Lord, to see them through their struggle. Louise asked her husband when they could go to Africa? She was up for the task, and wished to serve on their assigned placements with MCC.

"I want to go into service too," John affirmed. He smiled lovingly at his wife, who seemed more her bubbly, energetic self today. "But, Dear, I only want the Africa work if you are also there, doing what God gives you. I won't go without you, Louise. I can find a temporary job in Akron until you have sufficiently recovered—even if such takes years. I hope we can still do what we intended, rather than quit this dream and return home to Canada."

"I'm with you John, regardless how my parents won't agree," Louise assured. She hugged her knight in shining armour, though John suddenly appeared weather-beaten and sad behind his plastic smile. He frowned when she divulged, "They came here today like police and tried to kidnap me! Dan brought them and was in league with my mother as she demanded that Nurse Jane and Orderly Bob immediate release me from this place. I would not go with them until I talked to you, John, and we consulted with Dr. Jones, so my outlaws left in a huff, yet vowing to return. They are mad at our foolishness, but totally shocked at my illness. It simply doesn't compute for them that I refuse to return to Canada, until we complete our MCC assignment!"

"You are brave, Louise. God is with you, no matter what happens," John praised her in solidarity. "We'll go to Nigeria if you receive medical clearance, and when we get our work visas."

John was troubled by this unilateral "family" intervention, but he did not know how to deal with it. Her parents seemed selfish and naïve, yet they were old and wise; Mr. Poettcher was an ordained minister! How could he argue with them? He sought wisdom from Orville, but MCC's main man in KC grimly counselled John to pray on the heavy matter, and then watch and wait. He should know that Louise's parents had already petitioned Rod and Bill in Akron to terminate the young couple's MCC contract as the Lord had a better purpose in mind.

"Sheesh," John cried. He wanted to puke! "For *them*! What is that better purpose? Why did not God reveal our right purpose before we left jobs and possessions behind, after our home congregation commissioned us to serve the Lord in Africa, encouraged by many supportive friends, including our folks? If Louise is unfit for the task because of mental illness, why was I not told until we were ready to go?"

That night, he heard the mournful whistle of a passing train, despite dwelling in an upscale community far from any industrial yard or grain elevator that would require railroad tracks. Although haunted by apparitions, he vowed to remain positive and follow God's guidance. It made no sense; nothing did! Should they just give in, scrap their plans? Was it wrong to make plans?

◆ ◆ ◆

John saw progress when, at last, but *not* by chance, he met Dr. Jones one day while the psychiatrist was checking on Louise and, afterwards, could finally consult with him in the privacy of his hospital office. Louise feared this judge who filled her with drugs and decided her fate but she, supervised by Nurse Rose in John's presence, allowed the calmly discerning doctor to treat her. She envied her husband's opportunity to speak separately with Jones over her, but Louise cooperated when promised they would be able to consult together soon, depending upon her way towards wellness—which, by the doctor's calmly soothing demeanour, should come soon.

"Mr. Brightwood, your wife is bipolar, what we in the psychiatric field used to call manic-depressive. She has a form of mental illness which, while not curable, is treatable," Dr. Jones toned. He was bluntly matter-of-fact but sensitive of his client's reaction.

The omnipotent psychiatrist wore classic shrink gear: starched white gown, black horn-rimmed glasses, and carried a clipboard full of dense notes, yet exuded learned modernity as he eyed John solemnly, while the two men sat together in comfortable chairs among potted plants of a spacious office. Soft lights pleasantly augmented with sunlight glinted through open windows.

"Treatable?" John quizzed. He feared the worst. "How? Must she stay in this facility forever?"

"Certainly not," Dr. Jones assured. He refuted Brightwood's drab notions that he would be shackled to visit his beloved in some isolated and dreary hospital until death would mercifully part them, like he had read in *Jane Eyre* or envisioned the doom of families and patients, locked in long-term care at the old mental institution he had visited as a boy with his father. "Louise's temporary episode was caused by an imbalance in her body's electrolytes. She is prescribed lithium to correct this imbalance. You see how well your wife responds to the medication. If she regularly takes lithium as prescribed, Louise should be able to stay in balance; she can leave Johnson Gardens and do well in mainstream society. A stable, low-stress quality of life will help sustain her, augmented on a daily basis by a healthy diet, regular exercise, and adequate rest. Such lifestyle is intended by God for all human beings, although some special people like Louise are more fragile and thus more susceptible to breakdowns, when her electrolytes falter."

John, as though he did not believe or understand the learned doctor's chemical reasoning for his wife's difficulties, trotted out their naïve visit to the cult across the road from Grey Owl as a potential cause. John and Louise, together with Larry, a charismatic Christian friend visiting from Edmonton en route to the Holy Land had, for a lark, checked out the pillared, white mansion and its beautifully landscaped grounds one sunny afternoon back in June. Thinking it was a public park, they had buoyantly snapped photographs of one another as they clowned about, smelling beautiful red roses, feeding peanuts to goldfish swimming in a pond, and splashing in a fountain to cool off from the sweltering heat. They had met an elderly gentleman in bib overalls who had suddenly appeared from behind a hedge; assuming him to be the gardener, John had complimented the oldster on his awesome "green thumb" handiwork, while Louise had apologized for the trio's boisterous behaviour. The old workman, staring at her with unblinking black eyes, showed a rack of jagged white teeth as he smiled and suggested they go meet the "old woman" who lived inside the mansion. He explained, almost cackling with morbid anticipation, "Ma Baker owns this spread; she's expecting you kids."

Dr. Jones listened intently as John, his anxiety growing more weirdly, related how the gardener tracked them like a wolf, lagging stealthily behind but watching intently with lolling, glassy eyes, as they strolled to the mansion's ornate front door and whacked its heavy knocker. The naïve young trio were welcomed inside by matronly, grey-haired Ma Baker. She grinned broadly at her guests, before shutting out the daylight and her silhouetted sentinel of a gardener by closing the heavy oak door behind them. Ma Baker led the goo-goo-eyed trio down a polished hallway lined with dark paneled walls that occasionally sported heavy-framed portraits of sternly gazing ancients, but no windows or plants were seen in the gloomy house. Nonetheless, she hospitably sat her visitors down like Hansel, Gretel, and Pinch-Me in the dining room, at a large, intricately carved oak table and directed her uniformed maid, a sombre thing, to serve them lemonade and bumbleberry pie.

— Enduring Art, Active Faith —

While they ate, Ma Baker explained that she hosted a religious society three nights per week in this very room, around this same table, where they studied scriptures—the most important being the Golden Rule, by which the society functioned. When Larry, emboldened after eating his third slice of pie, arrogantly informed Ma Baker that Christians already knew the Golden Rule from the Ten Commandments that God gave Moses, chiseled on stone tablets atop Mount Sinai, Ma Baker stoically responded that her society knew the Bible, but meditated upon higher words of wisdom uttered by its own immortal prophet to the gathering when piously they assembled in the prayer room, located behind the kitchen. Yes, the Immortal Prophet knew Moses, for they had played together as children in Egypt!

"This, I gotta see. Show me your prayer room," Larry impertinently challenged, an obvious unbeliever but a zealot for Christ who would call down fire and brimstone from heaven to smite this ungodly idol. Louise, enthralled by strange theology permeating the mansion, had begged Larry to be quiet, to show respect, even if it was not his religion.

Ma Baker congenially agreed, quoting her mantra, the Golden Rule, over and over as she led the curious trio from the dining room and further down the hall. She stopped in front of a veiled archway and, devoutly drawing back the curtain, motioned for her gawking guests to peer into a church-like sanctuary, complete with oak pews, pulpit, and flickering candles but no windows or lights. At first glance, the room seemed empty but, upon closer examination, John had noted, with a start, a dark, long-haired figure hovering in the far corner of the stage. He was crisply attired in a military officer's uniform reminiscent of early struggles between French and English colonials in North America. This personage, taller and broader than burly John, silently gazed back at him with dark, vacant eyes. His grim, indigenous face seemed painted for battle!

"He is our Immortal Prophet," explained Ma Baker with breathless devotion. "He will not speak to you, however, since you do not believe. Our society members will gather tonight at the appointed hour in this room to pay homage, when they will receive his blessed wisdom.

You three should leave now, as the sun is setting and our prayer time draws nigh."

The trio, spooked by the mummy whose sombre eyes seemed to follow them, moved quickly together as Ma Baker urgently led them through a warren of dark hallways to the front door of her mansion. She let them out, her face ghostly illuminated despite gathering night, as she directed that they leave the premises at once. Her homespun friendliness must be a ruse for underlying danger far more sinister, John thought as he led his wife and friend on their purposeful march down the shadowy driveway and out the open gates. He noted in their flight how several ghoulish-looking beings sat on park benches or hovered amongst the shrubbery, warily watching these infidels pass by. John and Larry urged each other and Louise, who laughed merrily in breathless pursuit, as they raced across the well-lit and traffic-busy street, and took refuge inside the Grey Owl. The colourful hex sign hanging over the front door, which John bought for a lark at the farmers' market . . . like many he had seen in homes around about, would ward off evil.

"No," sternly replied Dr. Jones, rebuking Brightwood's strange encounter with the occult as a curse that had been placed upon his wife. He had laughed at his patient's husband for referring to themselves as Hansel and Gretel but now insisted that John stay real and current, accept clinical science, rather than give credence to medieval superstitions or fairytales!

John should read his doctor's memo! Louise's mental illness was part of her human psyche, a permanent feature that currently had broken out due to her electrolyte imbalance, probably brought about by stress. Dr. Jones did not like the Biblical term of "thorn in the flesh," but he acknowledged that her bipolar condition may have been inherited from her father who, she had divulged, also suffered bouts of "sadness."

"I thought Louise was disappointed when we stayed behind after all our colleagues in MCC orientation shipped out for their various assignments. Over the past six months, we have seen five other sets of recruits go through while we stay stuck in limbo, having failed to obtain our Nigerian work visas. She and I are also disappointed over our loss of a pregnancy, particularly when her sister Jean recently gave birth to a third child," John shared. He empathized with Louise's despair. "We tried to take our setbacks in stride, and do other things to help around headquarters, but we never know when or even *if* our travel overseas will happen. Louise's parents, even some of our friends, claim that God has closed the door; we should accept reality and come home, to pray and wait for what alternatives he plans for us. We were happy when Jean gave birth . . .. Louise rejoiced at the opportunity, even in our quandary, to visit her sister, but I never knew she was still grieving *our* loss of a child. Her miscarriage happened a year ago—the pregnancy was just weeks along."

"These are extenuating circumstances that could contribute to her current fragile state," Dr. Jones acknowledged. He nodding, encouraged John to understand. "Stress and disappointments can trigger an episode of electrolyte imbalance for a bipolar person. Luckily, her condition came to light before you folks went to Nigeria, where treatment of mental illness may not be—shall I say—as positive? Louise, with proper treatment and support, can function quite well in society here or over there, but both of you should be adequately equipped for relapses.

"While lithium is helping Louise regain normalcy, please remember that she must refrain from ingesting this medication if she becomes pregnant, which is a good possibility. Lithium can cause side effects in the child she would be carrying, but you should also remain vigilant, should Louise's mental health suffer during the pregnancy. Regular ingestion of a salt is vital throughout life but can, over time, affect the patient's thyroid glands or kidneys. You will want to keep your wife's best interests at heart. Her goals are important, even to go overseas."

"Of course. I love Louise," John vowed.

Dr. Jones nodded approvingly. Before wrapping up their session, he gave John his business card, inviting that he telephone him if ever he needed counsel regarding Louise . . . or even his own mental health. The good doctor sensed that John bore a heavy cross, and while assuring him that Louise was in good hands, her better half also needed to take care of himself. The young man promised to stay strong.

His commitment was tested yet again when, upon arriving next day to visit Louise, John found her room already full with her parents and brother-in-law. The seemingly placid mood quickly turned to rancour when John—deemed the cause of Louise's woes—arrived on scene!

"Louise needs to get out of this madhouse *today*!" Mrs. Poettcher insisted, glaring at John like he vindictively kept her daughter imprisoned against her will. "We intend to take her home with us."

"Where's home?" John dared ask. He sat politely on the bed beside his wife while the others assembled like bailiffs before them.

"Edmonton, of course," Louise's mother declared. She frowned at her son-in-law like he was totally daft, if not bogus. "Her parents love and know what's best for her."

"That may be," John acknowledged, "But I also love Louise, and I see that she is receiving excellent care here. I talked yesterday with her doctor. He believes that Louise can soon be released, but he advises that she regularly stay on the medication, and follow the lifestyle guides that he has recommended. She and I will discuss with MCC directors as to what our future holds."

"Her father and I have already discussed our concerns with this Dr. Jones, as well as Rod and Bill, and they all agree that Louise should come back home to Edmonton. There is nothing good for her here, and MCC offers only uncertainty, while she can refresh herself among those who care about her. We are her parents; we know what is best for our daughter, John Brightwood!"

"Louise and I ought to learn for ourselves what the options are. We need to decide what's best for us, but that comes after discussing our status with MCC, who currently employs us."

"John," interjected Dan, bluntly attempting to reason with his fellow man from outside the Poettcher family, and looking less of a black sheep than John for his courteous loyalty to Louise's parents. "You've got to do the right thing, man, what's best for Louise. Why pursue this crazy dream of working in Africa—it doesn't make sense anymore, even if you grew up over there. Louise doesn't really want to go anyways . . .. She misses her family too much."

John's angry eyes turned towards his wife, but softened with sympathy and frustration when he realized she was crying. He begged her, "What do you want to do, Dear? You told me the other day you still hoped to serve in Nigeria; we agreed that was what we both wanted . . .. What changed?"

"I still want to serve the Lord, at your side, John," promised Louise, smiling feebly. Ignoring Dan, she nodded deferentially to her parents, "Where ever he calls us. My parents are getting older, and they miss us. They're staying with Dan and Jean now, but it's been a long time, and Kansas City is pretty far from Edmonton. My parents want their children and grandchildren to be close so we can visit more often. Going halfway 'round the world doesn't help."

"But it's what *we* want and have worked patiently for. Didn't your parents travel all over the USA, following *their* dreams, even when they left parents and relatives in Alberta?" John asked. He hated to argue with Louise in front of her righteous family. He appealed to Rev. Poettcher, who seemed to understand his growing despair, "You guys came back to Alberta on visits, yet made your own way. If you had not worked in the USA, how would Jean meet Dan? We're just going for three years, not forever. God dwells in West Africa as well as he does in Alberta or US."

"We don't need to decide now, John. You and I can talk privately about our future." Louise offered an olive branch to her distraught husband, but she glared at her mother, demanding, "OK?"

"It's all good," Rev. Poettcher promised. He chuckled as he uttered an off-beat truth, "We don't need to break jail today."

"I feel like a failure if I just give up," John admitted gloomily.

"It's not about *you*," Mrs. Poettcher jabbed, vexing his spirit.

"Mom!" Louise raged in harsh rebuke.

"I think we should give these kids a break for today, Katherine, don't you think?" suggested Rev. Poettcher to his embattled wife, placing a comforting yet determined hand meaningfully upon her shoulder as he arose to stretch his stiff legs. He would not countenance her scowl, but turned good-naturedly to his refreshingly dutiful host, "Say, Dan, maybe we can check out that pie shop you mentioned while we were driving here. John, do you want to come along for some pie?"

"Uh, no," John wearily begged off. "Maybe another time, sir. Louise and I should talk."

"Well, how ar'ya gonna get back to where ever yawls staying, man?" demanded Dan. He regarded this older, shabbier dude with disdain. "You still walkin' and stayin' in a motel?"

"No Dan, I've moved out of the 'hood," John explained. He surprisingly matched his brother-in-law's sassiness. When the others stared at him, askance, he regained some confidence by explaining, "I'm lodging with Orville Metzler, the local MCC representative. He gives me free use of his car, so I'm good to go."

"See, Mom and Dad," Louise pointed out proudly. "MCC is looking after us. We're fine."

"Okay, son, we'll see you later," promised Rev. Poettcher, congenially shaking John's hand. He gave Louise an affectionate hug and promised to visit again, before he shepherded his pouting wife out of the room.

Dan trailed after the oldsters but not before he gave John and Louise some stern advice. "I know some about mental health. You two better stop fooling around, and do what's right."

"Goodbye, everyone." Louise cheerily waved this stumbling block from the room, glad that her husband continued to stand beside her, in sickness and in health . . . .

John and Louise avidly talked late into the afternoon and even had supper together in the hospital cafeteria, a blessing for her—she quipped with gusto—to get a break from plastic institutional grub served on trays by grouchy candy stripers. While strolling about the pleasant grounds in the cool of the day, they discussed their futures and present struggles, their daily adventures and learnings, joys and frustrations with visits from family and newcomers from Metzlers' church. When the sun set in its crimson glory, gilding wispy clouds with peaceful farewell but the promise to return in the morning, the couple returned to Louise's room, where they read scripture and prayed together for God's guidance as they waited upon him. He would provide the ram for their sacrifice, make straight their path, which now seemed twisted by uncertainty.

John left, feeling buoyed with hope, but his inner struggles resurged like storms upon tossing seas to accuse him as night fell, and he again heard the mournful wails of stalking trains. He felt like an arrogant, self-centred stumbling block to family peace, for foolishly pursuing his fruitless dream of returning to Africa, stealing Louise away with him against her will, to spite her unsupportive parents. On the other hand, Dan behaved like the perfect son-in-law: polite, dutiful, hospitable, caring, chivalrous . . . despite having been complained about by Louise's parents, since John's first day among them, that Dan was unstable, selfish, rude, abusive . . . .. Now, *John* was the nut case, not Dan or Louise. Why did Dan and Jean still not invite him over, at least to visit, eat a meal if not to stay for the night—especially now that their parents were in town to support everyone? He could help buffer against rough edges. Was he not part of the family? He tried to telephone Dan and sort things out with his group over there, but was curtly told that he was calling too late at night and disturbing the household. The ringing telephone had awakened the baby, who was crying now and distracting Jean, while she struggled to bed down her other two children.

"What's wrong with you, John?" Dan demanded. Briggs, sick of his whining, harshly called out John's contrary behaviour. "Stop thinking so much about yourself, feeling so hard done by! Get with the program, man. You should be more accommodating to our parents, but I don't feel comfortable giving you access to Donald and Katherine when you act like a self-righteous jerk. As for seeing Jean and my kids—they think you're a bogeyman! I gotta protect my fort, just like you—know what I mean, John?"

"Don't shut me out, Dan," John pleaded. "We're related, and thus should help one another, especially when the going gets tough."

"That's when the tough get going," Dan guffawed. He quoted President Nixon's attorney general John Mitchell, disgraced with his boss by the 1972 Watergate scandal. John gasped incredulously, while Dan hummed and hawed, but not for him . . . .. His wife or mother-in-law demanded his attention in the background. Finally, Dan offered, but seemingly under duress, "Talk to me tomorrow, John during business hours—you dig, man? I gotta go now and read my kids a bedtime story, since their grandma can't get it done. Bye!"

Early the next morning, Rev. Poettcher and Dan met John for breakfast, where they mended fences over ranchero style steak and eggs, complete with coffee, orange juice, and Texas toast. Jean, Katherine, and the children had gone to the park in Brigg's gated community for the morning, so were safely out of the loop where John found a sympathetic ear from his normally austere brother-in-law and august pastor/father-in-law, who patiently allowed him to unpack his baggage stuffed with frustrations over an uncertain future. John apologized for any harsh words spoken, and vowed to be more patient and understanding. He also promised to stand by Louise, and consider *all* their circumstances through consultation with God and their family. Rev. Poettcher acknowledged that both young men did him proud as sons, as well as husbands to his two precious daughters. Dan, admitting that his wife and children were wondering about Uncle John, invited the wayward sojourner over for supper at his house. John, tired of suffering alone, thanked Dan for this small mercy; he also gave kudos to Dan in front of their often critical "old man" for helping him better understand what mental illness was. The men later played horseshoes at a park and then toured Crown Centre before Dan returned John, feeling well-tended, to his tranquil abode among the walnut groves and clocks.

The rest of the week, indeed the sojourn in KC, went by positively. Louise, feeling better, was allowed day passes to accompany her parents and John on outings to the Kansas City Zoo, American Jazz Museum, or Metzlers' church come Sunday—to thank fellow Mennonites who had been so kind to her husband during his time of need. She begged off going to Jean's home, but was pleased that her sister, with children and mother in tow, visited her often at Johnson Gardens. John made his peace with Katherine, but remained stoically polite when she complained of her kids' willfully snubbing her from the church pulpit during congregational sharing of joys and concerns. John nonetheless died to himself, giving up his claim of an MCC African assignment to God, in promising to do what was best for his loved ones. Bolstered by Brightwoods' promises to keep them in the loop regarding their future plans, the Poettchers stepped down from demanding that Louise return to Edmonton upon her release from the hospital. Dan and Jean said pleasant goodbyes when their visitors left KC but, shrugging with typical aloofness, made no promises to meet up with anyone, anytime soon.

Dr. Jones duly discharged Louise from hospital care four weeks after she had first been admitted. He praised her for collaborating so well to regain her mental health, thanked John for his humble support, and promised the rejuvenated couple that, while he would put them in contact with a psychiatric colleague in Ephrata for ongoing assessment, he was always available for consultation. Mental illness, cautioned Dr. Jones, was an ancient condition that, despite many advancements in understanding and treatment, remained mysterious, with considerable societal stigma still attached. He counselled Louise to continue taking her medication, balance work with rest, and follow her regimen faithfully; they must take one step at a time, re-learn to crawl and then to walk, before they tried to run. The couple must be gentle, but vigilant for each other, and not give up hope in life. Louise could live richly, do as well as anyone else swimming in mainstream.

Louise came to live with John at the Metzlers' for two days, where the couple made tender love for the first time, it seemed, in aeons. They participated in that all-important telephone conference call with Orville, Rod, and Bill, regarding their future with MCC. Rod and Bill invited the couple to return to headquarters, where Louise could convalesce, and regain her strength. There were many local services that John could choose from to fulfil his purpose, and when Louise was able, she could also work in the community for MCC. Openings in health care and conflict resolution in nearby Lancaster city came to mind, but they could look at these or other service opportunities with MCC USA officials when everyone was ready. There was no hurry to decide; the poor were always with us, and the health of John and Louise Brightwood was now equally important to life's equation. They did not need to leave the organization, and return home now; they could stay on indefinitely, confident that they had purpose and support, until doors to Nigeria or some suitable, alternative profession would open. As for Louise's huge medical bill, and the cost of airline tickets back to Pennsylvania, the couple should not fret about payment or feel like a drag on MCC finances—they had proven their worth and were covered, no questions asked.

Orville, not Dan, drove John and Louise to the airport. While they chatted amicably, and looked forward to good days for everyone present and, in their prayers, John also found inner peace when he spied a freight train chugging beside them along the way. Despite Metzler's shiny new Cadillac being one of thousands of vehicles plying the busy interstate, the black engineer jauntily waved at John, and drove his powerful locomotive alongside their car for a good mile, as though escorting a kindred spirit heading out on his vital mission. Was this his angel? John smiled in appreciation, causing Louise to wonder at his strange pleasure. He could not say whether this was the very train that had called his name during so many sleepless nights past in Kansas City but at least now he knew where the trains ran, and had actually seen one in broad daylight, driving forward on schedule. John did not fully know his destination, yet he had a gained a better understanding of his wife, and how important mental health was, to each of them as well as to their loved ones. They would journey onward together, led by God's guiding hands.

THREE TREES — REFLECTIONS ON PLURALISM

BY VALERIE PROUDFOOT AND DONNA ENTZ

Try to imagine a forest of trees that are strong and healthy. The roots go deep into rich soil, the tree trunks are tall and straight, and the canopy of leaves grows a lush deep green. A closer look reveals that these trees are the Abrahamic faiths: Christianity, Judaism, and Islam. They are all vibrant, healthy, and thriving. This is a refreshing view of pluralism!

It is beautiful to see that each tree of faith stands full and complete, nurtured by its own traditions and understandings. The faith represented by its tree is the perspective the people of that faith could likely have about their own faith, and about the other two faiths in the Abraham tradition. The other two faiths are the short branches visible on each faith tree. From the perspective of the Christian faith tree, for example, Islam and Judaism are seen as short branches; they are perceived as faiths from the same roots in God, the trunk perhaps representing the sharing of similar or identical stories, but these two faiths are just not rich and full like the Christian tree. Likewise, when nurtured in Judaism or Islam, the small branches of the other faiths are not seen as vital from their faith perspective. Depending on one's perspective, and what faith tradition we have been nurtured in, it is very difficult to see that those of another faith can really be experiencing the richness of faith that has been the experience of my faith tradition.

This diagram helps us celebrate how our own faith has been nurtured through our faith community, the Bible, worship . . . all those things that make us spiritually strong. We needn't be apologetic about enjoying the Christian tree, but as we get to know those of another faith, we realize that the same experiences happen to them, and they experience their faith as powerfully as I do mine. It is reassuring that God loves us each in our own tree of faith, and all can be nurtured for the glory of God. When faiths are confident and secure, there then can be dialogue and celebrations between us that encourage peace. When, being truly respectful, and willing to learn and experience aspects of another's faith, we learn to see that their tree is as healthy as the tree of my faith tradition. We want to expand our vision where we can see the beauty of the tree beside us instead of it being a small dead branch on our own tree.

(Please regard the *Three Trees* drawing, prepared by Alicia Proudfoot, as you read and reflect.)

— Enduring Art, Active Faith —

(Three Trees 2017)

ICEBERG

BY ANNORA PROUDFOOT

We are all floating alone in a sea of society waiting to impress,
Afraid to undress,
Only showing a portion of our true selves to the world.
The rest is seven leagues below the sea waiting for a discovery.
The next ship is leaving soon. I am coming to meet you.
This is our expedition.

We start off with introductions, a smile,
A whisper of promised expectations.
Movies, phone calls, and coffee . . .. This is so simple, so easy.

But we are heading towards an unexpected fog. Hold on, Marco Polo.
Where did you go? Maybe you will answer if I sing you a song?
There you are. Forgive me? I went too far. I was wrong.

Back on track, I can see our horizon yet.
Our boat is patched and battle-worn, but it is stronger than before.
Talk turns to dreams, fears, and future. I am swimming deeper,
More careful with my words,
For now, I know that I can cut you like a sword.

People think we are twins or siblings:
Always together through thick and thin.
Your house is mine. I am there all the time,
But you and I are getting restless.
We need to spread our wings and see other things.
Life gets in the way: school, work, other friends, and lovers . . ..
When are we going to see each other?

Call out of the blue. It is you. We should get together; it has been forever.
Nervous about the time spent apart. Will it be hard?

The distance has made no difference. You're the same as I remember.
You regale me with tales; I tell you how I have broadened my sails.

Then a peaceful silence fills the air as we sit and listen to the atmosphere.
Later I realize that we are different than before we drifted apart,
But that does not hurt my heart.
Even though we're older and wiser, we still need each other.
No matter where we roam, there will always be a home.

TEST DRIVE

BY ANNORA PROUDFOOT

I spot him as I walk into the dealership. Is this the perfect relationship?
First, I check out the exterior: smooth, flashy, right colour.
Yes, everything seems to be in order, but what about the interior?

This is just the beginning of the journey. Who knows the end of this story?
An experiment, a test drive? This *must* be the right guy.
Only time will let me know, if he can carry me to where I need to go.

Getting in, I look around. Do I feel safe, warm, and sound?
How about the seat belt, the airbag . . .?
Will *he* catch me when I crash and sag?
Do the brakes slow? Will he stop when I say no?
Is he brand new or is he used? What is his mileage? Has he been abused?

Does he have room for me, the bags I carry?
Can I find the right paint to help him shine?
And wash away the scars and scratches of time?
Give the right fuel to get him through the day, or here alone, will I stay?
All this I wonder as I sit here with the doors closed.
I give the key to the dealer, and smile as I walk home.

TOTEM POLE

BY ANNORA PROUDFOOT

You go to the restaurant expecting to be let in,
But you are going to have to make a reservation.
Did you expect that you'd be able to start at the top?
This relationship starts from the ground up.
When in a relationship, why can't I take my time?
There is so much pressure coming in from all sides!
Just because I don't love you doesn't mean I won't soon.
You say you want to marry me? You're over the moon.

This is a test drive, an experiment, to see if you are different.
Remember, we are only kids trying to figure out what's right.
Relationships have never been black and white.

Our generation's feelings have faded to grey.
Everything's fast and easy; they don't know how to wait.
Our generation, will it ever understand,
That when it comes to love, nothing's drawn in the sand?

— Robert G. Proudfoot —

There you go again, Mr. Smooth Boyfriend,
Shooting lines out of your mouth when I just want you to be yourself.
Let down your costume!
Let me see the real you so I know what I've got myself into.
You don't understand why we fight; you and I are different, that's just life,
But day comes after night, and I want you here to see the morning light.
This relationship will never be perfect,
But we will climb the hill, and scratch each other's itch,
'Cause you know what they say: Rome wasn't built in one day.

Our generation's feelings have faded to grey.
Everything's fast and easy; they don't know how to wait.
Our generation, will it ever understand,
That when it comes to love, nothing's drawn in the sand?

TWO SIDES

BY ANNORA PROUDFOOT

She's a dog, a playful puppy tripping over herself to please.
She jumps up into your arms, giving freely; loving unconditionally;
Leaving herself open to whatever may come.
Forgives readily and keeps trusting.
She desperately wants to be your friend, and in her excitement,
Leaves puddles on the floor waiting for an unexpected accident.
She does not mean it, and she will try again to get it right.
She is man's best friend, always loyal to the end.

She is watchful, ever vigilant.
Looking at the chess board pondering, considering every movement.
She is buried deeper, only revealed
When the eggshells have all been obliterated.
Aura is a cold intelligence. Status: protector, mother.
She is battle weary,
Travelled across the empty tundra of experience.
She bears fruits of knowledge and judgement from her journey.
She is proud, but scared, a closed book,
For she knows that, in the wolf pack,
To toss caution to the wind is to welcome death.

— Robert G. Proudfoot —

The Mother was born old, the puppy permanently young.
They struggle within the bowels of the earth, switching roles of control.
The Mother is afraid to love, to be hurt again,
And thus, is jealous of the innocence of the puppy.
The puppy presents first, for she is easy to love,
And outsiders instinctively gravitate towards her.
She reminds them of their own strivings for approval, so they welcome her,
But when the puppy is content,
The mother bursts forth to assess the situation.
While the puppy loves without discrimination, the mother judges others,
And decides who deserves it,
For she was born from careless love, and knows the price.

The two halves must work together if they hope to survive.
Without the Mother's careful discernment,
The puppy blunders in blind love.
Without her joyful, loving puppy,
The Mother loses motivation to venture forth from her high, lonely tower,
Into the warmth on the other side of the door,
Where the healing can begin.

This is the cacophony inside of me that eventually must meld,
To make me whole.

PART III
ON A LIGHTER NOTE

(Crab Apple tree in bloom at Proudfoot Residence, Edmonton, Summer 1986.)

(FMC, Edmonton Canoe Party at Missinipe, SK, July 2009. Valerie and Annora are standing in front row, right side, with Robert Proudfoot behind them.)

DRUNK WITH SPRING

BY NORMA PROUDFOOT

She was heading across our garden, looking back over her right flank at the space from whence she had come. She was hunting: a cunning little vixen whose life and that of her cubs depended upon her success. I was watching her from my many-windowed, split-level home nestled into the river bank. She instinctively knew I posed her no harm.

The mother fox had come into our yard from the west along a path ancient in origin, but more deeply etched into the hillside by our five boys, their two sisters, and a myriad of friends commonly known as the "riverbank kids." This path had gained many an advantage for friend or foe as, armed with bow and arrows or simple slingshots, they played their way through "Cowboys and Indians," "Cops and Robbers," or the more recent maneuvers of dirt bikes in a kind of "Fox-and-Hounds" chase.

The vixen's passage was uncommonly quiet, approaching as she did on padded paw that could bring her within inches of our dog Toffee's food dish. It was a game they played together: both of them knowing how long his chain would reach, she tried to sneak up on him while he waited until she was almost there, before bounding towards her, to give her a chance to use her fast get-away skills. How splendid they both looked in their sun-drenched furry coats, his that of a golden retriever, her's variegated blonde and tawny. She was hungry, and I could not help wishing he would share his food with her.

The vixen's chosen path that morning led her down the slight slope to our front door patio, at the edge of which was situated the tiny kennel of our terry-pooh dog, Muppet. Of course, she knew *that*, and was almost eating from his dish when an angry little bundle of grey fur, not much more than three good bites for a hungry mother fox, emerged in a snarling frenzy to protect his own space. Probably more amused than afraid, she moved on across the patio to rummage 'neath the crabapple tree.

This was a special crab, one that my husband had planted early in the forty years of our life spent on the bank of the North Saskatchewan River. In spite of regular pruning, apple-laden branches stretched beyond human reach to remain a table of treats for birds, wasps, and squirrels—all of whom we also watched in summer from the dining room window. Many of those crabapples had fallen to the grass, laying beneath winter's deep snowdrifts. Now it was the vixen's turn to find them midst her rummaging. From the close proximity of my dining room window, I watched her chew, with her daintily pointed nose in the air, savouring each mushy-sweet bite.

My husband, son, and grandson, on their Sunday ramble just three days ago, came across the vixen's front dooryard of a cozy den under a fallen tree root. From the many tracks in the soft sand, they knew there were hungry little mouths to keep both parents busy. This pair of foxes moved into our four acres of river valley two summers ago, finding a bounteous table to feed from. Elegant pheasant cocks fought for and gained territorial rights year after year, and in their kingship, followed the morning ritual of coming up the very path the vixen now used, their many-coloured feathers a metallic display athwart the rising the sun. From coarse call and rapid whirling wing flaps, the trained eye of the hunter knew to seek out the hens sneaking along the sheltered edge of the yard. Seed eaters, they sought wild berry bushes, weed patches, and flower gardens. A yard-full of rabbits often gamboled under the full moon of a winter's night. When the grandchildren erected a large trampoline in our backyard, it did not run interference to the mating rituals of these many bunnies, who simply chased intruding hopefuls around and underneath it as the children stood unnoticed, in awed silence.

The natural way of controlling the law of supply and demand has been met. The cunning hunters have had their harvest. Last winter's snow banks revealed only the tracks of foxes crisscrossing each other over the surface. The lonely call of a cock pheasant is sometimes heard as he wends his way along a bush-sheltered path. Crabapples, although tasty morsels, are hardly an adequate diet for a nursing mother.

These thoughts were occupying my mind as I watched, now from my kitchen window, the progress of the vixen down the garden. Suddenly, she seemed to sway, sprang to the right, and raced in circles through the freshly cultivated rows . . . then to the left . . . and leapt into the air as if to catch a passing butterfly or busy bee! Then, as suddenly as it had begun, her frenzy was over, and she was wending her way intensively down the hill. I was left to ponder: were those crabapples fermented into wine or was our vixen simply drunk with spring? I hoped for her it was the latter.

BIG CHIEF'S SECRET

BY ROBERT PROUDFOOT

Ken rode grimly into town to finish the job he had been sent to do. This young desperado cruised dusty streets in his shiny pick-up, stalking a coffee shop amongst folksy parlours for ice cream or western wear. Suddenly, he swerved across the path of a rickety farm truck, and snatched the last stall for Family Friendly Pizza. Ken glowered at the incredulous old timer he had rudely beaten to the draw. Then, gripping his briefcase like a trusty Colt 45, the made-for-action surveyor descended in stiff blue jeans and polished work boots from his steed. He slammed its door, and swaggered into the crowded restaurant.

"I'll have a Denver omelette, black coffee and . . . *you* babe . . .. Ha, ha," Ken suavely propositioned his waitress.

She giggled, a mere child in a candy cane uniform, as she scribbled his order. Yet, her pearly smile meant business as the waitress primly cautioned, "We don't serve coffee here, sir."

"What!" Ken griped. He quickly tired of the teenybopper's coyness. The girl's dazzling engagement ring hurt his eyes.

"Would you like milk instead?"

She directed him to the hand-printed sign, hung stalwartly above the till, which professed the management's discretion. Rather than make a scene for curious locals, the stranger relented, grumbling nonetheless, "Bring me a tall glass of OJ! You got today's *Sun?*"

"You mean that dreadful Calgary rag with the pin-up girls? Not on your life! I'll fetch you Saturday's copy of our village newspaper if you wish, sir."

"Forget it!" Ken muttered. Waving this angel on her way, he wondered who on earth cared about pie eating contests or fish derbies? "Go fry my eggs 'n' bacon. I'm in a hurry!"

The outlaw re-read his land files, and psyched himself up for another heavy day, scouting right-of-ways to design new irrigation canals. Work, like this town, was weird, a pain in the butt: dozens of folksy landowners to deal with—sometimes five per quarter section of bald-assed prairie! Each owned his pie-sliver horse pasture, complete with duck pond, garden, six kids, and trampoline. The whole place seemed related through party-line or church, if not by genealogy!

Everyone smiled in this hilly paradise but Ken! Had not his boss at the engineering firm back home in Calgary leaned on him to cover the territory by week's end? That task was huge, and with buckets of rain dumped on these black, rolling soils of late, it now seemed hopeless!

"Excuse me, sir. We don't accept credit cards," the pretty cashier chirped as Ken drew forth his plastic.

"Not even for scrumptious home cookin'?" Ken scoffed as he scrounged all his loose change to pay the bill. As he slapped money down on the enamel countertop, and watched the married, twenty-something cutie scoop it up, Ken sardonically vowed, "I'll tell my wranglers to come rough 'n' ready next time."

The cashier grinned tongue-in-cheek as she informed Ken of the "cash only" notice scrawled on the bulletin board behind her. Quickly appraising him, she drawled, "You're a stranger in these parts, huh!"

"Yes, Ma'am," he replied adventurously. "I'm en route to Waterton Lakes to do some scuba diving. That mountain water is as clear as glass, but it's so cold I gotta wear a wetsuit."

Ken smartly tipped his white Stetson hat to the lady before stepping briskly outside. He scanned the street for gunslingers, then high-tailed into his truck . . . . The stranger had convinced nobody of his trail savvy; he winced to read that *other* sign:

WANTED, DEAD OR ALIVE!
Driver of new Dodge 4x4 who trespassed
on my land and trampled the oats last Friday!
Two gates were left open! Am still rounding up
stray cattle. Reward given for catching rustlers!
(**signed**) Ezekiel Smith

Ken locked the doors of his spanking new Dodge, and roared out of town, worried that those friendly folks promenading the boardwalks suddenly knew who he was! As he motored through rolling chaparral, Ken wrestled mentally to recall: was that really *oats* or just tall weeds he had driven over, working last week? He thought he had closed all gates . . . but then, as his boss had tersely instructed him, he must not let tight wire or nosy farmers impede promptly efficient completion of the project! Better avoid "them old cowpunchers" than waste hours listening to their gripes against the government!

"All the same," a strange voice boomed. "*What* have you been doing out here: prowling canal banks and fence lines, darting into farmers' fields to steal soil samples for lab analyses far away—without permission?"

"Who's that?" Ken demanded, unnerved.

He checked the radio, but it was strumming some country hurting song about jaded love. He glanced furtively from chrome-green range to massive Rocky horizon, focusing finally upon a huge rampart that locals called Chief Mountain. The mountain, grey with stony omnipotence, regarded Ken as it would a grasshopper. Ken gasped! Did Big Chief know what he had done? How could that giant Indian see anything terrestrial when, in full headdress, he lay peacefully, eternally on his back and studied the Heavens . . . or, Ken feverishly reasoned, did Big Chief merely sleep beneath an endless sky?

"Hah, it's just a big pile of rocks!" Ken snorted. He cursed himself to grab onto the reality of his tough but doable task at hand.

Following a route previously transcribed onto aerial photos with a grease pencil, the surveyor turned onto gravel, then swung purposefully into somebody's pasture. The rutted trail was puddled with water, yet flanking virgin turf held as Ken toiled across its rolling contours. White-faced Herefords chewed their cud and gazed docilely after him. Ascending a bluff, Ken stopped, and used a hand auger to probe the soil for depth to underlying bedrock.

He breathed invigorating highland air as he studied the valley yawning below. Ken decided to descend, and sample those glacial clays and gravelly stream terraces en route to a pasture beyond. That far lea, where now some lovely black horses pranced through a breezy tag game, would take him onto another road. Ken's only real obstacle remained a creek, but fording it would be a cinch, he relished, with his monster truck!

To birdsongs of buntings and woodpecker's drums, Ken examined his crossing. He was favourably impressed: although swollen by rain, the current was shallow and glinted from underlying gravels. Relying on these shoals to buoy him up, Ken charged into the water—where, aghast, he ran aground!

The truck floundered in spineless sand, sputtered, then finally died to the relentless stream. Ken, flustered that he could not gun his steed into action, jumped from the cab into knee-deep, icy water to dig it out. His curses echoed above the laughing brook when he realized that he held no hope of budging the carcass. Indeed, valiant efforts to free his truck only eroded the precarious ledge to which it clung.

"What a mess!" Ken gnashed. He slumped dejectedly upon the bank and watched his precise work flow helplessly downstream.

"I knew I'd catch ya sooner or later," an old land man drawled. Emerging slowly on the far bank from his battered, 1950s-era farm truck, he chuckled with the black horses that sauntered behind him, "These beauties tipped me off. Whatcha doing', panning for gold?"

Ken chose his words carefully under the sombre glare of shotguns racked in the old timer's truck cab. He politely explained to everybody— the rancher, his horses, and the toothy bird dog all staring at him—that the local irrigation district had hired his company to investigate the feasibility of expanding the water delivery system into their valley.

"That's new to me, bub."

The gnarled oldster stuffed his calloused hands into hip pockets of his bow-legged, bib overalls like some contented king of his castle—albeit a rustic one, like, homesteaderesque! Ken gulped; this was the same guy he had cut off at the pizza joint just two hours earlier! He seemed deaf to Ken's highfalutin jargon about regulated water management and irrigable soils yet spoke his simple mind with pride.

"Irrigation water rights have been in our family since Grandpa helped build the first canals in Mountainview after the war. I flood a few acres of bottom land for these horses' hay when weather's dry, but the good Lord provides all the water we need. Mom's geese like swimmin' in that slough back of the home-place."

Ken feared to tell this good old boy that Mom's geese pond would be gone as soon as the irrigation district, prompted by his report, replaced its aging, leaky lateral with a drum-tight steel pipeline. Ken expounded instead upon virtues of improved water delivery for stock ponds, lawns and flowers, cooking, drinking, bathing . . .. The old coot agreed, pointing upward to an impressively new main canal that skirted the valley rim like a moat between parched hilltops and their lush Garden of Eden. Yet, that water was used by plains folk farther east; he refused to be taxed for *their* comforts when large-scale irrigation did not pay *him*!

"Besides, it's too cool up here to grow big-shot crops like wheat and sugar beets! The good Lord brings us rain in due season. He taught my Pappy what to plant."

Ken marveled at how the other's simple faith kept his humour as they floundered in icy torrents, hauled chain, built ingenious catwalks, shoveled mud, and raced their engines in futile effort to beach the stuck truck. When even his muscular tractor failed, Ken's host shrugged in mild chagrin.

"I've been meanin' to build a bridge across this crick. It's the only way into the back pasture. I got stuck here myself last spring, checkin' on my sorrel's new colt."

Zeke suggested, almost as an afterthought, that they call a tow truck from Cardston. He studied the sun (while Ken thumbed impatiently through his wallet for his AMA card), and correctly surmised that it was noontime. "I hope Jim don't mind drivin' out here during the lunch hour. He usually eats with his family."

Gramps' washboard face scrubbed hard beneath his greasy ball cap as he pondered how best to accommodate both his kinsman and this stranger. He finally offered, "Let's go up to the house, wash up, and see what Mom's cooked for lunch. You can phone Jim from there."

Ken had hoped to munch his bag lunch alone, in tranquil view of Chief Mountain. Instead, he was forced to listen to Gramps' incessant jawing as they rattled back to his ranch. The city slicker's frustration heaped further when his captor greeted a neighbour strolling home from the post office. Only after an irritatingly chummy conversation about crops, church, and family did these country gents part company.

"I appreciate your boy's help in catching my steers, Norman. See you come Sunday," the driver adieued.

"You bet! Glad to help, Ezekiel."

So, *this* was Zeke Smith, the rural crime watch, Ken shuddered as they pulled into the busy yard of the oldster's quaint hilltop home. Although Zeke remained silent about stray cattle and trampled oats—of some yahoo insulting him in Cardston—the old codger *must* have recognized Ken's rig stuck in the stream!

Only kind, bubbly words were spoken as they entered the homespun kitchen where, indeed, Zeke's plump wife Mabel had cooked up a savoury stew for her grandchildren. While three freshly scrubbed boys dressed western read *Tom Sawyer* or took crayons to colouring books, the young blonde woman sitting opposite them at the dinner table turned from dotingly feeding her youngest in the high chair to jovially greeting their awkward, reticent guest. Realizing that she was the cashier at Family Friendly Pizza whom he had been so fresh with earlier that morning, Ken smiled back with chagrin, and faced the music, yet inwardly wondered: *how* could this be?

"You bet, stay for lunch—and supper too, son," Mabel gushed. "We don't often get city folks as table guests . . .. You must be new here—skidding around the land in a fancy truck, when it's sopping wet from six inches of rain this past week!"

Embarrassed at his folly, Ken preferred to compliment her cooking, and quietly dug into some serious eating. Why draw attention to his work and get nabbed as a duck pond threatening, cattle rustling, gate-crashing oat trampler?

Zeke rescued Ken from his amused farmwife and inquisitive daughter by relaying good news he had cranked out of their wooden telephone. "The dispatcher caught Jim at home. He'll be along this afternoon to yank out your truck."

With the Lord blissfully present at the table, the Smith clan served Ken much good food and meaningful conversation. They espoused the valley's close-knit community spirit: neighbours depended upon one another, and gathered for church socials and town hall meetings to keep in touch. Ken warmed these gentle hearts by confessing his own small faith in God.

The home folks were especially amused by Ken's discovery of one of their valley's best-kept secrets.

"Those veggies are *mountain* radishes," Zeke chuckled. Ken played uncertainly with a pale, grainy mash heaped by Mabel onto his plate. "I grow 'em myself in the garden. I'll show ya after lunch."

This gruel tasted more like turnip, but Ken was surprised when Zeke unearthed red taproots bigger than rutabaga from deep, black garden soil behind the house. These had furry foliage and crisp, white flesh of radishes, but looked more like the fare of a giant's table than for mere mortals as him!

"You can boil these babies like spuds or eat 'em raw. They taste great fried or in salads." Zeke offered boisterously. He washed and bagged 20 burly gems for the surveyor's yuppie pantry. "You bet! Take a chunk of great mountain livin' back to your city people, son. They don't get enough there, even when Chinook winds blow!"

"But *how* do your radishes grow so big?"

"Must be all the spirituality around here, I guess. Everyone in this valley attends church on Sundays, and keeps Bible ways durin' the week. Them Bloods too, they found the Great Creator through vision quests atop Chief Mountain long before any white man came around here. This is God's country—don't forget it!"

Ken did not forget, even months after Jim's tow truck came, and easily pulled his Dodge from the stream. Neither did Ken forget to revisit his adoptive parents, next time he passed through their pristine valley.

JOYOUS PIANO TUNE

BY ROBERT PROUDFOOT

Jim's face glowed in the embered sunset as he departed Lethbridge with a busload of fellow Christian singles bound for a fun ski weekend near Kalispell, Montana. Jim was Pastor Buck Norris's hesitant guest, but he joined the group's bubbly laughter and travelling songs. He sought pretty Christian ladies and exhilarating alpine slopes. Surveying these revelers, Jim cherished his chances of success!

His adventure sweetened quickly: a smiling, shapely blonde alighted beside Jim, and warmly welcomed him aboard.

"So, you're the *friend* that Pastor Buck is bragging about," Nancy chirped. "I hope the Lord blesses our time together."

"Me too," Jim replied. Flashing a pearly smile, he enjoyed being the talk of the town—Buck's rumours were honey to this bee buzzing about him!

"We're glad you came. Where do you worship Jesus?"

"Oh, I'm a good Catholic boy . . . though a bit lapsed of late. You ski much?"

"I'm beginning but willing to learn."

— Enduring Art, Active Faith —

"Well . . . "Jungle" Jim[71] here will teach you all the basics," Jim chuckled. He suavely caressed Nancy's shoulder. "I ski moguls myself, but the bunny hill will do me fine for a morning if you're on it!"

"Good," Nancy smirked. Her doll-blue eyes winked mischievously. "I'll learn a lot then!"

Their snappy conversation lasted longer than others', yet also waned over cumbersome miles of brown, wind-blown prairie between Lethbridge and Pincher Creek; it became punctuated by pondering silence, and useless attempts to doze or read in the gathering dusk. Cheers arose as the bus passed the boulder fields of Frank Slide and the gritty coal mining towns of Blairmore and Coleman, but the stunted peaks guarding Crowsnest Pass were barely dusted with snow. Everyone knew there were still hundreds of kilometres to go, with an international border to cross, before they would reach the winter wonderland of Big Mountain.

At a pit-stop in Fernie, Nancy took advantage of the welcome shuffle to join her friend Janice up front. Jim, returning from the gas station with two coffees and chocolate bars, was miffed to find Pastor Buck waiting in Nancy's seat.

"Enjoying the trip, brother?" the grinning Norris broached.

"Of course, man! You've got a fine bunch here."

---

71 A reference to "Jungle" Jim Hunter, member of the Canadian Men's Alpine Ski Team, nicknamed the "Crazy Canucks", from 1970 to 1977. 'Jungle' Jim Hunter earned his nickname due to his aggressive skiing style, and was considered to be the original Crazy Canuck. Hunter represented Canada at two winter Olympics in downhill, giant slalom, and slalom events: 1972 in Sapporo, Japan and 1976 in Innsbruck, Austria. He won a bronze medal in the 1972 World Alpine Skiing Championship, the first medal in alpine skiing won by a Canadian male skier. Hunter placed among the top ten contestant skiers in 17 World Cups; he earned bronze and silver medals in 1975 to 1976 championships. Hunter competed as a professional in, and won first ever downhill event on, the World Pro Ski Tour in 1977. He was later inducted into of the Canadian Ski Hall of Fame.

"They *are* good folks, though they've all got their problems—just like you and me."

"You'd probably know," Jim dodged. Buck's piercing gaze unnerved him.

Why, Jim grumbled, did Norris strive to spiritually purge him? Knew he the murky secrets of Jim's supposedly "Christian" life: that he chased women in bars, and occasionally purchased *Penthouse* magazines to salve his bachelor loneliness? Those gleaming eyes, that confident smile—he hated them!

"Every person here is uniquely important to the Lord, and he helps them work the kinks out of their lives . . .."

"I'm fine, Buck! Really, life is *good*!"

"Glad to hear it," the pastor replied. He mellowed some as he sipped on the coffee Jim had given him but Norris playfully chided as he tapped Jim's shoulder with his fist. "And you thought our little 'Bible excursion' would bore you silly!"

"Hey, man," Jim protested good-naturedly. "You know I'll go for broke in those powder bowls tomorrow!"

Climbing through snowy, forest-clad hills south of Eureka, the bus driver slowed in response to a barrage of red lights flashing ahead. Inching forward, the group discovered an overturned pick-up truck being towed from the ditch. Smokies stolidly directed traffic as medics lifted a wrapped accident victim into their ambulance. The travelers groaned at this calamity. Jim heard Nancy praying for God's healing mercy.

"That's a mess," Buck murmured. "Now, if that fool had refrained from racing with ten beers under his belt . . .."

"We don't know what happened", Jim rebuked. "It's snowing hard; the road's icy. Maybe, he just lost control."

"If he controlled his life better . . .."

". . . He'd be skiing tomorrow, like us righteous?"

"Something like that," Buck nodded. He troubled his guest with a smugly knowing thought, "Accidents happen when you least expect them. It could have been you or me on that stretcher; we must stay tuned to God."

"How morbid," Jim growled. He rolled his eyes.

Jim stared straight ahead but, while Kalispell's lights glimmered in welcome, he found no relief at the end of the tunnel. Pastor Buck had purposely left behind his wife and children so that the pair could bunk together for a tormenting weekend of Bible judgement!

Captive Jim dreaded some interrogation even while everyone re-assembled around the ski lodge fireplace for a cozy nightcap of praise singing and cocoa. Nancy temporarily rescued the newcomer and introduced him to her lounging mates. Aside from one odd, bug-eyed fanatic who questioned whether Jim was "born-again," this was a hip group! If Jim could only grab some sleep and remain sane around his spirit-filled roomie—a great weekend lay ahead!

❖ ❖ ❖

The fun came early! After a hearty breakfast, Jim and Buck hit the slopes with skis waxed and poles flying. They took the main chair aloft and made ten fast runs before the others had showered! Jim spotted Nancy once en route, heavily into ski school, so he stuck with Norris and tackled some expert runs off other chairs until lunch.

When Jim spied Nancy, man-less, sitting at a table with Janice in the crowded cafeteria, he abruptly took leave of his buddy. Scorning Buck's dismay, this macho man declared, "I'll catch ya later, big guy. We'll ski the back bowl this afternoon."

"Don't be late for going over the summit on that crazy T-bar," Norris muttered. He was cool to his guest's cavalier attitude and hated shouting to him above the din of crowd conversation and ski boots thunking across the floor. "Storm clouds are moving in. Let's not get trapped in a blizzard up there!"

Jim ignored Buck's pouting retreat. Nancy waved the young powder hound over, and presented him with the seat reserved beside her. *They needed no chaperone, Pastor!*

"Where have you been, Jim?" the ladies giggled in airy, rosy-cheeked unison.

"Oh, Buck and I broke trail at sunrise—checked out all the mountain's black diamond runs," Jim exulted. "God was everywhere!"

"Amen," Nancy chimed. Then, winking playfully at her female cohort, she leaned over and whispered a secret in Jim's ear. "We've learned how to ski!"

"Good work! When will you show me your new curves?"

"Could we try a few beginners runs after lunch?"

"No problem, ma'am. Jungle Jim is at your service!"

"Just don't lose us, J.J.," bantered Janice knowingly. "I can't return home to my kids with a broken leg!"

"You won't, Jan," Jim parried. Nancy watched adoringly. "Those greens are so flat, it's almost better to cross-country ski them."

Jim tried to include Janice because she was Nancy's confidante. Yet, the idea of this older, dumpy-looking mother playing "frisky singles games" rubbed him wrong. Nancy, conversely, was cleanly free—like himself! *They* would plot their breakaway, riding the doubles' chair together.

Nancy learned quickly, and stayed close to Jim as the trio snowploughed sinuously down a wide-open run. Janice, however, nervously fought her boards: huffing and puffing at a snail's pace, she often fell, delaying her companions at every turn. They jokingly took this inconvenience in stride: Jim showed off, telemarking or performing stem christies[72] but also clowned about, doing headstands in the snowdrift for Nancy's applause and laughter while waiting for their slowpoke companion to catch up. Janice despaired at her own mounting failure.

"I think I'll go soothe my bruises in the hot tub," Janice wearily surrendered. Not wanting Nancy to feel bad, she encouraged her roommate, "You guys stay out here and enjoy yourselves."

"If you insist." Nancy, hesitating, hugged her frustrated friend. "We'll all eat a fancy supper downtown tonight."

---

72 Stem Christie or stem turn in skiing is made by turning the downhill ski inward and shifting one's weight upon it while bringing the other ski into a parallel position.

Jim sighed in relief after this dowdy casualty trudged away—finally, he was alone with Nancy! She caught him lolling at her hourglass figure—shimmeringly revealed by her skin-tight, designer ski suit—and flashed him a daring grin as she taunted, "You want to soak in the Jacuzzi too, Jim?"

"Naw, rest and relaxation are after-hours stuff," he deked. His athletic figure was poised for action. "We came to Whitefish to ski!"

"You bet! Mush you to the chair!"

They relished more runs, filling their lungs with crisp air and expelling it shouting as they swooped and spiraled down echoing, forest-clad trails. They affectionately held hands, and sang folk songs while riding leisurely upslope, dangling their skis freely in the pristine air as the sun warmed their already glowing faces.

Bobbing downhill again with renewed energy, Nancy missed a turn and fell, face first, into the powdery snow. Her pride hurt more than her body, she nonetheless allowed her companion to chivalrously untangle and upright her.

"Always place your skis downslope and push back up with your poles to rise," instructed the manly St. Bernard. "Don't be afraid to fall down if you need to."

Then, smoothing back Nancy's tussled golden hair and gazing into her sapphire eyes, Jim stammered, "I really like you, Nancy and hope to see much more of you."

"And I, you, Jim. I enjoy your company."

"I've waited a long time for someone as beautiful as you to come along!"

"I'm no spring chicken myself . . . but Jim, if you're interested in me, you'll also want to date Amanda."

"Who's *she*?"

"My three-year-old daughter. Amanda comes with the territory."

"For God's sake, Nancy!" Jim moaned. "I thought you were *really* single! I'm sorry for being so stupid!"

"Wait, Jim. What's stupid?"

Jim, in his embarrassment, bitterly refused to wait. He slalomed fiercely to the bottom, leaving Nancy to pick her way brokenly down the slope.

❖ ❖ ❖

"Where ya been, Bucko?" Jim snorted. He jostled Norris in the queue for the summit T-bar.

"I've been waiting for you, brother. Had a good day?"

"Just great!" Jim gnashed. "You promised me a party here—lots of pretty girls!"

"Well, aren't there?"

"All these dames have pasts, Buck—they're used goods! I don't need divorcees or single mothers hassling my tail! They've all got kids, for Pete's sake!"

"Not *all;* some folks have never been hitched, while others stay celibate for God. Anyway, he doesn't create junk! My ladies and gentlemen are fine single Christians, despite and because of their troubles. God loves each one!"

"I'm single—I've never had a steady girlfriend, let alone a wife. My needs are different from your groupies. Why didn't you read me the fine print, Norris?"

"You chose to chase Nancy like a hound dog! You are embarrassing me, Jim!" Norris growled. "Nancy's a young widow—understand? Her husband Bill, previously an upstanding member of my congregation, but a bit of a daredevil like you, died last year in an ultra-light plane crash! What's your problem with *her?*"

"I want my own history, not some other dude's!"

"You're a selfish hypocrite! Jim, who are you to judge anyone?"

Buck fervently admonished Jim, but the latter took it hard, like a harsh rebuke from the Almighty himself. In turn, they silently boarded the T-bar, a spindly, single-seat, pie plate contraption that threaded precariously over the mountain.

"Hold on tight! Don't sit down!" the snowy lift operator lectured. He slung sullenly obeying Jim into line, then cast him away into the cloud bank.

Jim, engulfed by billowing snow, neither saw the end nor heard the putting donkey engine that dragged him over glacial wastelands. He tenaciously followed two ski ruts carved by other adventurers gone before. Plate-seats, creaking past empty on his flank, testified frigidly to others' presence somewhere beyond the saddle. Gales howling through this alpine netherworld obscured jagged peaks—even Norris's black dot ahead—with white-out.

"Stay in harness, Jim, or you'll lose your lifeline . . . oh, God!" Jim wailed through frostbitten lips. "Don't let me fall!"

A seeming eternity later, Jim felt his cramped legs extending onto solid snow. Norris stood beside the exit ramp, frantically waving him off.

"Let go of your bar!" Buck hollered.

Jim obeyed at the last second and skidded into the pastor's strong arms as his pie plate sprang away. They clung to a windswept ledge dizzily overlooking the powder bowl far below.

"And I thought the trip up was hell!" cried Jim. He implored his buddy, "Where do we go from here?"

"The operator said, 'Follow the ledge trail carefully to the right, and descend into the bowl. Go slowly, and trust God!'"

They hugged the drifted course and crept downward, unable to decipher milky sky from landscape, until they skirted the bottom of the cliff. There, sheltered from driving winds, they knitted through soft, neck-deep snow among scattered spruce until they joined the service road. Buck and Jim gladly skied out for the day, pursued in gathering darkness by patrollers anxious to get such stragglers safely off the mountain.

Jim gave Buck a joyous high-five as they stacked their equipment for the night, then headed indoors alone for some well-deserved rest and relaxation. Jim declined the group's invitation to paint the town.

Sleeping in, Jim nearly missed the bus for church next morning.

"How *was* your quiet evening alone?" asked Buck sarcastically as Jim charged aboard, necktie loose, and shoes in hand, just as the driver pulled into traffic. "I beat you home!"

"So, I quaffed a few beers, and danced with some strange women," Jim muttered, glaring with bloodshot eyes at his unchosen mentor. "I hope *you* weren't naughty, Bucko!"

"The food and company were fine, but you would have made them better, Jim. Nancy surely missed you," Buck reported sombrely. Then, rising stalwartly, the pastor addressed his people, "Where do we want to worship this morning?"

"With spirit-filled brethren," declared the bug-eyed fellow, whom Jim had not seen since late Friday night. "There's one meeting downtown, right now."

Supported by an enthusiastic show of hands, "Bug-eyes" directed the bus driver to park behind a vacant warehouse. Then, this unlikely shepherd led his sheep through an open side door, and down a narrow flight of stairs. They discovered a small, but lively worship service already underway in the basement.

"Welcome—join our circle, all! It's never too late to worship God!" beamed the youthful, casually attired pastor from behind his makeshift pulpit. Deacons eagerly ushered the newcomers into unfolded metal chairs, while a grinning player with huge, "coke-bottle" glasses but *sans* sheet music, gaily pounded "Come and Go with Me to that Land Where I'm Bound" on an old upright piano, and everyone sang the hand-written praise chorus projected onto the wall. The pastor, pleased by this jaunty influx of believers, effervesced, "The Lord blesses us today! Amen!"

Jim, languishing in disgrace with a throbbing head, could hardly wait! He was not disappointed, even after stumbling through some well-meaning but idealistic liturgy with these zealots in their drafty, threadbare chapel. He then heard the strange pastor preach a message encouragingly for *him*. The text, Ephesians 2, verses one to ten, Jim hardly knew, but it became wondrously alive to him through illustration by the joyous piano tune!

"Before we met Christ, we lugged our sins around like this piano. They were a heavy burden—almost unbearable!" the pastor gasped. For emphasis, he crouched beneath the piano's keyboard, and struggled to budge the bulky instrument.

Then, he sprang lithely to the top of the string chamber, and sat there smiling, contentedly cross-legged. He buoyantly proclaimed, "Jesus laid down his life for each one of us, *while* we were yet sinners. God, through his mercy and grace, also raised *us* from death. Even now, we celebrate with our heavenly father—playing "O Happy Day!" instead of "Taps"—Amen!"

"Hallelujah, mighty Lord!" praised the congregation as one. They broke into angelic song, blending many spiritual tongues in praise.

Jim wept shamelessly then, convinced that God still loved his children: Nancy, Janice, Bug-eyes, Buck, other skiers, and their frayed but welcoming hosts—even himself! The Lord *was* faithful; *he* knew their every need. After the service, Jim gave each of his new friends a hug, but reserved the last and warmest one for Nancy.

BUS DRIVER

BY ANNORA PROUDFOOT

There are many paths in this life.
Some lead to love, some to strife.
We are just hitchhikers stubborn to make it alone.
We come to a cross in the road.
Where do we go? Both ways look so cold.
A bus driver pulls up, and offers us a lift.
Do we take Him up on it?

He is older than time; He knows all the ways to the end of the line.
Through the wind, through the rain, He will persevere again and again.
Our fare is trust and faith; He will get us to the right place.

Sometimes, we look around, and think He has taken us the wrong way,
But we are His precious passengers, and He will never lead us astray.
For, when we are taken out of our comfort zone,
And into the unknown,
We grow by the things we have never done before.

— Enduring Art, Active Faith —

Along the way,
Different people we might not want to meet will take a seat,
And we will think they do not deserve it,
But He sees every heart, and believes they're worth it.
For we are the passengers . . .. He is the driver,
And if we want to survive, we have to work together.

So, hop on, come aboard! It's long and hard, but you will be amazed
By how much you have grown,
As He carries you all the way along the road.

HOW OLD ARE WE REALLY?

BY ANNORA PROUDFOOT

Age never matters.
At any age, you can be at any stage you want to be.
You find your mirror in someone older, and your dreams in children.
What connects us all is this: laughter, music,
And a good game of *Dutch Blitz*.

TOPSPIN FOLLIES

BY ROBERT PROUDFOOT

Steve Powers captured my imagination when he stealthily emerged from the shadows to conquer all comers during my first crack at tournament table tennis. This magician controlled his tables with such icy composure and rapier skill, even top-rated opponents marveled at his invincibility. He was, they claimed, just toying with us nameless journeymen en route to joining Canada's national team.

"He's superb!" I applauded in awe with other also-rans as "Power" Steve surged to golden victory over the defending but hopelessly outclassed Alberta provincial champion. "Just wish I could play half as well!"

Several seasoned table tennis players nodded in agreement, amused by such breathless understatement from a tournament greenhorn. I had warmed the sidelines since being mercilessly knocked from play during the first round early that morning. Yet, energized by finally escaping mundane, rumpus room ping-pong for the blazing adventure of competitive sport, I absorbed every blurring detail of others' games in an effort to learn their winning strategies. I vowed to cultivate Steve's secrets of ultimate success.

My weary travel mates raved about Powers' greatness as we limped home through the wintry prairie night in a pooled car, bearing naught but wounds to salve our deflated debut into big league tennis. Seizing opportunity to advance my own fervent dreams of excellence, I proposed that we club together, and practice Steve's winning formulae for future tournaments.

"Jim, you want these young stars to eat us for intermission?" Joe scoffed. He was the best player among us. "I could be their dad, man!

"Chalk today up for experience, then let go! Steve has been rigorously trained since he was in diapers by Chinese masters. We'd never beat him in our prime, let alone now, when we're just good old paddle boys looking for some fun!"

"There's no good athlete who's unbeatable," I argued. "I'm not gunning to take Powers on . . . . I simply want to improve my own skills to where *someday* I could give heroes like Steve a decent match. Let's invite the guy to our club, and learn from him awhile."

The others laughed at such folly. Why did I, who could barely beat the lunch hour ping-pong boys at the shop back in Lethbridge, think I even belonged in the same gymnasium as Powers? Had not the champ's blazing paddle enlightened me that I had no grasp of competitive strategy? My peers insisted that they had nothing more to show the "professionals," and refused to labour in vain for *my* improvement.

These detractors all displayed glistening hardware from youthful athletic exploits in "manly" Canadian sports like ice hockey, slow-pitch, and football in their home dens. *They* were playing ping-pong in old age now for fun and recreation, and wanted no more hassles. Did they not realize that I, who had no medals to prove *my* worth for peers or descendants, had finally found a game I loved and could win at, too?

"Let me win, also," I begged in vain, upon deaf ears.

I was misunderstood and ridiculed as a whiner. I became a prophet without honour in my own playroom. So unqualified was I in my dear sport that my driving enthusiasm worried other noontime smashers. They brusquely relegated me to hack around with raw beginners on a makeshift plywood table in some ill-lit corner as penance for my unseemly lobby.

Forsaking others' discouragement to shape up or ship out, I travelled forth alone, seeking my own victories. I burned passionately within to drink my fill of that exciting new wine that Steve had unknowingly poured for me. I must find him, as my vision meant nothing without the champion's help; I fantasized about this young god training diligently beside me as my mentor, drawing card, and friend. Though we moved in different circles now and I knew next to nothing about him, Steve strangely had acknowledged me at the tournament. Where had Powers been all my life? Did he not also realize that we were meant for each other?

Just when I had exhausted my own efforts to bring Steve on-board, golden words came down from the provincial sports council, inviting my wife Jane to join our Southern Region's badminton squad for the Alberta Winter Games. Jane hesitated to accept this honourable but 11th-hour plea to replace a superior sportswoman who had suddenly taken ill, but *I* saw Providence at work and demanded that she accept our one shot at glory. I promised to leave comforts of home and office to cheer Jane from the bleachers of some northern bush town gymnasium, if only she would get me in with her teammate, Steve.

I basked again in the sunlight of superior athletes engaged in blistering table tennis competition. Their polished play mesmerized me with grand displays of relentless smashes, magical spins, and unyielding defense. Momentum surged and waned with consistency and drive. Position and accuracy, speed and fitness collaborated with strategy, controlled emotion, and aggressive power to win the struggle. Elating victory and agonizing defeat were excruciatingly real, yet were soon lost in comradery, which came through confidence that *all* competitors belonged.

I watched Steve drive mightily yet fall short of medal glory to superior foes. He seemed mediocre as he despaired over petty losses backstage while I hobnobbed like a celebrity with the rich and famous of his athletic world. Dark horse Jane had impressed in this, her first Alberta badminton championship, and I, her coach, was suddenly friend to all her southern teammates.

I made my historic move on Steve with all the daring bravado of a circus showman. Catching Powers lurking outside, mourning the ping-pong squad's losses over a marijuana joint with his fellows, I brazenly declared my plans to form a new table tennis club in Lethbridge. He seemed unnerved by my stranger's boldness, yet sombrely considered the solicitation, and promised to call me next week. O happy day!

I smoothly produced my telephone number and address, but Powers discreetly brushed me off, stating, "Jim, we live in the same town . . .. I'll find you."

I fervently pursued the case, even while chained to my telephone awaiting his reply. Steve's vague promise in hand, I stumped our community's verdant ping-pong basements in search of players and equipment . . .. Verily, Lethbridge was crawling with smashers and choppers eager to play in my organization! I sifted bids on rent and times from several rec-halls, like some powerful agent hired by hundreds of card-carrying members. I explored funding opportunities with several levels of government, discussed future tournaments and clinics with established clubs in other towns. "Letting my fingers do the walking through the Yellow Pages" I ordered an expensive, red-and-black, Butterfly competition racquet by VISA from Toronto!

Weeks passed without sight nor sound from Steve, but I had faith that he also wanted the project. I zealously forged ahead to lay its groundwork before dutifully reporting back to his lordship.

I nearly fainted when Steve suddenly materialized in my office one sunny August morning so far removed from the tables of winter. Powers was dressed in work overalls and rolling tattered furniture away for repair from my government citadel when he recognized me, and stealthily padded into my air-conditioned cubicle.

"You got that club organized yet?" Steve demanded. He lounged in a chair, and propped his work boots upon my desktop. His gleaming eyes seemed to case my file cabinets for valuables to lift, when he divulged shamelessly, "I meant to phone you last Saturday but went drinking instead . . .. So, what's up, Jim?"

Refusing to register such crude impertinence from his grace, I effervesced instead with developments about our club. I promised Joola match tables, Butterfly three-star tournament balls, and seed money. I crisply relayed rental terms from several community associations, which I felt had sports facilities favourable to our needs.

"Top flight, man! Let's check 'em out tonight," Steve decided abruptly. "You make the arrangements, Jim, and I'll pick you up at seven bells."

I recollected that I had some church committee meeting on tap, but Powers was so ripely available now that I felt the committee could forgivingly wait in favour of his higher calling. I barely gulped my agreement before Steve vanished.

We barreled onto Mayfield Hall in Steve's polished hotrod, stereo blaring and high hopes flowing for the royal tour, but our enthusiasm evaporated as we languished instead on the periphery of some black-tie banquet taking festive precedence inside. Unbowed by this glaring miscue, Steve donned his invisible stocking mask, and prowled the inner premises in brazen defiance of diners gawking after us. We waited out our rivals downstairs, then made ourselves at home measuring their hurriedly vacated party room. The place was too small, so we moved on.

All was grimly locked, dark, and silent at our next appointment: with the soup kitchen director. A lady volunteer finally showed to touch up preparations for tomorrow's service, but she fearfully bolted the door against my smooth talk about table tennis. An urgent ring to the director's house found him sick in bed.

"I guess you'd hardly believe these guys promised to strut their stuff for us tonight," I giggled with chagrin. "Maybe God is trying to tell me something!"

"Those jerks let you down, Jim!" growled Steve. His brooding face was an ugly Incredible Hulk green in the dashboard light as we aimlessly cruised the streets.

Suddenly, he veered into a pub, and suggested we take five from our labours over some Blues.

"Set the record straight . . . .. You gotta jump on some guys to sell yourself, Jim. Nobody cares about table tennis, here in the land of ice hockey. That broad at the flophouse thought we were psycho-rapists, for Christ's sake!" Steve guffawed. He wolfishly loped ahead.

Upset by worldly cynicism in one so young and promising, I subconsciously rebelled when Steve slammed the bar door in my face. I gnashed my teeth in frustration: this arrogant prick gave no glory to our Lord! He rebuffed what sacrificing effort I had given for the club because nothing had panned out tonight . . . because I was a *Christian*? Well, *that* sealed my fate as a bumbling clown in Steve's jaded eyes.

"What did you say?" he demanded. Turning back to find me still fumbling with the door, Powers impatiently halted and crossed his arms. "What the hell's wrong with you, Jim?"

"I can't find my wallet," I muttered, sweating profusely. "I must have left it in your car."

"Go get it!" Powers snarled. He threw his keys at me as though I was some incorrigible child. "Nobody sponges off me!"

I turned tail like a whipped pup and raced into Steve's muscle car; yet, after practically ransacking it, found *nothing* of mine! Angry at my wasteful buffoonery, I paled in helpless chagrin when Powers jeered towards my wallet dangling precariously from his nimble, pickpocket's hand! *Nobody* fooled around with Steve!

"Your billfold feels empty, Jim, for a rich government mandarin," this punk scoffed. His entire household seemed stashed in a gym bag behind his car seat. "I'll buy your beer!"

Reduced to nothing in Steve's regally defiant eyes, I glumly wondered why as I followed my liege to a dim corner table. This footloose youth exuded confidence in accomplishment beyond his years, which he deserved not. I, five years Steve's senior, envied his virile success. He seemed to carelessly flaunt it, so self-certain he would never fail. I, who laboured tenaciously down life's rocky roads thirsting for victory, yearned to savour even a drop of its sweetness.

"What's happening, Lord?" I wept inwardly as Powers refused even my most congenial small talk. "Do your angels behave like Steve?"

— Enduring Art, Active Faith —

I felt I had blown everything and craved to slither away. Citing the grossly loud band music, acrid cigarette smoke, and shameless hustlers, I offered to walk home, but Steve seemed to read my mind.

Suddenly coming to life, he brandished the big question, "Well, Jim, where do we go from here? I thought you had lots of potential ping-pong facilities in mind."

"There is another," I offered. Taken aback, I broached my best cautious effort to restore Steve's confidence in me. "It's probably the best place of all, and I *know* we can view it tonight. It's a Sunday School hall in the basement of my church."

"I used to attend church. Let's check it out, man."

My battered spirit leapt joyfully within me, and I cherished Steve's naked testimony as we sped across Lethbridge to that vibrant cathedral I called "home." Powers shared that he had been a stalwart Christian during his teens: he had ingested Bible studies, and fervently witnessed Christ's redeeming grace to high schoolers hanging around pool halls and drug dens. Now that Steve had graduated beyond that phony religious phase, he became his own god! He lived with a lady he vaguely hoped someday to marry.

I burned to ask Steve why he strayed so far from Christ's loving presence when this brute halted before my church and entered. Left hanging on my own turf, I scrambled to follow his strong lead.

"Skipping out on the big budget meeting tonight, eh Jim?" admonished Janice Jones. The sparky congregational secretary was toiling in the duplicating room as we skulked past, but her shrill voice accosted us in our tracks, and held us there until she emerged, unfettered by her stack of papers, to jokingly read us our rights. "I *knew* I saw you out here . . . .. Good thing too . . . .. Some little old ladies at the meeting thought you boys were thieves and wanted me to call the cops!"

Steve shared Janice's morbid amusement, while I desperately sought a plausible alibi for shirking my ecclesiastical duties.

"I thought we were meeting *next* week," I stammered.

"That's the Christian Education Committee," Deacon Folsom corrected. His body screamed disgust as he dumped a sheaf of notes into

221

my hands on his way doorward. "Anyway, the Finance Committee just finished sitting now. I played secretary for you tonight, Jim, but I don't understand where *your* commitment is to our congregation."

"Sorry, Ed." I grimaced sideways at Steve. Ignoring his extreme preference to remain anonymous, I introduced this aloof fish out of water to my scrutinizing churchmates. "Steve Powers, a good table tennis buddy of mine. We're contemplating the use of the auditorium as a practice gymnasium for our club, come September."

"The *Lawrence MacPherson Hall*?" Folsom demanded. Frowning incredulously at me, like I had just mooned some sacred congregational heirloom, he rebuked, "Our Sunday School chapel is no place for ping-pong, even if church members are involved!"

"Jim, you should bring a written proposal to the next board meeting," Janice advised. "You *know* what the proper channels are."

"Do everything decently and in good order," Folsom lectured smugly. "By the way, Robinson, Pastor wants these minutes typed up and distributed by Friday."

"I'll try," I croaked. Without turning back, Ed left with Janice for the coffee room.

"Jim, I like that last space," Steve offered finally, as he dropped my shell-shocked carcass on my doorstep. "I might even attend your church if things work out."

"That'd be great, Steve!" Jane chimed in from the doorway. "You're always welcome at Hillcrest."

"Really?" Powers fished. He smiled warmly for the first time all evening.

"Yes, *really*," my wife reiterated. Her sweet hospitality mended all the fences I had broken. "Why don't you come by here for a visit sometime. We could eat supper together."

"Sounds good," Powers grinned. "See you folks later. Jimmy, it's been a slice."

"Thanks," I agreed. Steve sped away into darkness, leaving me confused by our twilight zone adventure.

— Enduring Art, Active Faith —

◆ ◆ ◆

The clanging office telephone shattered airy pleasantries of an important client interview.

"Sorry, Jim," the receptionist giggled. "I know you're working hard, but your boyfriend's been trying to get through all morning."

"Jimbo, Steve here." Powers broke in, as though shouting from outer space. "When're we gonna draft that letter, man?"

Embarrassed, I squirmed before three baleful farmers as I tried to remember the context of Powers' burning question. I stalled by promising to get back to him tonight but no dice . . . . Steve had his own rough draft ready, awaiting my immediate review.

"Great, Steve," I cheered, albeit discreetly. No need to hassle my sombre visitors, who probably *never* played games. "Ed and Janice will be very happy with your efforts."

"Ah, *those* bozos," Steve sneered, "They don't want me hanging around their righteous temple . . . . It's because of such hypocrites I left the church, five years ago!"

"Hey, let's talk about it over lunch," I whispered. "Bring the letter, and we'll type it up together."

"Sounds wild," Powers muttered, signing off.

I was *not* relieved to set down the phone, as intuition told me that lunch with Steve would be a heavy affair. Yet, my own work demanded my immediate attention: crops were ripe and ready for harvest, but how few were the labourers!

"Is talkin' on the telephone all you ivory-tower, gov'ment boys do with our tax dollars?" one leathery farmer teased as I turned sheepishly back to our business at hand. "We don't got all day to chew the fat, eh."

Neither did I. Steve met me for lunch in my office before noon, and we typed the letter on a government word processor to Hillcrest's Board of Managers, requesting use of Lawrence MacPherson Hall for three hours every Thursday night, commencing September 25. To mutual surprise, our proposal passed with ease!

We met several times in subsequent weeks to plan publicity and structure for our growing baby. Shared excitement of its debut into Lethbridge's sporting culture spurred us on: we rounded up six tables for the church and made ourselves legal by opening a bank account. Old, doubting Joe raced into the stable like a young stallion, bringing with him several curious ping-pong cronies from the noon-hour shop "for extra practice." The club came together beautifully, launched by some thirty players of all ages and walks of life. We drew enough old pros, ambitious journeymen, and teachable novices during our maiden year to benefit every member's learning, growth, and enjoyment.

❖ ❖ ❖

Steve and I lived table tennis during our memorable season together. He refined my raw talents and unyielding determination into a winning package. Powers worked long hours alone with me at the church, on my own basement table, in barroom playpens, and at various tournaments, patiently rebuilding my awkward defensive style with textbook strokes for attack and counter-attack. He carried me along to big tournaments across Alberta, where he coached me to hard-fought singles victories, or we played stellar men's doubles together, before Steve showed me how it was done, by whipping the ranked opposition at his own championship tables.

Steve dared me to become his worthy sparring partner and tournament sidekick.

"Okay, Jim, try to score ten points this game." Steve baited one night in my cavernous basement, dancing a powerful topspin at me with a book, rather than his vaunted designer racquet. "Look, I'm even playing left-handed!"

Left hand or not, the book practically shut me out! Not to be discouraging, Powers handicapped himself further for his next trick—a softball! He razzed me to frustration with that weapon, before ghoulishly displaying ultimate weakness to emphasize his strength by wielding a banana peel! I stole twelve points against *that* gimmick, then wryly

— Enduring Art, Active Faith —

suggested that we break for coffee rather than have me hang a licking on Steve. He agreed but only after lecturing me not to get cocky!

"Jim, you're getting better, but you've got far to go!" was Steve's big theme. "Heck, it took me ten years of solid training under various savvy coaches to achieve my current high calibre."

While we discussed club goals and rehashed old tournaments, our often-deep discussions invariably circled back to Steve's dispute with Christianity. His story remained unflinchingly enforced, typical of our generation: he had been a staunch believer back home in Edmonton until self-righteous church fathers condemned him for living in sin, shacked-up with Helen.

"There's no compassion, love, or understanding among you hypocrites!" Steve railed at me during an emergency lunch hour meeting to discuss Hillcrest's demand our club to pay increased rent for additional custodial maintenance, as complaints from parishioners mounted that we were excessively scuffing the hall floor and leaving adjoining bathrooms untidy. "You thump your Bibles, and claim to have all the answers regarding morality and fate! You don't know *everything*, man!"

"Our denomination takes a strong stand on couples engaging in sex outside of marriage because we honour God's admonition to keep our bodies pure, as temples for His Holy Spirit. Yet, we also value God's mercy, grace, and free will he offers his created humans."

"Ah, you're just another 'company man'! Get real, Jim.... Why would a loving creator condemn to hellfire billions of folks from other faiths or even pagans who don't agree that Jesus Christ is the Son of God?"

"Man condemns himself when he chooses to disobey the Lord."

"The Bible clearly states in Romans that God has chosen whom he will save," Steve retaliated. He was weary of me and my stuffy rhetoric. "I'm among countless not chosen; that's why I will never accept the Bible as God's holy book!"

Jane and I befriended Steve and Helen as a fellow couple but, during many autumn evenings we spent together, we encouraged them to embrace the virtues of holy matrimony. Steve's depressing stumbling block of predestination I countered with the Lord's overflowing love reiterated in First John. Helen openly listened, but Steve, the calm intellectual, remained a tough nut to crack. We all reasoned as best we could through personal testimony and Bible study, but getting nowhere, finally agreed to disagree. Steve privately complimented me for accepting Helen, a black woman, as my friend and his beloved spouse, but he bitterly vowed that they could not publicly marry unless narrow-minded churches and Lethbridge society became tolerant of mixed-race unions. Jane and I gave our friends up to God, but continued to labour for them secretly in prayer.

Steve was certainly the best table tennis athlete I knew, but *he* grimly surmised that all his glistening trophies meant nothing when so many whiz-kids rising to glory out there prevented him from realizing his dream: a regular spot on the national team, where he would use the highest quality equipment, have access to top-notch coaches, and get paid to play for Canada in international table tennis summits around the globe. He was discouraged by his inability to grasp that extra tenacity and polish required to win every qualifying match—discouraged enough to drink! He blamed his failures on others' superior coaching, venues, and contacts, but Steve was the one who failed to deliver the big wins. He hated, as smug complacency, my happiness with far lower sights: do well enough in tournament play to remain rated above 500; win or at least place in various realistic classes, and thus attain respect among our fraternity of competitive table tennis players around Alberta. My desire to play with composure, and unified spirit of mind and body, unnerved this aggressive and turbulent competitor.

Powers' frustration with failed aspirations in his "empty" life exploded upon me during our last tournament together. That long, wintry road to Edmonton for the Alberta Open gave him ample excuse to upbraid me for "quitting" Sunday's portion of the competition.

"Don't you care that I persuaded the judges to make you eligible for those events?" Steve growled. "You're always bitching about getting slaughtered when forced to play over your head, so I got the tournament rules bent for you. Jim Robinson, you may now compete in the under 900s. You'll win in a breeze, man!"

"I didn't ask you to fix anything in my favour, Steve," I argued. "I want to worship the Lord on His Sabbath, even if that means curtailing my own pursuit of fleeting glory in some two-bit game. I'm more into the big game of life."

"Is that all our friendship means to you? I fought for you cuz I admire your great determination to learn, to win. Jim, you have potential to get where I am now and more, but success in our sport doesn't come without sacrifice! It will take you five more years of hard practice and full tournament experience to gain 1,600 points. You're 36 now, Jim! You don't have time left to climb on top before these young punks take over!"

"What's the use then?" I cried against his tirade. "Why go through the motions on Sunday in the gym if my heart is elsewhere?"

Anguish coloured my greater joy of having the Lord to rely upon for my every need. Although this big tournament was my last chance to earn a 1,000-plus rating, and to compete next month for the south in the Alberta Winter Games before the provincial sports council, touting a youth movement, limited entry to kids under 19 years . . . while an impending job promotion would soon take *me* away to Toronto . . . I refused to break my decision to rest with God.

Fighting back tears, I declared, "I wouldn't win there anyways but, with Jesus, I've already claimed total victory."

"Yeah, you're one of God's chosen few!" Steve scoffed. "I'll go play my hand with the other lost souls. I'm up for winning—done paid my dues!"

"The Lord loves you, man; He desires not that you perish."

"I know, Jim. I have peace with God and don't fear *his* justice," Steve replied solemnly. Then, just as suddenly, he defiantly shouted, "It's the man-made Bible and church I can't stand! They're so full of hypocrisy that they lead many gullible seekers astray. I won't be misled again!"

We found nothing meaningful left to discuss after that argument. In fact, we stayed on different wavelengths that weekend, and have since drifted apart. I slept soundly in preparation for Saturday's grueling schedule, whereas Powers drowned his sorrows in beer, and tottered into competition like death warmed over. While I gained new friends and respectability by scraping out three victories, this multi-talented veteran was blown from contention by some upstart kid! Steve charged into Sunday mean and hungry yet fell short of the podium. He was glumly dressed for home when I arrived after church, expecting to cheer him on to the prizes!

I laid Steve Powers on God's altar that Sunday, and continue to pray for him from afar. My fervent hope remains that the Lord will open Steve's ears, and soften his heart to a most wonderful love by grace. I was strengthened during a fleeting moment by Steve's compassion with sharing table tennis secrets, which I can hone during the rest of my athletic career. I thank God for his interest in me, yet I hope that I was also able to plant good things in my friend's life of struggle. I believe Steve's many talents will enrich the Kingdom!

HALF AND HALF

BY NORMA PROUDFOOT

The old man slumped on a wire bench in a shopping mall. The bench back was curved and slanted just right to fit the tiredness of his body. Christmas shopping was okay for the young, but he would let them do it. He was warmly dressed for the below-zero temperatures outside, but his coat was unzipped, and his scarf and gloves lay idle beside him. His daughter and two grandsons had given him this outing as a change from sitting indoors looking out at the falling snow. He had walked and talked with them, enjoying the sights and sounds of a busy commercial mall well-prepared for Christmas shoppers. Now, he would rest quietly while they made one last stop at the pet shop to select a special treat for their dog, Boxer; that was a cacophony he could do without! Instead, the oldster rested his head on the bench back, listening to festive Christmas music.

It was easy to listen to Christian music played quietly and peacefully, as befit the remembrance of a season ushered in by the special act of the Prince of Peace born quietly in a lowly manger. The resting grandfather shifted his position slightly, to suit the thoughts that came next to his mind. He did not consider himself a particularly religious man. It was hard to reconcile oneself with religion when there were so many unsolved problems in the world—but that was just the problem! The world was the problem, so full as it was with people who spoiled ideals like peace. People made war, rather than peace, and the precipitations of war were poverty and hunger, cold homes and colder hearts, selfishness and greed . . . a world where the gift was never big enough!

Suddenly, the old man became aware that he was not alone on the bench. Somebody small and insignificant, who could hardly waver the steadiness of the bench as he sat down, had moved his scarf and gloves for a closer look into his face and, doing that looking, were two of the biggest, most innocent eyes he had ever seen.

"Are you a grandfather?" the boy asked whose eyes were honest as well as innocent . . . eyes that needed answers, not only to the questions at hand, but to all the questions that lay in their limpid depths.

"Yes, I am a grandfather, a very tired one at that."

"Oh, I'm sorry. I didn't know you were napping."

This boy is well-mannered but disappointed, the old man determined. He sat up and leaned towards the boy, muttering, "I was just listening to that beautiful music. My two grandsons had me walking these halls a bit too long for the old legs of a grandfather. Do you have a grandfather?"

The boy flashed a most winsome smile that begged him to say more. The shrug of his shoulders gave away more than his words. "Sort of half and half," he shared with a shy giggle. "Well, it's quite simple, really. You see, I just have so many steps."

He got out his fingers to help with the logistics of his answer. "My mom married my stepdad"—that took care of his thumb and one finger— "And my dad married my stepmom" —and now there was only the baby finger left.

They both had the same thought at the same time, and they laughed together as they identified who was the baby finger. It was in the midst of their laughter that a stout, rather overtaxed young woman arrived on the scene. She was obviously too pregnant with someone else to share an already half-and-half grandfather.

"Matthew! I'm sorry. I couldn't remember which bench I had asked you to sit on!" She glanced cautiously at his laughing companion, who continued to smile, leaving all explanations to the boy who owned them and was completely capable of providing them.

"Oh, he's okay, Mom. He's not just any old stranger—he's a grandfather."

Mother and son then wandered down the mall, leaving the old man alone, with more questions than he had answers. Was this Mom or Stepmom? He would never know, but somehow the music had more meaning for him after his close encounter with a pleasant little boy, with whom it was so easy to laugh.

He was still smiling when his own two grandsons arrived as one at his knee. They were rosy-cheeked and sparkly eyed. They did not have to share him with anyone except their grandmother.

"Grandpa, were you dreaming?" Bill asked. A dreamer himself, Bill thought this was the answer for the smile on his grandfather's face.

"Of course, not," more realistic Simon protested. "Who'd ever be able to sleep in this busy place?"

The old man looked at his daughter with a sudden pleasure. Bonny was chubby, just as rosy-cheeked as her sons and still as sparkly eyed as she had been when a child. She was leading a busy life, working part-time to help with the household expenses. *Thank God it was a good life*, mused her doting father, *full of stability and love.*

They arrived home at the same time as his son-in-law, Pete. He had "a grandmother" in his car. He had picked her up at her son's home where she had been busy babysitting her only granddaughter. Kate was a real bundle of joy at two, but much too much for Grandfather to keep company with for a whole day. Now that grandmother gave full attention to her two grandsons, both talking at once. Grandmothers were great copers!

There was much joy in greeting! Even Boxer bounced into the melee. There were fun stories to tell one another. A wonderful meal was ready to eat, graciously presented by unflustered Bonny who, on her precious day off, had prepared her father's favourite shepherd's pie before she picked him up to go shopping.

This is my religion, the old man thought to himself. *This is the life God has given me to enjoy. I fought for this, so long ago on Vimy Ridge, in the war we were assured would be the "War to End All Wars." It didn't work for everybody. Many soldiers were wounded, and some died, never to return and enjoy the nebulous peace they fought for. But it worked for me, and I can surely learn to appreciate life.*

"Grandfather, why are you smiling?" Bill asked. The dreamer climbed upon his grandfather's knee with a favourite book that only Grandfather knew how to read.

"I've had a lot to think about today, Bill: happy thoughts, and sad thoughts . . . things I understand, and things I must still sort out. When I get it all together in my head, maybe I can better explain to you the real reason behind a grandfather's smile. For now, let me tell you, it has a lot to do with a grandson who still wants his grandfather to read to him."

Grandfather liked that book too. He read it to his own children when they were little, and contrary to the psychologists who worry over children's minds somehow being warped by animals who think and talk, he believed that the lessons one could learn from the antics of Jimmy Skunk, Reddy Fox, and Peter Rabbit were still appropriate. Their escape techniques, stress-coping strategies, and survival tactics could stir imaginations of smart little boys like Bill and Simon, who always came for his part of the attention.

Grandmothers know when it is bedtime, for little boys as well as for grandfathers.

"We must get your father home now," she said to Pete. "He's had a long day."

So, after all the goodbyes were said, Pete took them home to their cozy little cottage on the edge of town. Grandmother said it again after they drank their hot chocolate, and enjoyed a few soda biscuits that had been heated in the oven just long enough to melt the pat of butter on top.

"Why don't you come to bed now?" she called to him as he sat for a moment in the glow of the streetlight that shone through the window.

Why did it seem to everyone else that closed eyes and a smile should indicate some degree of exhaustion? Did it ever occur to anyone that an old man could be doing some serious thinking? It was that "half-and-half" grandfather that had stirred his thoughts. He had heard the expression before. He heard it first when his wife was busily making the tea dainties for her lady friends who would come to call for afternoon tea. He was to pick up "a few things at the corner store," before making himself scarce while the women visited. He did not like shopping, and went as few times as possible, but this time he was being useful—until he came to the last item on her grocery list!

"Half-and-half," his wife had written as plain as day in her bold hand but what could it mean? Half and half *what*? Finally, a sales clerk who noticed him puzzling, came to his rescue.

"Oh, that's an easy one, sir," he said. The clerk led him to the shelves of dairy produce. Smiling broadly, the young man had handed him a carton of cream clearly marked "half-n-half," as well as a bit of ready advice, "You'll just have to come shopping more often. You are getting out of touch."

There was also the funny story he liked to tell from during his younger years, when he had been a travelling salesman, selling towels and similar products for Caldwell Knitting Co. He had met a lot of friendly people in those days; some even invited you in for a meal and offered you a bed for the night.

That was how it was with the English couple, Charles and Min. They were the friendliest people, always looking forward to his next trip up their way. "Their way" was farming and a very unusual way it was. Charles and Min were so typical of the English who were often the butt of pioneer stories, whether true or fabricated, who came out to the colonies to farm without any idea of how to do it. During one visit, Charles took him to the barn to show what was, for him, a rare treat: a beautiful horse with a newborn filly beside her in the straw bed. It was on the return walk to the house that he noticed the peculiarity of the chicken-coop door.

With the straightest of faces, Charles gave his explanation. "Well, d'ja see, that's whot ya calls a 'alf 'n' 'alf door. The middle bar is stable. The flaps up and below were built that way for a reason, the reason being: when a fox sneaks in through the bottom 'alf, the 'en flies out through the top 'alf!"

Charles, being a great storyteller, gauged his timing just right. Anybody could laugh at the way he related, but he waited for one to puzzle at his reasoning. Then he laughed loudly, "You may not believe this, seeing you're my friend, but I really believed in a 'alf 'n' 'alf door when I built it."

Salesman and farmer were still chuckling when they reached the house, so Min guessed the cause.

"Oh, Charlie," she cackled just like a hen, "You told him about the 'en whot flew the coop!"

The old man smiled contentedly as he sat thinking about them all. The big, serious eyes of the little boy on the bench in the mall would always haunt him. There were a lot of "half 'n' halfs" in this world. It was certainly not a perfect place. Peace was an elusive thing—hard to attain and maintain! To him, it appeared now as a state of mind that one could have if one willed it to happen. Too many people settled for half 'n' half . . . half war, half peace; half contentment and half none; half rich and half poor . . . for individuals as well as for larger groups, even nations and churches.

His church, which was over a century old, had just completed a survey of its congregation, only to find that it was comprised of several halves—half over and half under? —which probably precipitated the second, where half enjoy traditional music, and half want more of the modern. The Quebec Referendum vote on sovereignty[73], he speculated,

---

73 The separatist Parti Quebecois (PQ) provincial government introduced two referenda, each closely defeated through voting, on whether Quebec should become an independent country, but maintain a political and economic agreement (sovereignty association) with Canada. On May 20, 1980, the PQ proposal to pursue sovereignty association was defeated 59.56% to \0.44%. On October 30, 1995 the "No" side won by a much slimmer

in spite of its flaws and political capers, could probably have been predicted to be too close to call . . ..

His wife was beside him now, also seated in the streetlight glow, while he told her about the small boy he had met earlier on a bench in the busy shopping mall.

"I'm ready to go up to bed now," he concluded. "I think the lesson I have learned today is that each person must find his own faith, and believe in it strongly enough to fit his life around it, in such a way that allows him to be tolerant of others, and learn to cope with the differences."

The grandmother climbed into her bed with her mind now filled by many varied thoughts that he had put into it. Her turn had come to marvel at the peaceful smile on his face while she learned to cope with half-and-half sleep.

---

margin of 50.58% to 49.42%, carried by 54,288 votes during the largest voter turn-out in Quebec history (92.5%).

THE SPECTATOR IN RETROSPECTION (ARTIST'S STATEMENT)

BY ALICIA PROUDFOOT

The Spectator in Retrospection is a curious character that jumps to mind when I imagine the performing, living body. The interactive sculpture I am proposing considers the spectator as a performer, who is in a relaxed viewing position, but still strongly supporting the oversized theatre glasses on its shoulders.

The glasses are interactive, yet the inner mechanics offer a nostalgic surprise of a View-Master toy with silk screen slides of historic photos of Hinton's cultural diversity with performing arts in the reel. The handle operates the reel change, inviting active participation. Following the Public Art policy, the work takes a responsibility, encouraging all ages to access art as well as culture through the safety and delight of play. With a responsibility to cultural policy, this work invigorates a healthy community of play and learning of Hinton's local artistic heritage. This piece is intended to be an outside sculpture on the new West Fraser Performing Arts Centre's site, standing at approximately 6ft x 9ft x 4ft. sculpture is to be constructed from re-purposed metal, cement, and ˥ses to withstand Hinton's varying weather.

— Enduring Art, Active Faith —

There is a layering of viewership to this proposed work. The visitors view the performing spectator who, in turn, view the slide reel in the theatre glasses. The work draws awareness to the key role that the audience holds and reflects on their responsibility to the performance.

(*The Spectator in Retrospection* sculpture, front view, installed on September 29, 2017, to commemorate the opening of the new West Fraser Performing Arts Centre in Hinton, Alberta.)

(View-Master Reel held on back of *The Spectator in Retrospect* sculpture.)

PART IV
FAMILY MEMORIES

(*What We Leave Behind*. A stone lithology 2017.)

WHAT WE LEFT BEHIND (ARTIST STATEMENT)

BY ALICIA PROUDFOOT

The drawing is an abandoned wasp nest in an empty space. The way it is drawn is thin and delicate, making the nest appear fragile. Simultaneously, the print instills a feeling of relief that the nest no longer hosts such annoying insects, as well as a feeling of sorrow that the nest is a home that has been forgotten. Home does not mean the same for everyone, and most times it holds a mixture of contradictory emotions. It is easy not to acknowledge the melancholic mournfulness carried with the vibrant remembrance of nostalgia. The nest is a reminder of a home from the past, and when threatened, the swarm leaves. Human behaviour is not as simple as with these insects. Humans fear, over-analyze, and financially worry about leaving home. It is an investment to the extent that we collect curios of nests, apply human narrative to them, and wonder.

ROOTS, VINES, AND TENDRILS

BY NORMA PROUDFOOT

"He was a funny old fella, my Great Uncle Peter," Dad was wont to say on one of those long winter nights just made for storytelling at the farm home in the Peace River Country. "Some of them of his generation didn't worry about it, but my Great Uncle Peter wanted to learn the English.

"'If it's to be living in this country we are, we best be learning the language o' 't,'" was Peter's advice to all of them. Of course, he had nobody to talk to at home, they all speaking Gaelic together, but Great Uncle Peter didn't let that stop him. He'd get himself all done up on a Saturday afternoon, and walk the seven miles into Montague.

"He had a special wardrobe for the trip: Highland tweed from the "auld country," jacket, britches, and a cap jauntily pulled down over one eye. His gold watch on a long chain lay elegantly across his chest to drop into a pocket there. Homemade leather boots he laced up past his calves with leather thongs, and a hardwood cane, with a handsomely curved staghorn handle, fit into his right hand as if it were born there. He didn't need the cane for any reason at all, other than that he loved to twirl it in the air as he walked along, singing Gaelic songs he had learned as a boy. My Great Uncle Peter couldn't sing in English.

"The storekeeper knew him well, and was always glad to see him. Part of the Saturday afternoon entertainment was to get Peter talking the English to give those gathered around a chance for a good laugh."

"They really were not being very kind, were they?" Christie said. Thinking seriously big for only twelve years old, she was not so much asking as telling. Christie protected all those who were teased, the butts of jokers. Christie did not like to think that people stood around, laughing at Dad's Great Uncle Peter.

"Well, he was quite funny," Dad explained. "He'd have the words, but he'd speak them in the wrong order somehow."

"Tell us what he'd say," Blanche pleaded. Blanche, the middle daughter between Christie and their kid-sister Eve, liked a funny story.

"Well." Dad always started his stories like that. "Great Uncle Peter had this old pipe that he smoked whenever he had something to put in it. Tobacco was really a luxury for P. E. Islanders of his day, so he'd make one tin go a terrible long way. At home on the farm, he'd smoke things he gathered and dried, like different kinds of bark or leaves off lamb's quarters[74] and such. Pete'd fit these into the bowl of his pipe, then top them off with enough tobacco so's he'd get the occasional whiff. Sometimes, he'd just hang the pipe in his mouth empty."

"But what can you do with an empty pipe?" son Gordon asked. He thought such to be a very strange idea indeed.

"Oh! You don't know my Great Uncle Pete! He could hold the stem just lightly in his teeth," Dad explained. He demonstrated with a pencil. "Then he'd roll his tongue around the end of it, moving it from side to side or up and down. He could make it roll over without putting a hand to it. Pete'd be talking the whole time, the pipe putting the punctuation marks into his sentences."

---

74 A greyish-green, annual weed commonly found in farm yards and fields where ground is disturbed.

"I get it!" Eve chimed in. This youngest daughter, behaving like a school teacher even then, was excited to contribute. Illustrating with her curling tongue, she continued, "To the left could be the first comma. Then, the right side could be the second comma . . .."

Her tongue was long and very juicy.

"Ya!" Blanche jumped into the limelight, as always. "The exclamation mark could start right up at the top and come straight down."

Even Christie was giggling by this time. Gordon continued through his giggles to reflect on all these empty maneuvers, "But why bother? What pleasure could you get out of a dry pipe?"

"Great Uncle Pete's pipe was never dry! All that tongue action would force enough air and moisture through the stem to cause all sorts of strange little windy and gurgling sounds."

"Henry!"

Although she enjoyed listening, Mom could interrupt quite sharply when she thought it time to bring Dad back to his story.

"Oh, yes! I was telling about the Saturday trip into Montague. Great Uncle Peter always saved up enough tobacco to fill his pipe just as he entered the store. He did it with a flourish, ceremony enough to allow the people time to gather round . . .. Then, when his pipe was full—tamped to his satisfaction—Pete'd put it to light with an expansive gesture designed to keep his audience from knowing it was his last match. Just as the smoke puffs were rising in even circles above his head, the storekeeper, whose name was Little Willy Butt (as distinct from Big Willie Butt), would say, '"Good afternoon, Peter. Yore tobacco is shore burning well the day."'

"Right on cue (and it was also cue for Dad as well, who liked to act out this part of the story with his own equally long legs), Great Uncle Peter took his stride, which was a long one acquired from walking all over Prince Edward Island, right up to the counter, and asked with typical charm, '"Got'cha any matches, Willie?"'"

There was no doubt that the same snickers went through Great Uncle Peter's audience as did through Dad's, and there was also no doubt that they had the same non-effect on both charmers.

"Little Willie Butt was not finished." Dad could be both narrator and actor with ease. "Reaching under the counter, he pulled out a tin of tobacco. '"Wud ye like a new tin o'tobacca, Peter?"' he asked. '"'Tis noo in this mornin' and, *ach aye-ee*, what a lovely aroma it has. Just get a whiff o'it, Peter,"' and Little Willie Butt removed the cover and shoved the tin right under Great Uncle Peter's nose.

"Great Uncle Peter took a long whiff. '"*Ach-aye-ee*,"' he murmured. His eyes and the pipe rolled over at the same time. Then he remembered that he was Peter MacDonald of Forest Hill, who could not afford that whole tin of tobacco. '"Well noo, Willie, it's thankin' ye I be for that satisfyin' sniff, but ta hame I ha'e me own tobacca can."'

"'"But yore pipe is empty the noo, Peter, and ye be a lang way this side o'hame. Let me jest gi'e ye a few puffs to tide ye o'er."'

"'"Ach and that wud be dacent o'ye, Willie. Me sma' pouch I ha'e right here in me pocket,"' Great Uncle Peter replied. He gratefully produced the well-worn pouch that Little Willie Butt knew he should have, and Willie filled it the way that Uncle Peter knew he would. '"I'll jest be goin' the noo and I bid ye a good day, Willie."'

"With that, Great Uncle Peter doffed his cap around the room, turned on the pivot of his staghorn cane, took up his stride, and left with a sympathetic, laughing crowd behind him." So, incidentally, did Dad.

"'"But Willie,"' exclaimed Dad for Norman Cox, who always worried about such things. '"He didn't pay you for the matches, or the tobacco."'

"'"But he paid us a satisfying visit,"' Little Willie Butt concluded."

❖ ❖ ❖

Fifteen years later, Dad leaned back in his chair after a satisfying meal, and announced that he was thinking of going to Prince Edward Island the next summer. He explained, "I want to look up my memories, and I'd like to take Blanche and Eve with us."

"I can take leave without pay," Blanche offered. She worked as a teller at a bank, but was ready for a change.

"I suppose you'll want to take your books," Dad teased Eve.

"I certainly will not! I'll run on the beaches, splash in the waves, look up Green Gables, and forget all about university." Then, in honour of the memory of Dad's many good stories about him, she just had to ask, "Will there be anything left of Great Uncle Peter?"

"No. He's long gone now, but memories play wonderful tricks. You know, Peter was the one who took me in when Dad and Mother took their four youngest kids, and came out West. That would be in the fall of 1903, when I was only 13. Jack and Dan, my two older brothers, were to take care of me.

"'"Them fellas'll forget a'about ye, sae ye best be keepin' company wi' me,"' Peter insisted. Dad relived how his great uncle had mentored him about value of family while he spent his youth under his great uncle's roof. "We were kindred spirits, Pete and me.

"'"'Tis understandin' I be how ye feel, me lad, 'cause y'see 'twas on me own I went back ta see t'auld sod for mesel', leavin' me family on this side t'ocean . . . but 'twas older be ye that I was when I chose ta do't."'

"Great Uncle Peter moved his long legs, which were stiffened from the sitting, adjusted his chair and leaned towards me," Dad recalled. The dour storyteller became misty-eyed as he piped out his departed ancestor's tale, crisp with Scottish brogue not heard since his youth.

"'"D'ye see, lad, I had an Uncle Peter mesel'. He didna came ta t'New Land wi' t'rest o' us. I were a sma' laddie o' six, red haired an' freckled like himsel' an' he favoured me . . . took me aside he did.

"'""Peter,"' says he, '""Ye be only a laddie an' 'tis crossin' t'water ye be. 'Tis hopin' I am an' prayin' I'll be that ye'll return the day. Come back, lad an' see where ye came from. A man has ta ha'e roots, d'ye ken? An' yore roots be here, waitin' for ye amang t'heather o't'moors where t'peats be gathered for t'fires. I'll nae be here, lad but some'll know ye."''

"'"So ye see, 'twere as much for me Uncle Peter as for mesel' that I returned ta t'auld sod."'

"How did you live, Great Uncle Peter? What did you do?" young Dad inquired.

""""Ach well, I were interested i' sheep pasture spread out afore me, changin' betimes only for t'hills an' t'deep glens . . . an' t'sheepfolds! Sae many, sae clean, an' as purty as a picture o'er t'green land. But I had somewhat ta do for me uncle, Scotty MacPherson.

"""""Ya'll be tastin' a dram o' whiskey for me, lad,"""' Scotty tellt me as he shook me hand o't'dock. """"Ya'll be nae tasting t'like o't this side t'water, wi' or wi'out t'pro'bition."""'

""""Scotty couldna ope' his ane e'e. He kep' 't kinda funny like. Nae op'n an' nae clos't. Ye couldna tell did he see ye t'noo. When he talked ta me, I couldna keep me ane e'e on't, 'twas tha' queer!"'

"""""Gae ta Tamdhu m'lad, an' tak' a dram f'auld Scotty. Touch 't ta yore lips an' let 't run thro'. *Ach-aye-ee*! 'Tis smoky, like barley roasted o'er peat fire, an' smooth, pure as t'water tha' comes doon fra' t'sky as rain."""'

""""Sae I went ta Tamdhu, ta a sma' pub there. It be dark, an' fu' o'tobacco smoke, wi' menfolk a'over t'place. I moved mesel' ta a table i'ta corner an' I orderet a dram. I touched 't ta me lips like Uncle Scotty said ta do. But ach aye! I didna like t'taste o't. Tha' burnt me lips an' tha' burnt me throat an' me e'en the' waterset somethin' terrible. As I coughed an' sputtered there, a man sat him doon b'side o'me."'

"""""D'ye nae like t'whiskey, then?"""' he asked me.

""""Tha' I don't an' 'tis sorry I be, for I be tastin' 't for another man.""""

"""""I ken wha' ye say, for I canna' like 't mesel'. There be some as do an' some as don't an' we be t'other ane. Wh'be yore name, for I know ye ta be a stranger."""""

"Great Uncle Peter's oil lamp stuttered and died, but that didn't matter to either of us. He could talk, and I could listen in the dark," Dad marveled. He piped richly and deeply into his great uncle's brogue as he continued to speak for him and other brave Scotsmen who had lived in both the old and new worlds.

"""""'T be hard for ye ta be believin', Peter,"""' this one said ta me. """"But I think we be kin. I be Neil MacDonald mesel'. Grandpa Neil, whose name I bare, sailt ta t'New Land wi' me Uncle John—who shorely be yore father—an' me Uncle Alex an' me Uncle Donald, who shorely be yore ane kin. Me father be Angus, the wild ane he said o'himsel'. He didna gang awa'. He couldna d'ye ken, for he had me, a wee cripplet laddie.""'

""'"Neil stood ta his fu' height which was sma' and I stood ta mines, which was ta tower o'er him.

""'""We be goin' ta where t'roots be, Peter an' 'tis proud I be ta be showin' ye,"""' Neil said.

""'"There be sheep everywhere. Lambs bein' born afore our very e'en . . . an' only t'wee black an' white border collies movin' i'an' ou' among them . . . an ta shepherd whustling ta them fra t'big rock where he stood. As we walked along, I asked him, ""'"Wha' did happen ta ye, Neil?"''

""'""Ach, well, me Dad, Angus, got a taste o't'Scotch i' him. He bein' ta t'mainland ta buy t'sheep for t'laird[75] but t'market be close ta t'pub—this here pub—d'ye ken. An' t'deals wi' t'buyers an' sellers be made b'yon hill. Angus, me Dad, be only a shepherd fra Skye an' he ha'e nae t'heart ta sae them nae. When t'dram be passed, he took ane, an' another ane, an'—ach Aye! He be tha' sick, near ta death.

""'""Me mother ha'e nae help wi' t'birthin' an' I came out wi' me foots a'tangled up. Me father couldna forget 't. He worked wi' me day after day. Ye couldna cross t'ocean wi' a cripplet lad but ye could tak' him out ont' t'hills an' teach him an honest day's work for honest pay.

""'""An' when me father lay on his death bed, t'auld laird came by. He leant low on't his cane an' whispert, """""'Tis carin' for Neil I'll be, Angus, like he be me ane son. An' me ane son after me."""""'

""'""An' he did tha'. His son be Malcolm fra doon t'Great Glen an' I be here selling t'ewes for him. 'Twas sayin' goodbye ta t'other ane I be when I saw ye. There be work for ye, Peter, d'ye be wantin' it: work wi' ye ane kin,"""' Neil promised

""'"Tha' be hours ago an' Neil an' me be walkin' wit' t'pace o' a cripplet man, seein' t'sights o't'land an' I be thinkin', 'tis nae me ane

---

75 Scottish pronunciation for Lord, the owner of the land to whom the various crofters paid due and helped manage his sheep.

beautifu' wee island back hame, restin' like a cradle ont' ta blue waters o'a sunny day. Here there be mists, wi' cloudy skies tha' turn ta sea inta themsel's but O! T' smell o't, t'feel o't wind blusterin' thro' t'glen!

"""""Sit ye down a wee, Peter and listen ta't. Turn yore ear ta t'wind. Tha' be them lairds be doin' back then—emptyin' t'glens for sheep they be. T'auld ane tha' didna gang awa' wi' ye, the' sit here be times. The' hear t'voices i't'wind. 'Tis t'greeting o'those ane wha' sailet awa' ta tha' New Land—Highlanders grievin' for hame, the' be. A braw ferlie 'tis, t'greetin' ont' t'wind i't'glens tha' be empty o'people t'noo."""""

""""I heard 't mesel' as I sat there on t'hill. I'twangs t'strings o'me heart, Neil, an' turns me mem'ry ta t'day me father took me hand an' walked me up t'gangplank o't'big ship name o' *Polly* . . .. There be sheep, Neil, far as me e'e can see; nothing but sheep! 'Tis thankin' ye I be for a' yore kindness, but I couldna stay here.

""""So, I got in the boat and went acrosst ta t'island name o'Harris, which be west o'er t'sea. There tha' be crofters still, growers o'wool, an' cutters. The' spin an' the' dye the wool. Then the' weave it. I ha'e seen a man once't fra o'er there, Henry. He be dressed a'i'tweeds like mesel' an' I wanted mesel' ta ha'e sic a suit."'

"And you got it, Great Uncle Peter. Tis a fine suit o'tweeds ye be wearin'," Dad had emphasized. Enthusiastically retelling it now to his raptly listening wife and daughters, Dad rolled his sides with laughter. "I said it with brogue for him because I knew he'd like hearing it!"

In his long-winded story to justify going back home to PEI, Dad resumed playing his dapper but eccentric, storytelling great uncle in response to his own assertion of youth, """"Yes, lad, I got me a fine suit an' sic a lot mare. I worked mesel' up in t'business. I did 't step by step. T' owner was bein' a very fine man, by name o' Kenneth MacDonald he be, tho' nae kin o'mine . . . but a very fine man for a' tha',"""" Great Uncle Peter laughed. He heartily enjoyed his own joke.

""""""'Tis a fine worker ye be, Peter,"""""" MacDonald tellt me. """"""'Tis watchin' ye I be an' when ye get ta t'top, I'll be tha' proud. Ya'll be a partner someday, me lad."""""

Great Uncle Peter stood up and began to pace.

"Did you get to the top, Great Uncle Peter?" Dad asked him.

"'''Tis tha' strange how yore values change, me lad,'" the oldster replied. His eyes, in focus again, turned upon me. "'It be jest tha' moment, d'ye ken, tha' I knew it t'will be me family I'll be missin'. I couldna let go o'tha'.

"'"Sae I counted me wealth an' I had't. T'same as had me father when he set sail o'er t'water. Sae I said ta Mr. Kenneth MacDonald, '"'Tis thankin' ye but I be a lonely man t'noo, Sir; wi' money i'me pocket tha' I earnt an' 'tis hame I be goin', crost t'seas ta a wee island name o'Abegwait.

"'"Mr. Kenneth MacDonald said goodbye ta me like ta his ane son, did he ha'e ane, ga'e me t'staghorn cane, he did, ta carry wi' me.

"'"""Peter," said he, """"I know ye'll ne'er be back. I'll miss ye, lad. There'll ne'er be ony ta' yore place. Think o'me betimes an' write ta me, 'cause 'tis wonderin' I'll be how are ye."'

"'"Ach, well,"' Great Uncle Peter reflected. He sadly took his head in his hands, '"I ne'er did write tha' letter. Me hands jest couldna pen 't, but I did think o'him often an' often. E'erytime I put o'me tweeds an' walk t'red roads, swingin' me staghorn cane, d'I think o'Mr. Kenneth MacDonald, an' tha' other life tha' might o'been."'

"Great Uncle Peter never married. He lived by himself in the old family home that was the first one they had on the Island. He cared for me. He could cook, especially trout caught fresh from the brook and fried in a pan with butter, onions—and mushrooms gathered on the way home that very day. And *bannock*[76]!" Dad extolled, teasing his now wryly knowing daughters. "He could make a better bannock than any woman I ever knew, even your Aunt Blanche, who was pretty good. It was as we ate our last meal together that Great Uncle Peter gave me his fond farewell before I left for Canada's western prairies myself in 1906.

---

76 Scottish griddle cake, usually unleavened and made of oat meal, barley, or wheat flour. This food has also been adopted by many indigenous peoples in Canada.

""'I'll be do it here, tonight, Henry 'cause I wouldna be wantin' t'boys sayin' I favour ye. Learn ta tak' care o'yoresel', lad, 'cause none'll be doin' 't better. Keep a holt o'wha' had ye. New things'll come an' go, new ways—auld things'll pass, but ye be brought up a Presbyterian, ta fear God an' honour him fore'er. Remember 't, lad an' may God bless ye.'"

"My Uncle Peter shed tears, just for me . . ." Dad recalled wistfully.

◆ ◆ ◆

One day, while reading the history of the Presbyterian Church in Canada, Eve had come across the story of the Highland Clearances,[77] and the voyages of the Selkirk Settlers[78] to Canada; some of them settled in Prince Edward Island. Bells started to ring for her as she remembered

---

77 Forced removal by British landlords of Scottish Highlanders during the mid-1700s to 1800s to the coastal areas so that their farmland could be repurposed for raising of sheep. This hardship began after military defeat at the 1746 Battle of Culloden of the Jacobites, led by Scottish prince Charles Edward Stuart and supported by Highlander warriors, by British forces loyal to King George II. The British government encouraged Scottish Lowlander and English lords to acquire the vacated highlands, while former inhabitants were made to harvest kelp, go fishing, work as crofters for the lords, or emigrate. The Highland Clearances destroyed traditional Scottish clan society, suppressed Gaelic culture, and caused loss of language and depopulation of the Highlands, as thousands of destitute Highlanders left Scotland for the New World.

78 While touring the Scottish Highlands in 1792, Thomas Douglas (Earl of Selkirk) was so moved by the plight of local farmers who were being uprooted to make room for sheep pastures that he worked for the next twenty years to prepare a colony for the poor and dispossessed in Canada, starting in 1803 at Belfast, southeast of Charlottetown. The Earl of Selkirk, with support from the Hudson Bay Company, brought the first Selkirk Settlers to the Red River valley in the Canadian prairies (then part of Rupert's Land) in 1812.

parts of the stories Dad had told about Great Uncle Peter. Her family history was falling into place. She asked Dad about it.

"Well, my Grandpa John told me that his family came to The Island in 1820, when he was eight years old and that they came in the *Polly*. They disembarked at Orwell Bay and settled first in the Belfast area. When Grandpa and Grandma married, they were given part of the land for their own. Some of the others moved up to Valleyfield, and on to the Forest Hill area. It seems to me that the old ones got fairly good farms and the house that Neil lived in, which was the same one where I lived with Great Uncle Peter, was a nice big home. When the sons married, they were given parcels of land. I guess the first farm seemed like a terrible lot of land to them.

"I don't think my dad did much with the piece he got. He was a better carpenter than farmer, and went off to Boston to make his living. Checks were supposed to come home, but many was the time Mother sent me to the corner box to find nothing there. Dad was good with his hands though, and could make beautiful things out of wood . . . probably a family trait that was passed down. Great Grandpa Neil had been one of the builders of the first Belfast Presbyterian Church in 1823. Grandpa John helped build the one that still stands. Dad built the one where the family settled out West, and I helped build the one in the community where we lived. The piece of land owned by Grandpa John was a long, narrow piece that extended down to the sea. I remember that there were sharp cliffs and treacherous rocks below. It was a stormy point and Grandpa, being the kind old man he was, worried about ships that '"could run foul o'those very rocks, bein' nae able ta see i't'height o't'storm."'

"Often, on a stormy night, he'd put on his slicker and cap, light his old ship's lantern that could remain lit through a storm, and walk'd down to the cliff. Grandma would stay, worrying the whole time, by the window until she'd see the lantern coming back through the fog. Then, she'd go about her business, pretending to be surprised when he came in."

— Enduring Art, Active Faith —

❖ ❖ ❖

Once Dad made up his mind to something, he usually set about doing it, so it was a special morning in May when four excited travelers began their journey in a big, shiny black Mercury. Their hearts and minds were set on that small island at journey's end that Blanche and Eve had always heard called "The Island," as if there were no other in all the world. Now, they would get to see "the *cregilechi* in the creek," which was an expression for the blue heron, and follow the echoing footsteps of Great Uncle Peter as he trod gallantly along the red-brick roads.

"They *are* red!" Eve exclaimed, as the Mercury disembarked from the *Abegwait*, the ferry that had taken them away from the mainland.

Everyone was quiet, unable to express the beauty of the countryside as they drove over the highway that would take them to Charlottetown. To *talk* about emerald green fields bordered by the shapely, darker evergreens, topped by a soft blue sky filled with billowy white clouds, cut here and there by the even bluer bays and inlets and crisscrossed everywhere by roads and furrows of brick red, would simply do injustice. This was a sight for the eyes, to be appreciated and enjoyed.

"Hey! All of you listen to this," Eve called. Her eagerness brought Mom and Blanche into the sound of her voice as she read, "Centuries ago the Indians had their own names for this bit of land. When they felt poetic, as they often did, the Mi'kmaq called it *Abegwait*, which means "cradled in the waves", but when they thought of it as a home, they called PEI—now get this—The Island!

"Imagine that, Blanche!" Eve laughed. "Here we thought that Mom, Dad, and all the other Islanders had made that up when in some egotistical frame of mind!"

"Well," Dad said. The day began to warm up. "I'm off to find an old relic. Who's game for it?"

"Count me in!" Eve was definite, thinking that this would surely be something to do with the Mi'kmaq, but Mom and Blanche had to get the facts.

"What would *that* be?" They wanted to know, and both laughed when Dad failed to find the "big hill" he had walked down and up again with Great Uncle Peter to fish for trout in the brook. It was for Dad as if both hill and brook had completely disappeared.

"I'm going to look for my old home on Forest Hill. The way houses face the elements in this country, I have the feeling it will still be there."

It was.

"Well, gee whizz!" Dad exclaimed as he drove into the yard. "The house looks just as I remember it, 41 years ago."

Dad stepped up to the door, where he knocked gently. An old lady opened it a crack, but seeing a strange man wearing a hat and a big, black car in the yard, she closed it again. Dad's foot was in the crack. "*Timerah Hashin' anew*," was how his words sounded to those waiting in the car but were meant to say in Gaelic, "How are you?"

They worked. The door opened wide.

"Oh! Come on in and bring yore family with you," the little old lady invited. She didn't remember Dad's family, but she did make a fine cup of tea, which she served with delicious scones and jam.

Dad walked zig-zag to the car, so busy was he with looking around. As we drove away, he expressed a feeling of awe. "I was born in this house in 1890, and people are still living in it! I would have liked to lift the rug and find the bare floorboards, where we knelt each morning for family prayers while my Dad read from the Gaelic Bible that we didn't understand."

❖ ❖ ❖

Now it was the summer of 1991, the summer of Eve's return to her roots "from away." She could hardly wait to show her husband George this little piece of Canada that loomed so large in her long memories. The *Abegwait* dropped its travel-worn passengers on Prince Edward Island's red soil, just as the last rays of the setting sun were leaving the countryside awash in a kind and gentle light.

Eve was driving towards Charlottetown, seeking lodgings. Both she and her passenger were quiet, absorbing the scenes around them. Out of the corner of her eye, she could watch George's head turning as if on a swivel. Finally, overcome with curiosity, she asked, "Well, what do you think of it?"

"Lovely, just lovely. Everywhere you look, there's a picture."

Many of the motels were not yet open for business, this being only June 29! As the days passed, Eve and George found this unrushed atmosphere without stress, void of urgency, to so much be the cause of PEI charm. Yet, work had to be done by many folks: building and painting, ploughing and planting. In the fields, acre upon acre of dark green potato plants grew in rows, reaching their way through brick-red soil uphill to the sky and downhill to the sea. The fishermen who brought in their lobster limits in such a short season must have to rush in order to remain competitive . . . and, there *was* stress . . .. Those beautiful fields of the memorable PEI spud carried a blight that had rendered the product unacceptable to the big USA market in 1990. Thousands of bushels had hit the compost heap. Would this happen again? Who could tell?

The manageress of St. Peter's Bay Campground gave Eve encouraging news. "Just follow Forest Hill Road, and yore shore to find yore dad's old home. If you have any trouble, turn into the farm below the hill where the roofs of the buildings are all painted red. The MacLeods live there, and they know the history of the people."

Eve was surprised at the short distance down the hill before she felt the tug of recognition. "My instincts tell me to turn in here," she confided in George. "But these buildings with the red roofs look much too new and cared for."

"What about this one on the left?" George asked.

There, an old gable roof reached out of a fancy skirt that had obviously been added to its foundations. The peak looked right to Eve, but it was on the wrong side of the road! There were two farmers in the yard talking, each astride his own tractor.

"Are you Mr. MacLeod?" Eve asked the more likely of the two.

"I am that," he replied.

Eve spoke out her quest, but there was no sign of recognition. Just then, Betty MacLeod appeared. As Eve presented to her the story, Betty's husband Wendell had a few flashes of memory.

"Will you believe this? You are standing in yore Dad's very yard! When we came here to live, we took off the old kitchen and moved her 'crost the road. She's been added onto for to make a summer cottage. That little old lady was Josie MacDonald."

While everyone else stood in amazement, George called for pictures. When they left, they carried a verbal invitation to attend the lobster supper that would be held the following day at Dundas Church, as well as the name of Norman Matheson from the neighbouring farm, who now lived in the Souris Home for Seniors.

Mr. Matheson was a dear old man who, at 94, had his mind clear as a bell, but was too young to remember Dad's family. He did, however, remember "the big hill," down which Eve's father had walked as a lad with his Great Uncle to fish for trout. Best of all, he knew "the Big Church."

"It's not a *big* church—just a *little* church—but we always called it 'the Big Church.'"

"Was it a Presbyterian Church?" Eve asked.

"Oh, yes," the ancient was that definite. He seemed so pleased to be able to help Eve with at least part of her search, and also that she and George had plans to attend the lobster supper. When they offered to take him with them, however, Mr. Matheson declined, crustily explaining, "My legs don't always know they have to take me there *and* back."

Eve said goodbye to Mr. Matheson as if to Dad, dead these past five years. He had touched her heart strings.

The Archives were not very helpful to Eve, with so many Mac or McDonalds on file but Eve remembered Dad's words to her when she asked if his great grandpa had been a Selkirk Settler. She felt that tug of familiarity again when she and George stopped at the Selkirk Campgrounds to splash their feet in Orwell Bay. They could see, touch even, the red sandstone rocks that showed so clearly through its blue waters. Eve's fertile mind had no trouble rolling back a century plus three-score-years-and ten—the unspoiled coastline permitted that to happen! The Belfast Presbyterian Church, with its high tower reaching up as if to prick the sky, remained tall and straight for its age. Eve, and even George, felt right at home in it . . . and there, kitty-corner from the church's front door, stood the evidence Eve needed.

"It's a fine stone, George." Eve called. She leaned against a tall, narrow marker that came up to her shoulder blades, representing the end of their search. "They just used it better than most."

At the top of the stone Eve could see the inscription: *Memory of Neil MacDonald of Glasnu, died 22 May 1852, age 81*. About three-quarters of the way down the face she could see another: *John MacDonald 1812 to 1907*.

Looking back from the Wood Island ferry a few days later, Eve watched the little crescent-shaped piece of red sandstone disappear from view. She realized she might never see it again, but she also knew that she had stood on the same soil her ancestors had trod, looked upon their ocean, lakes, and streams, and reddened her feet in the soil that her Dad's bare feet had printed on their way to a trout stream, since become a trickle. She had found her roots in a beautiful little place that, for her, would forever be "The Island."

THE MERCY FLIGHT

BY NORMA PROUDFOOT

Snow began to fall that Sunday afternoon of November 22, 1953, as Gateway Aviation's Cessna 180 rolled to a stop at the terminal door of the Grande Prairie airport. The single-engine silver airplane had been chartered earlier in the day at Edmonton by Mrs. Lloyd Williams to fly to Grande Prairie, to see her husband, seriously ill with polio. Now it was returning with the patient.

Pilot Gordon MacDonald was a former Wanham resident. He had grown up on the MacDonald farm two and a half miles east of the Wanham school. His father George and mother Olive had arrived in this southwestern district of the Peace Country, northwest Alberta, in 1919. Both parents had been active in all community affairs. Their daughters—Margaret, Ethel, and Norma—along with Gordon, were all part of a special family. They attended South Slope School in Wanham before going on with their careers.

Gordon joined the Royal Canadian Air Force on September 26, 1940. He received his wings on March 17, 1941, while still under twenty years of age. He left for warfare overseas on April 6, and piloted Blenheim bombers over Nazi territory; Gordon later won the Distinguished Flying Cross for extreme bravery while flying in Burma against the Japanese. Following World War II, Gordon returned to Wanham with his wife

Phyllis, and took over the MacDonald family farm. They later moved to their own farm, located just east of the Wanham-Belloy cemetery. The urge to fly prevailed; Gordon and Phyllis moved to Edmonton, where he was employed by Gateway Aviation as a commercial pilot.

Gordon had flown Mrs. Williams to Grande Prairie on November 22, 1953, and telephoned his parents who were living then in Wanham. She and Lloyd's doctor decided that, because of her husband's serious condition, he would be flown back to Edmonton that same evening, where a hospital respirator was available for him. Dr. Don Wilson, a Grande Prairie physician, would take care of the patient during the flight; Mrs. Williams, because of room limitations on the aircraft, returned to Edmonton by car.

At 5:28 p.m., the airplane left Grande Prairie as a vicious blizzard swept into the Peace Country. The storm came suddenly. The howling wind, drifting snow, and bitter cold that night caused residents to nudge their thermostats up, and cancel any plans they had made to leave the warm comfort of their homes.

Shortly after take-off, Gordon radioed that his aircraft was icing up, and he was returning to Grande Prairie. A few minutes later, he radioed again that he had decided to resume course for Edmonton, flying at lower altitudes. Nothing more was heard, but later that evening, the airplane was reported as overdue in Edmonton. The RCAF sent a Dakota aircraft aloft to "track crawl" the route of the missing Cessna. Nothing was sighted. On Monday, November 23, a full-scale search began.

The news reports that Wanham residents heard on the radio that Monday morning shocked everyone. Gordon was their boy; his family was part of the community! Everyone lived with the hope that "their" airplane would be found . . . and found soon!

There followed a series of sighting reports that brought emotional highs and lows to the families of the missing men. A *Grande Prairie Herald-Tribune* newspaper report of December 10 chronicled some of these:

The search for three men missing on a flight from Grande Prairie to Edmonton continued Thursday. Nineteen days ago, the light aircraft disappeared as it carried its pilot, a polio patient, and an attending doctor to Edmonton. One of the most extensive air searches ever conducted in Canada has seen aircraft put in more than 11,000 air hours, and cover thousands of square miles. There have been hopeful reports, most recent of which came from a Debolt farmer who reported seeing an aircraft fly over his farm in November, not long after Gateway's Cessna disappeared. He saw a fire to the northeast, which lasted about twenty minutes. Twelve men formed a search party, and tramped through rough bush country following a line pointed out by the farmer.

On December 17, a report was received that a plane flying at tree level was sighted in the Mayerthorpe area. Residents from Mayerthorpe organized a ground search, and reported that a single set of footprints was discovered in the snow. Two men working in a lumber camp brought in the report that what they called 'signals' were seen from the Mayerthorpe forestry tower.

Investigations of reports of flares north of Edson, south of Crooked Creek and south of the Wapiti River were checked out. The cruelest was a message 'HELP' stamped out in the snow near Greencourt; this message was found to be the work of children.

Hopes rose and fell as each report was checked out by ground search parties from Wanham, Grande Prairie, and all through the Peace Country. A search and rescue fund to pay fuel costs of private pilots reached $3,700. Rewards totaling $3,000 for information leading to the discovery of the missing airplane were posted by the families of Dr. Wilson, George MacDonald, and various Grande Prairie businessmen. Nothing was learned; expectation that the men would be found alive disappeared.

On August 5, 1954, some nine months after Gateway Aviation's ambulance plane went missing, a private pilot named George A. Andrew reported sighting an airplane wreckage, some three miles north of Whitecourt, and about one and a half miles north of the Athabasca River. This crash site lay in bush country, a few miles from the new Valleyview to Whitecourt road. The *Herald-Tribune* reported that a ground party of Royal Canadian Mounted Police (RCMP) officers from Mayerthorpe removed the bodies of three men from the wreckage: Dr. Don Wilson of Grande Prairie; polio patient Lloyd Williams from Edmonton; and pilot Gordon MacDonald, formerly of Wanham. An RCMP spokesman said that death had come instantly to the victims. None of the emergency flares had been fired. The aircraft did not burn; it apparently struck the ground with terrific impact. The wreckage was scattered over a wide area. Body identifications were made through the men's wallets.

The *Herald-Tribune*, on August 12, 1954, subsequently covered MacDonald's funeral:

> Wanham (special) – The community, where he was born and raised, Tuesday paid final tribute to Gordon MacDonald, pilot of the ill-fated ambulance plane which crashed near Whitecourt while on a mercy mission last November. Nearly 300 mourners, many of whom battled muddy roads to reach Wanham, attended the Legion-sponsored memorial service in Wanham Hall at 2 pm. Tribute was paid to Mr. MacDonald, son of Mr. and Mrs. George MacDonald of Wanham, by Father Thomas, as a man who had died serving his fellow man. Prayers were offered by Rev. DL Campbell of Wanham. Mrs. Clarence Webber, a cousin of the pilot, received a wreath from Norman B. MacDonald, an uncle, and laid it at the base of the cenotaph in front of the hall.

World War veterans who attended the service in a body filed past the cenotaph dropping poppies at the base. The MacDonald family, away in Edmonton to attend a family memorial, was represented by Mrs. HC Hamelin of Rycroft, an aunt of the crash victim. During the service, a solo 'O Paradise' was sung by EJ Harrington. Also participating in the service were Bud Ireland and D. Palmer, president of the Legion. Accompanist was Miss Clara Hauser.

The afternoon of the same day, a lone Gateway Aviation airplane swooped low near the wreckage of wreckage of the ambulance plane, from which ashes of the three victims were scattered over the bushland[79], which had claimed their craft (but not their souls) during a mercy flight from Grande Prairie to Edmonton.

---

79 George and Olive MacDonald (pilot's parents), and Dr. Wilson's wife Agnes, and son Fred, were subsequently buried at the crash memorial site. The aircraft debris was removed from the site by Alberta Environment & Parks staff in November 2017.

— Enduring Art, Active Faith —

(1953 Gateway Aviation airplane crash site near Blue Ridge, Alberta, in 2010. Plaque commemorating the crash victims and gravestone for George and Olive MacDonald are visible within a fenced enclosure in lower photo.)

(Close up view of plaque commemorating the victims of the 1953 Gateway Aviation airplane crash: Gordon Webster MacDonald, DFC (pilot); Lloyd Everett Williams (polio patient); and Donald Broadrib Wilson, MD (medical doctor attending Mr. Williams) 2010.)

WHY I WEAR A RED POPPY ON REMEMBRANCE DAY

BY ROBERT PROUDFOOT

Although, as a Mennonite, I believe in peace and justice, I come from good men who took up arms in war—an uncomfortable truth with which I struggle, especially on Remembrance Day!

John Webster, an ancient ancestor, was an officer in the British army that recaptured the French fortress of Louisburg on Cape Breton Island in 1758, and later occupied Prince Edward Island (PEI), then known as Isle Saint-Jean, and previously by its Mi'kmaq name of *Epekwitk (Abegweit)*. In 1758, Captain Webster assisted in the brutal deportation of approximately 3,000 French and Acadian settlers from the island and helped erect the British Fort Amherst upon the former French fortifications of Port la-Joye. As commissariat, Webster resided at Fort Amherst as officer-in-charge of troop provisions until after the Treaty of Fontainebleau in 1763, when France formally ceded her Canadian territory to Britain. He later served in similar rank at Fort Edward, established across the harbour in 1768 when Charlottetown became the colonial capital of St. John's Island, known since 1799 as PEI.

My grandmother Olive Webster, a descendant of John Webster, married fellow Islander George MacDonald who, in 1919, had returned from the battle trenches of the First World War. Lieutenant MacDonald fought with Canadian forces at Vimy Ridge (1917); he was wounded twice and suffered chlorine gas poisoning but was also awarded the Military Medal and Bar by King George V for risking his own life to retrieve wounded fellow soldiers from the battlefield. Gordon Webster MacDonald, my grandparents' only son, served in the Royal Canadian Air Force during World War II, where he distinguished himself as a bomber pilot and squadron leader against Japanese forces in Burma. Flight Lieutenant MacDonald flew 119 combat sorties between 1941 and 1945 and was awarded the Distinguished Flying Cross in 1944.

My ancestors were decorated war heroes, but I am inspired more so by their acts of kindness and compassion. Rather than quit Canada among withdrawing British troops, John Webster and his wife raised their family in Prince Edward Island and helped develop the colony. He was an elected government member in the PEI House of Assembly (1784–1786), and also served as sheriff for eight years. Mr. Webster defended the colony as commissariat at Charlottetown garrison during the American War of Independence (1775–1783) but was relieved of duties when it was discovered that he had loaned many provisions to the hard-pressed colonial governor. He was later exonerated and reinstated with full pay by the British Army.

My grandfather George MacDonald had been a constable with Edmonton Police Service from 1913 to 1915 but, after the war, he chose farming over further police work. Grandpa and Grandma homesteaded in the Peace River country of northwestern Alberta from 1919 to 1961. They raised four children and were active in their church and community. As an officer of the Veterans' Land Act (VLA), Grandpa also helped hundreds of returned war veterans obtain financial assistance for purchasing farms, livestock, farming equipment, or commercial fishing gear. He personally intervened for two widows of fellow veterans so that they could continue receiving their husbands' war pensions.

Grandfather was born in 1890; he was seventy years old when I first became aware of him. As a boy, I lived in awe of this strong and hardy pioneer/soldier/athlete/farmer, but I also spent time in his presence to learn wisdom and history from him. Grandpa played backyard football with my brothers and I, passing the ball while we pretended to be Edmonton Eskimos football greats: Parker, Getty, Kwong, Bright, and Miles[80]. My grandfather safaried with our family in southern Africa in 1970; together, we viewed big-game animals, and stood atop Victoria Falls. He recited poetry, and waxed eloquent of his pioneer family life, but he never discussed the wars. We did not see Grandpa's military medals or uniform on display. He refused to watch war movies on TV. How could he regale us with military victories, or describe the horrors of war to kids who had no idea of armed conflict?

World War II broke out when Uncle Gordon was 18. He was a farm kid and a potential university student, but like thousands of other young Canadian men, he felt the greater call of duty to defend his country. Grandpa tried to dissuade his son from joining such a brutal conflict. If Gordon would stay home to manage the farm, he offered to go in his son's place, to train new recruits at the army barracks, but Gordon could not abide with the idea that his father, then fifty years old, should serve in his place. Gordon enlisted straight away. When Uncle Gordon left the RCAF in 1946, he wanted only to go back farming with his Dad, "to feed and work with the animals, to feel the soil in his hands and with his bare feet." Like Grandpa and so many other soldiers then, as before and since, Gordon returned from war bearing scars of mind and soul as

---

80 Jackie Parker and Don Getty (quarterbacks), Normie Kwong and Johnny Bright (fullbacks), Earl Lindley (end), and Rollie Miles (offensive/defensive halfback) comprised the Eskimos' offensive backfield when the Canadian Football League team won the Grey Cup championship three years in a row (1954 to 1956). This team and its players, among the best in football, won many awards and accolades, and made positive, lasting influence on Edmonton and Alberta. Getty and Kwong served as Alberta's Premier (1985 to 1992) or Lieutenant Governor (2005 to 2010), respectively; Parker coached the Eskimos (1983 to 1987), but lost the 1986 Grey Cup game. Miles and Bright taught school and coached student sports teams in Edmonton. Mr. Bright later became a principal at Mackenzie and Hillcrest junior-high schools.

well as of body—invisible scars that are hardest to heal! My uncle never attended university. He married his sweetheart and tried farming, did a stint in the civilian air force, and worked various trade jobs but the young family could not establish itself. Gordon eventually went back to flying, this time with Gateway Aviation, for whom he flew advertisement banners and commercial flights around the province.

On the night of November 22, 1953, Uncle Gordon took an emergency flight that had been chartered to carry a seriously ill polio patient and his doctor from Grande Prairie to Edmonton, where an iron lung awaited at the hospital. The ambulance plane flew into a blizzard en route. Captain Gordon MacDonald radioed in that heavy icing on the wings and fuselage was impairing the flight. He initially tried to return to Grande Prairie, but then proceeded towards Edmonton, flying below the storm clouds. The blizzard did not abate, and continued icing caused the plane to crash into the forest near Whitecourt. All persons on board were killed upon impact. One of the largest air searches ever performed in western Canada ensued; the plane wreck was not discovered until August 5, 1954, right on course! My uncle, who had flown many successful bomber missions during the war, and had once returned to base flying a damaged plane on only one engine, had been overcome by bad weather in a struggle against a different foe—the polio epidemic. He left behind a widow with three small kids, his parents, and his siblings to carry on.

Every time I visit the graves of Uncle Gordon and my grandparents (buried near their son after they died in 1970 and 1986, respectively) at the crash site deep in Alberta's northern boreal forest, I am saddened that my uncle died too young, but I am also inspired by his bravery shown in laying down his own life for others. I believe this was a selfless act of peace. Gordon could have delayed the flight until the blizzard ended, or passed on it altogether; perhaps he could also have resisted the patriotic call to join up when war came. He did what he thought was best.

I never had to make difficult choices regarding loyalty like those presented during warfare to my ancestors; what would I do? Hopefully, I would choose what made most sense to me, do the best I could with purpose but compassion, and then would accept the consequences, with God's help. I loved my uncle and grandfather; I acknowledge that they and Captain Webster killed enemy soldiers or uprooted civilians during war but they were also strong men of their times, and I remember them respectfully.

These vital family stories about war and peace are why I wear a red poppy today.

(Norma Proudfoot, her children, and parents in Wanham, AB. Back Row (L to R): Olive and George (holding grandson David) MacDonald, and Norma; Front Row (L to R): Gordon, Maryanne, and Robert Proudfoot 1962.)

(Robert Proudfoot's Family on the dual occasions of graduations of Annora from MacEwan University, and Alicia from McNally Composite High School in Edmonton, AB. Left to Right: Annora, Robert, Alicia and Valerie. May 2012.)

(Norma at home with her dog Beverly, 1956.)

(Proudfoot home in Beverly, 1954.)

ABOUT THE AUTHOR

Robert G. Proudfoot is a professional technical writer and environmental scientist who has also been a creative writer most of his life. He has written several essays and short stories about his experiences and learnings, particularly cross-cultural (with African, Muslim, or indigenous people) or social struggles (justice with mercy, marginalization of people, and a fair-trade market place). He writes about things that are difficult to explore, share, and articulate, such as human rights abuses, mental illness, racism, and poverty.

Robert lives in Edmonton, Alberta, with his wife Valerie (a recreational director for people with disabilities) and elder daughter Annora (a massage therapist). They enjoy living in this vibrant, multicultural city, which intentionally walks in reconciliation and collaboration with indigenous peoples and newcomers. Alicia Proudfoot, an emerging sculpturer, creative writer and musician, is completing her Master's Degree in Fine Arts at Nova Scotia College of Art and Design in Halifax.

Norma Proudfoot (1926 to 2015), raised in Alberta's "Peace River Country", was a school teacher, mother of seven children, world traveler, and creative writer. Norma self-published her autobiography "Roses on Our Trapdoor", and co-edited "First Presbyterian Church, Edmonton: A History", written in 2004 by Dr. Kenneth Munro.

Robert feels that with the unique reality of three generations of his family actively involved creating art, they should celebrate by sharing with others and helping them to explore and expand their own artistic talents. He believes he and his family are humble creators, who understand that God has given them whatever talents they have to share with others and thus edify Him.

(Contributors Family Portrait, May 2018: left to right – Annora, Robert, Valerie and Alicia Proudfoot)

CPSIA information can be obtained
at www.ICGtesting.com
Printed in the USA
LVHW071205250319
611682LV00003B/2/P